CW00554513

MEXBOROUGH
TEL 01709 582037
5/10

CENTRAL
LENDING
TEL 734315

9/13

1 9 JUL 2010   23/4/19

- 4 JAN 2011

1 4 FEB 2011
1 2 MAR 2011

1 9 AUG 2011

1 5 APR 2014

1 4 MAY 2019

HL5

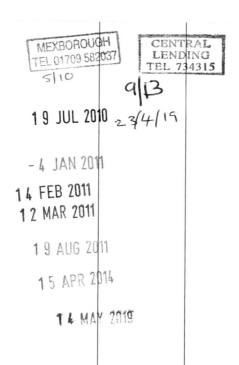

Doncaster
Metropolitan Borough Council

DONCASTER LIBRARY AND INFORMATION SERVICES

Please return/renew this item by the last date shown.
Thank you for using your library.

InPress 0231 May 06

DONCAS

3012

Air War Over
the Nore

Dedication

Dedicated to the memory of Keith Farman, a friend, neighbour
and contributor to the book who sadly died before its publication;
a Suffolk man to the core.

Air War Over the Nore

Defending England's North Sea Coast in World War II

Jon Sutherland and Diane Canwell

Pen & Sword

AVIATION

First published in
Great Britain in 2010
By Pen and Sword Aviation
An imprint of
Pen and Sword Books Ltd
47 Church Street
Barnsley
South Yorkshire
S70 2AS

DONCASTER LIBRARY &
INFORMATION SERVICE

30122031902881	
Bertrams	04/05/2010
940.544941	£19.99

Copyright © Jon Sutherland and Diane Canwell 2010

ISBN 978-1-84884-153-6

The right of Jon Sutherland and Diane Canwell to be identified as the
Authors of this Work has been asserted by them in accordance with the
Copyright, Designs and Patents Act 1988.

A CIP record for this book is available from the British Library

All rights reserved. No part of this book may be reproduced or
transmitted in any form or by any means, electronic or mechanical
including photocopying, recording or by any information storage and
retrieval system, without permission from the Publisher in writing.

Typeset in 11/13pt Palatino
by Mac Style, Beverley, E. Yorkshire

Printed and bound in Great Britain
by the MPG Books Group

Pen and Sword Books Ltd incorporates the imprints of Pen and Sword
Aviation, Pen and Sword Maritime, Pen and Sword Military, Wharncliffe
Local History, Pen and Sword Select, Pen and Sword Military Classics
and Leo Cooper.

For a complete list of Pen & Sword titles please contact
PEN & SWORD BOOKS LIMITED
47 Church Street, Barnsley, South Yorkshire, S70 2AS, England
E-mail: enquiries@pen-and-sword.co.uk
Website: www.pen-and-sword.co.uk

CONTENTS

Acknowledgements

The authors would like to acknowledge the assistance of a number of people who lived along the east coast of England during the Second World War. Notably we should like to thank Brian Provan of Hellesdon, Clyte Venvell from Knapton in Norfolk, Patricia Fogarty of Norwich, Geoff Parker of Great Yarmouth, E. Martin of Lowestoft, George Woods of Halesworth, Paul Rush of Norwich, Patricia Lilley of Great Yarmouth, Eileen Robinson (née Turner) of Lowestoft, Rosemary Hodgkin (née Whitehand) of Gorleston, Gary Brown of Gorleston, Keith Farman of Gorleston, Richard Kerridge of Bradwell near Great Yarmouth, Ivy Wright of Gorleston, Mary Dove of Bradwell and Graham New, whose father was in the police force in Great Yarmouth during the war. Special thanks go to Norman Bacon, formerly of Norwich and now living in Ipswich, for sharing his lifetime research on the Norwich bombings. Also, many thanks to Stephen Pullinger, the chief reporter for the *Eastern Daily Press*, Great Yarmouth, and to Matthew Gudgin of BBC Radio Norfolk for their help.

Introduction

The Nore is actually a sandbank, sitting in the mouth of the Thames Estuary and close to the Isle of Sheppey. It is considered to be the point where the River Thames becomes the North Sea. For centuries the sandbank has been a major hazard to shipping. Unsurprisingly it became the site of the world's first lightship in 1732.

The Nore is also a term that is used to describe the anchorage at the mouth of the River Medway, used for centuries by the Royal Navy. Indeed, so important was this entrance to Britain's capital via the River Thames that a Nore Command was established, later with subordinate commands at stations such as Ramsgate and Great Yarmouth.

By the Second World War Nore Command, now stretching from Bridlington in the north to Ramsgate and the beginning of the Dover Strait in the south, had assumed vital importance. The command would protect the coastal shipping routes along the east of England. It would act as a shield against German seaborne invasion. It would also be the scene of vicious and prolonged enemy air raids along the length and breadth of Britain's eastern flank. Ultimately, as the tide turned against Germany and her allies, the east of England would resemble a vast aircraft carrier and a staging-post, as Allied armies prepared to liberate occupied western Europe.

In the dark days of 1940, when invasion seemed only days away and the German *Luftwaffe* pummelled the south coast of England, the RAF's airfields and London itself, the east coast lay vulnerable and unprotected. East Anglia's defences were hopelessly under strength in terms of aircraft, searchlights, anti-aircraft guns and ground units to counter any potential invasion. In 1939 the Thames Estuary was undoubtedly the world's busiest waterway.

Indeed, the maritime tradition dominated the whole of the east coast, and this was despite the economic crisis that had taken place earlier in the 1930s. This was before there was any major decline in the importance of east coast seaports, ship building and, of course, the fishing industry.

The Commander-in-Chief of Nore Command, who at the outbreak of the war was Admiral Sir Henry J. Studholme Brownrigg, was responsible for the whole of the North Sea and the Dover Strait, between the east coast and the low countries of continental Europe. His headquarters was at Chatham and known as HMS *Pembroke*. He had four sub-commands, each under the command of a Flag Officer-in-Charge (FOIC). Each of these men had the rank of either rear admiral or vice-admiral.

Dover was commanded by Vice-Admiral Sir Bertram Home Ramsay, who had been in the Royal Navy since 1898. He knew the Dover Strait and the Belgian coast like the back of his hand. He had been brought back out of retirement by Winston Churchill and promoted to vice-admiral on 24 August 1939. He would protect against German raiders and enemy cross-channel traffic, and attempt to clear the Straits of Dover of enemy submarines. At the Nore itself, Rear Admiral Hugh Richard Marrack, another veteran of the Great War, was in command. FOIC London was Rear Admiral Edward Courtney Boyle, who had won the Victoria Cross as a submarine commander in 1915, and Rear Admiral Charles Frederick Harris was FOIC of Harwich Sub-command.

As late as April 1937, north of London saw just two fighter groups, Nos 11 and 12, covering the whole of north Essex and the remainder of East Anglia. Supporting the fighters was No. 2 Anti-aircraft Division, which had been formed in December 1936. It was supported by the 1st Anti-aircraft Division, centring on London. On paper the 1st Division would need 1,000 searchlights, but it only had 120 of them. It was armed with 3 in. naval guns, which were woefully inadequate and of First World War vintage.

The Committee of Imperial Defence looked at vital points along the East Anglian coast in April 1937 and identified an immediate requirement for 300 Bofors guns. They identified what was known as Vital Points; most were oil depots or power stations at King's Lynn, Ipswich and Norwich. A scheme was set up, and for the princely sum of £2 per year civilians would be attracted to the National Defence Battery, and they would defend their own places of work. But even this was considered to be too expensive a scheme.

By late 1937 it was decided to increase the production of the Bofors guns. It was hoped that a twin-barrelled 2-pdr would come into production within the next eighteen months and that the 3 in. naval guns would be passed on to the Army or the Navy. By January 1938 No. 2 Anti-aircraft Division had less than fifty per cent of its required manpower.

Prior to the outbreak of the war, in the summer of 1938, reinforcements arrived in the shape of Spitfires at Duxford, but it would take time for them to become operational. As the Munich crisis developed, Territorial units were mobilised and sent off to establish searchlight and anti-aircraft positions around East Anglia.

By May 1939 a belt of searchlights, stretching all the way from Newcastle to London, and then around the south coast to Portsmouth, had been established. It was manned by the Territorial Army, with over 23,000 officers and men. The Territorial Army manned the line on a monthly basis, rotating in four contingents. The new defence systems were tested on 11 August, with a home defence exercise. The defences were still patchy.

The first genuine alert took place at 0640 on 6 September 1939. Hurricanes of 56 Squadron lifted off from North Weald and climbed to 11,000 ft to patrol the air between Harwich and Colchester. More Hurricanes of the same squadron took up stations close to Ipswich. No. 74 Squadron also took up station. A single Heinkel He 111 was approaching to the east of the Thames Estuary. It circled and turned north and flew fifty miles out to sea. Air raid sirens sounded across East Anglia at 0730. The Heinkel turned north-east off Cromer at 0927. It was to be the first of many enemy aircraft to threaten eastern England.

The east coast and its vital shipping lanes were extremely vulnerable. This situation would become worse after the fall of France, yet the shipping lanes still remained busy, with coal coming down from the north-east to fuel London's power stations and homes. It was imperative that this vital traffic was not stopped. It would have been impossible for all the necessary coal and oil to be transported by either road or rail. In fact the first wartime east coast convoy sailed on 6 September 1939 when vessels had come from the Firth of Forth. More had joined at Tyne and at Sunderland, Middlesbrough and Hull, while others operated out of Ipswich. The system would become standardised; north-bound convoys would have the codename FN and then a number, and south-bound ones would use the same system but would be prefixed FS.

A series of buoys, light vessels and light floats marked the convoy routes along the east coast. Further out to sea they were protected by a vast mine barrier. There were gaps: one broadly adjacent to the vital Humber ports, another slightly to the north of Ipswich, in line with Orford Ness. There was a larger gap in the approaches to the Thames Estuary, out to sea from the Naze to the River Crouch. It would be vital that these gaps were monitored and protected from enemy surface and submarine craft. The channels were marked by buoys at intervals; for barges and coasters there was a narrower inshore channel. Most of the convoys would be guarded by escort vessels, mainly obsolete destroyers that were rearmed with anti-aircraft guns.

Systems of convoy, defence, and early warning and reaction forces were still in their infancy. It was fortunate that Nore Command and the east coast were spared from major enemy incursions or interest in the first few weeks of the war. In truth the Germans were as unready for a sustained campaign. The *Luftwaffe*, at this stage, was under instruction not to bomb British civilian targets, and this included London and the ports along the east coast. In any case its hands were full in Poland. This policy and the German preoccupation with the East would not last. The scene was being set for a major offensive and a period of unprecedented terror, which would slowly build and reach a crescendo in the dark months of 1940 and 1941. The east coast would become a tempting target for the *Luftwaffe*. Bombs, incendiaries, mines and anti-personnel weapons would be dropped across the length and breadth of the east coast. Fate had placed the east coast between Germany and more tempting targets around London and in the Midlands. The east coast would also be victim to coastal raiders, and later to V-weapons. In time, East Anglia would be dotted with airfields and defences.

The east coast's population of just 1.7 million in 1939 would see enormous increases as evacuees were shifted from London into the supposed relative safety of market towns and villages. Almost half of the population of East Anglia in 1939 lived in villages; Norwich had a population of around 118,000, Ipswich 100,000 and Cambridge 80,000. During 1938 Sir John Anderson's Committee had studied the thorny problem of evacuating civilians from London and other major cities in the event of war. The committee had designated certain areas as being neutral, which meant that they were considered safe from attack, and others excluded, which indicated that they were too dangerous to consider evacuating the population to in the event of a crisis. This left East Anglia in a difficult situation, as the *East Anglian Daily Times* noted on 12 January 1938:

> Whereas the towns and urban districts of both Essex and Norfolk are scheduled either for evacuation or as neutral areas, those of East and West Suffolk are classified as suitable for the reception of refugees. In view of past experience and known possibilities the arbitrary division of East Anglia along these lines is neither explicable nor defensible. There is neither rhyme nor reason in the belief apparently held by the Home Office that, of the entire coastal area from the Thames to the Wash, Suffolk is the least exposed to attack from the air. Everything, in fact, points in the other direction. During the Great War both Ipswich and Felixstowe suffered frequently from the attention of enemy air raiders, while Norwich enjoyed comparative immunity. Yet Norwich, and not Ipswich, is now listed as a neutral area. Again, while the Borough of Harwich is considered to be a danger zone, the adjoining Felixstowe Urban District and the densely populated County Borough of Ipswich – only two miles away as the bomber flies – are regarded as so safe as to be suitable for the reception of refugees. In no less a degree the same paradox applies to the position of Lowestoft and Yarmouth. Only ten miles (by air) separates them; yet one is officially safe and the other dangerous.

As we shall see, tens of thousands of evacuees, many of whom were children, would be packed off to various locations along the east coast. At each of the railway stations there would be an official reception officer. Some of the evacuees arrived on steamers from the Thames, disembarking at Lowestoft, Great Yarmouth or Felixstowe. Thousands arrived in cities such as Norwich and were then distributed into villages in the surrounding area. There were mothers and young children, and pregnant women. Some of the children came from Hungary, Poland, Russia and Turkey. A German scientist living in Cambridge who happened to speak Greek found himself in charge of a group of sixty Greeks in a local youth hostel.

At 1100 on 3 September 1939, war was officially declared. Less than an hour later, Flying Officer McPherson took off from Wyton, Huntingdonshire, bound for Wilhelmshaven. He was flying a Blenheim bomber of 139 Squadron. His mission was to discover whether major elements of the German fleet were still in the harbour or whether they were *en route*. McPherson saw the *Admiral Von Scheer*, the pocket battleship, along with the *Prinz Eugen*; they were both in Kiel harbour. An attack was quickly organised, but the raid was ineffective, and five of the fifteen Blenheims from Wattisham were shot down.

By the time war had been declared there were fifteen military airfields across East Anglia alone. Across the whole region buildings had to be blacked out; at the Norfolk and Norwich Hospital, for example, there were 1,600 windows to black out. Public transport was cut back, curbs, walls and corners of buildings were painted white so that people could see them in the darkness. Shops would close at 1900 and no later, newspapers shrunk in size to conserve paper, the Post Office cut back on daily deliveries, and across the region so-called enemy aliens were rounded up and people were prosecuted for hoarding. Every piece of available land was turned into allotments, and there was considerable confusion about whether the next major herring voyage, due for October 1939, would take place.

The scene was set. In East Anglia alone over 5,000 tons of bombs would be dropped. At least 1,000 civilians would be killed and over 4,000 seriously injured. The enemy would be last sighted on 30 March 1945 when German jets would be spotted at high altitude on a photo-reconnaissance mission. Before then, however, the east coast would have much to endure.

CHAPTER ONE

Nore Command 1939

A dark, ominous shape brought back terrifying memories of the First World War as it approached the east coast in August 1939. The second and less illustrious LZ130 *Graf Zeppelin*, the last of the great German rigid airships, had been launched to undertake an espionage trip (*Spionagefhart*). Its mission was to collect information on the British radar system. On board were forty-five crew and twenty-eight technical staff. They approached the east coast and slowly proceeded north to the Shetland Islands and then slowly flew back. They stopped off over Aberdeen, in order to investigate antennae masts. There was a bizarre meeting of times as the airship was buzzed by Spitfires. The mission had been launched on 2 August, and in just forty-eight hours the airship had covered a distance of over 4,200 km. Fishing vessels off Lowestoft excitedly reported what they had seen to the local press:

> Skipper W. Bridge, of the steam trawler *Witham*, said he had seen it so low over Smith's Knoll, the famous herring ground 22 miles from Lowestoft, that he plainly saw the swastika on its hull. Skipper Nelson Hood, of the smack *Lustre*, also saw it. Skipper Beamish, of the Lowestoft drifter *Peacemaker*, reported that during the night *Graf Zeppelin* had swept the decks of his and other craft with her searchlights.

The mission was actually a failure. Winston Churchill later wrote in his memoirs that the Germans discovered nothing because the British radar had been switched off. This was not actually the case. The German's own radio transmissions had masked the wavebands that the British were using for their radar. The British, however, lodged a diplomatic protest, and a delegation was waiting at the airfield to inspect the airship when it landed. The Germans fooled the British into believing that the airship would land in one place, when in fact it landed in another, giving the Germans the chance to strip out equipment and replace the crew. This gave the Germans the opportunity to claim that it was a meteorological mission. The airship was close to the end of its useful life, and in April 1940 the orders were given to scrap it. By the end of the month it had been cut up and the enormous airship hangars in Frankfurt had been levelled.

All too soon the east coast would face a far more dangerous adversary. Initially it would come in the form of reconnaissance aircraft belonging to *KG26* in the shape of He 111s. In early September a number of sightings were made off Sheringham, Great Yarmouth, Orford Ness and Clacton. British radar early warning stations were still poorly equipped and the personnel manning them were still in training. It was difficult for them to locate incoming reconnaissance aircraft. It would be the radar station's role to alert the RAF, which would then send up fighters to intercept or to protect likely shipping targets. Even though the RAF was responsible for the entire east coast protection, its responsibility only extended to five miles out to sea. It would quickly have to learn to expect a myriad of different German aircraft designs, all built for the specific purpose of levelling targets, subduing defences, knocking the RAF out of the sky or terrorising the civilian population.

One of the most common raiders, which were indeed versatile aircraft, was the Me 110, although the He 111 would in fact be the most numerous unwelcome visitor over the east coast. It was estimated that the Germans could muster twenty *Gruppen* of He 111s – upwards of 780 aircraft. It had a range of 1,650 miles, a speed of 200 mph and could carry over 4,000 lb of bombs. The Germans were building 200 of them each month. Another frequent visitor would be the Ju 88. It had a range of 1,865 miles, it could carry over 6,600 lb of bombs and had a top speed of 329 mph. The Germans also used Dornier Do 18 flying boats and Heinkel He 115 floatplanes.

Directly facing the east coast, based in Prussia, was German *Luftflotten II*, consisting of *KG26, 27, 28* and *4*. They were believed to have seventy-two dive-bombers and 312 fighters. In all the *Luftwaffe* could muster 1,180 bombers, 1,179 fighters, 262 long-range reconnaissance aircraft and 240 maritime aircraft. There was, however, considerable debate as to the primary targets for the *Luftwaffe*. The *Luftwaffe* preferred attacks on British ports, arguing that this would be the most effective means of isolating Britain.

Facing this potential enemy force in East Anglia was 23 Squadron, with twelve Blenheims at Wittering, 213 Squadron with fourteen Hurricanes, also at Wittering, Spitfire Squadrons 19 and 66 with thirty-two Spitfires in total at Duxford, supported by eighteen Spitfires of 611 Squadron. At Debden there were twelve Blenheim Is of 29 Squadron and eighteen Hurricanes of 17 Squadron. In reality only about half of these aircraft were ready for action.

To begin with the *Luftwaffe* would concentrate on British shipping and on the ports, and consequently the first recorded operation was launched on 14 September 1939. Three Do 18s were spotted just over a hundred miles to the east of St Abbs on the south-east coast of Scotland, in Berwickshire. They flew to some thirty miles east of North Foreland before turning towards home. On the same day another Do 18 was seen around a hundred miles to the east of Cromer, but it too turned back, making for Borkum on the German-Dutch border.

No. 611 Squadron was shifted out of Duxford on 10 October and moved to RAF Digby in Lincolnshire. This left room for 222 Squadron to move into Duxford. The Germans had deployed sixty-five Heinkel 111s (*KG26*) and twenty Ju 88s (*KG30*) to mount raids on British merchant ships and smaller Royal Navy vessels. October saw an increase in activity, with no fewer than nine sightings of enemy aircraft off Cromer alone. Three more were seen off Orford Ness, two off Southwold and one off Felixstowe. The closest any of these German aircraft came was ten miles. A single German aircraft was spotted at 0803, just ten miles off Lowestoft on 30 October.

The Germans were yet to unleash their potentially devastating force on the east coast. This gave time for the British to redeploy and reinforce. Three new Blenheim squadrons were created, No. 222 at Duxford, and 236 and 254 at Stradishall. Subsequently these two squadrons would move respectively to Martlesham and to Sutton Bridge. Their duty would be to protect convoys and their escorts. Further patrols would be assigned to ensure that the fishing fleet was protected.

Close contact with the German aircraft did not take place until 13 November, when a Do 18 was spotted. Hurricanes of 56 Squadron at Martlesham were scrambled. They encountered the German flying boat some forty miles to the east of Southwold. The German aircraft was shot up but managed to escape. The RAF would have to wait for its first kill.

There were more sightings four days later when it was believed that German aircraft had tried to penetrate the Thames Estuary. Some of these early sightings were undoubtedly incorrect, and probably friendly aircraft. In fact on 17 November, over Manchester, a Walrus had been mistaken for a German aircraft and chased. This had not been the only mistake that had occurred; three weeks before, on 27 October, the crew of HMS *Fleetwood* had opened fire on five British aircraft off Hunstanton. Ground crew, pilots, the Observer Corps and civilians all needed to know what was enemy aircraft and what was not. The authorities used wooden scale-models, Bakelite copies, silhouettes and hand-touched drawings and photographs. As it transpired, it was the *Daily Mirror* that came up with the solution. It produced a booklet of silhouettes and details of all major British and German aircraft.

The Germans were certainly off to a slow start, and had barely probed the defences of eastern England. On 20 November things would begin to change. Flying Officer Davies and Flight Sergeant Brown of 79 Squadron, Manston, responded to the sighting of enemy aircraft off Dover at 0940. They encountered a Do 17 which turned to escape, desperately manoeuvring, but the two pilots shot it down. Little more than two hours later another German aircraft on a photo-reconnaissance mission over the Thames Estuary was spotted. No. 79 Squadron again responded; it hunted the skies between Margate and Canterbury in vain. Then 74 Squadron answered a call indicating that the aircraft was further north, and Flying Officer Measures, Pilot Officer Temple-Harris and Sergeant Flinders encountered an He 111 at 27,000 ft at 1245. The target was flying at 270 mph and fifteen miles from Southend. They swept in to attack and the bomber dived away, trying to use cloud cover over Ramsgate. It flew north into Essex, skirted Ipswich and then fled for the coast near Felixstowe. All the time the aircraft was tracked and chased. Probably due to engine trouble the He 111 ditched a hundred miles out to sea, and the destroyer HMS *Gipsy*, which was to meet its own end just three days later, picked up three of the German crew.

On the same day, 20 November, another pair of German aircraft, probably an He 111 and a flying boat, were spotted to the east of Felixstowe. Squadron Leader Knowles and Flying Officer Holden of 56 Squadron out of Martlesham flew to intercept. They shot at the flying boat but it escaped into cloud. It is also believed that another German aircraft had tried to bomb HMS *Boadicea* some six miles to the east of Cromer. The Germans were building up for a major attack, with units of He 111s believed to be in excess of 170 aircraft (*KG26* and *KG4*) soon becoming available.

So far at sea, it was almost business as usual. At the outbreak of the war the cargo and passenger trade between Hull and the Scandinavian countries and Harwich and Belgium and Holland had been suspended, but these had been resumed. The Harwich ferries were now operating out of Ipswich and there were still enormous convoys assembling in the Thames Estuary with the intention of sailing through the English Channel. Having said this, the Germans managed to sink twelve merchant ships in the first ten weeks of the war. All of these victims were claimed not by direct enemy action but by mines.

The British had taken the precautionary measure of erecting booms across the Humber, Harwich and the Thames Estuary. But magnetic mines had already been sown. The SS *Magdapur* and *Goodwood* had been sunk on 10 September off Aldeburgh and Bridlington respectively. The mines are believed to have been laid by German U-boats (*U13* and *U15*). In fact on 10 September a submarine had been spotted in the vicinity.

Nore Command still controlled the Dover Strait, and by October cables, nets and mines had been laid across it. Electromagnetised cables had been placed on the seabed to detect U-boats that had been operating in the Atlantic from using the Dover Strait as a shortcut back to base. On 8 October *U12* was sunk and on 13 October *U40*. German submarines had not yet dared to make torpedo attacks but were still sowing mines along the coast. In fact in Nore Command during the whole of the war (with the exception of midget submarines) only two British vessels were sunk by German submarines. The first was sunk on 4 December 1939, and the other, a tanker, on 2 February 1940, both being lost off Withernsea just to the north of the Humber Estuary, and at the virtual limit of Nore Command.

In fact in the north there had been considerable success by the RAF against the *Luftwaffe*. On 29 September 1939 a single German raider had dropped three bombs off the Humber, on 21 October four Heinkel He 115s (there may have originally been nine) failed to press home a torpedo attack off Withernsea; all four were shot down by 46 Squadron. One of the three-man crews was picked up by the destroyer HMS *Gurkha* three days later, and three bodies were washed up at Happisburgh in Norfolk on 2 November.

The Germans seemed content to make isolated attacks on individual ships, hoping that they were outside Fighter Command's air cover and out of range of the radar. A prime example took place on 7 October 1939 when some fifty miles to the east of Great Yarmouth, at Brown Ridge, a pair of Harwich minesweepers, *Niger* and *Selkirk*, paid little attention to an incoming aircraft. They were under the misapprehension that it was an RAF escort; it was in fact a Do 18. The promised RAF escort had failed to arrive, and both ships were lucky that the Dornier's bombs landed harmlessly in the water. It had in fact been a mix-up; Rear Admiral Harris, the FOIC Harwich, had failed to get the necessary escort but had not told the captains of the two minesweepers. The Royal Navy rounded on Harris and on the minesweeper captains, who had not fired the necessary recognition signals. Just over a month later, on 10 November, almost exactly the same thing happened. A pair of Polish destroyers, the *Blyskawica* and the *Grom,* were hunting the same area for lifeboats. This time a pair of RAF aircraft were also involved in the search. A pair of He 115s approached and were not challenged. One of the Polish destroyers was lucky as it was narrowly missed by a German torpedo.

It is important to stress that throughout this time the fishing fleet, particularly off Norfolk, was still fully operational. On 17 December the Germans launched an attack and struck at vessels operating from the Humber, the Forth, Great Yarmouth and Lowestoft. Some seventy miles north-east of Great Yarmouth the first fishing vessel, the Grimsby-based *Pearl*, was lost.

There would be further shipping losses just into the New Year. Again the Germans picked on isolated vessels. On 9 January a handful of He 111s attacked a pair of small merchantmen to the north of Cromer. They sank *Oakgrove* operating out of Glasgow, and *Upminster,* operating out of London. The Germans also managed to damage SS *Chrysolite.* On the same day Captain W.J. Lees of the Trinity House tender *Reculver* was on his way from Great Yarmouth to nearby lightships with relief crewmen. The vessel was attacked and hit with bombs and machine-gun bullets. Lees and over thirty of the forty men on board were wounded, and two of them died. The *Reculver* was towed back into Great Yarmouth by the Grimsby trawler *Hammond*, assisted by the Gorleston lifeboat. On 11 January Radio Officer C.A. Coleman, on board SS *Keynes,* transmitted an urgent SOS as the vessel was attacked off the Humber. Seaman S.L. Brown fired at the raiders but it was to no avail, as the SS *Keynes* was sunk.

Coleman was later awarded the OBE and Brown the BEM. They were also the first to be given the Lloyds War Medal (a decoration for Merchant Navy crews, and the first to be awarded on the east coast). The Germans also attacked the Hammond Knoll light vessel on 13 January. The two survivors were saved by the Cromer lifeboat.

There were two further attacks on 29 January, even though the weather was bitter and operations were kept down to a minimum. The Germans sank the merchantman *Stanburn* off Flamborough Head and shot up the East Dudgeon light vessel off Skegness. Only one man survived, John Sanders of Great Yarmouth. A Latvian vessel was also attacked. The *Tautmila* was abandoned, and the captain and a number of the crew made it ashore and the vessel grounded near Cromer. On 30 January, off Caister, the tanker *Voreda* was sunk and two other ships were damaged.

There were other attacks: the trawler *Larwood* and the SS *Royal Crown*; the latter beached at Cove Hithe. The SS *Highwave* was particularly unlucky. She had broken down and had become separated from the convoy that she was with. She radioed for assistance from Harwich but the Germans had spotted her and she was sunk close to the Kentish Knock light vessel.

There was considerable outrage that the Germans were targeting clearly civilian vessels and lightships. In fact the British claimed that this was a violation of international law. A medium-term reaction to this was to replace many of the lightships with buoys or red-light floats. Some of the light vessels were removed completely. There was also outrage about the clear attacks on neutral vessels. The Italian *Amelia Lauro* was shot to pieces near the Humber on 9 March. Several of her crew were rescued, and Captain Lepaci launched a blistering attack on the Germans when two of the crew were buried at Great Yarmouth.

In retaliation any German merchant ship or vessel that was believed to be *en route* to Germany or trading with Germany would be seized. By late 1939 it had become clear that Germany was preparing to launch an assault in the west, and a new force operating out of Harwich was tasked with checking merchant shipping operating along the coast of mainland Europe. This would be part of the Allied blockade of the German ports. Seized vessels were taken into anchorage off Ramsgate, one of these vessels being the German SS *Phaedra*.

Despite the establishment of this new force, the Germans were able to launch Operation Wikinger on 22 February 1940. A number of German destroyers were to make a raid on the fishing fleet operating out of the Humber and fishing on the Dogger Bank. It was an ill-conceived German plan. A number of He 111s spotted the German vessels and mistakenly identified them as British ships. They launched a bombing attack, and two of the destroyers, *Leberecht Maass* and *Max Schultz,* zigzagging to avoid, ran into British mines; both sank and 600 German sailors were killed. This would be the last time that German destroyers would attempt an operation like this.

The persistent danger in these early months, and indeed throughout much of the war, was the innumerable German magnetic mines. Each time a seemingly innocent German reconnaissance plane buzzed the east coast it was more often than not dropping a magnetic mine. The danger was all too clear, as can be seen from the following example.

It was 0514 on 13 November 1939. HMS *Blanche* and HMS *Basilisk,* both destroyers operating out of Harwich, were escorting HMS *Adventure*, a minelaying cruiser. HMS *Adventure* was moving from Grimsby to Portsmouth. They had stopped in dense fog near the Tongue light vessel, some ten miles to the north of Margate. Suddenly there was an enormous explosion ahead of them. At 0525 there was another explosion, this time right under HMS *Adventure.* Sixty-two of the crew were injured, three of whom would later die. The ships stopped and radioed for assistance. The casualties were taken on board HMS *Basilisk* and sped to Sheerness. Meanwhile, the tug *Fabia* from Ramsgate began to tow HMS *Adventure* to safety. By this stage it was around 0800. HMS *Blanche* was standing guard in the shocking weather in case of attack. She had just got under way again when there was another explosion. There was catastrophic damage to the destroyer, and as she awaited a tug from Ramsgate to help she began to list. The crew abandoned her and she sank.

The British firmly believed that a German U-boat was at work around the Tongue light vessel, aiming to pounce on shipping heading for the Thames Estuary. HMS *Glowworm,* a Harwich-based destroyer, was stationed there to direct shipping away from the Tongue light vessel. It was a fruitless task. The merchantman *Pozano* and the *Matra* were both lost. In fact in the space of the next twelve months or so the British would lose another fourteen vessels in the area, including the trawler *Mastiff* out of Sheerness.

Soon enough the British realised that the enemy had sown mines, but they were initially perplexed that none of the vessels had actually struck a mine. The mines were in fact triggered by the hull magnetism. Numerous other vessels were lost up and down the east coast, and British fears were soon realised when 200 or more enemy mines were washed up on the coast of Yorkshire. It quickly became clear that many of the shipping losses were as a result of these mines. Added to this there were also a great number of contact mines that the Germans had sown in the Humber area during the hours of darkness on 17/18 October 1939. The Germans had used a number of destroyers and torpedo-boats to accomplish this mission. The Danes lost the SS *Canada* on 3 November 1939, and a public enquiry held in Copenhagen announced on 19 November that the loss of the ship was as a direct result of magnetic mines.

There would be considerably more losses over the next few weeks, the first of which was a Dutch passenger liner that belonged to the Royal Netherland Steamship Company. The vessel, the *Simon Bolivar*, due to head for the West Indies, was wrecked by a mine some twenty-five miles off Harwich at 1230 on 18 November. There were two explosions; the first stopped her and the second ripped open the hull, and 130 lives were lost. Rescue vessels left Harwich to pick up around 140 survivors, and lifeboats from Clacton and Walton searched the area for survivors. The area around Harwich was becoming hazardous, and within the next few days another six ships were lost, the largest being a Japanese vessel, the *Terukuni Maru*, a passenger liner that was sunk some ten miles off the Naze.

If the British needed confirmation as to how the mines were being sown it came on the evening of 21 November 1939. The 1st Destroyer Flotilla left Harwich harbour, its mission to hunt for U-boats around the Cork lightship area. It spotted a pair of enemy aircraft, certainly floatplanes, at around 1900. The aircraft dropped to around 150 ft at the harbour entrance and dropped a number of objects by parachute. After machine-gunning an observation post they disappeared out to sea. The British had not fired at the aircraft, believing, having seen the parachute, that the crew was baling out. A small craft was sent out to investigate what had been dropped, but nothing was found.

The 1st Destroyer Flotilla proceeded as planned. Leading was the Polish destroyer *Burza*. It was followed by HMS *Griffin*, HMS *Gipsy*, *Grom*, HMS *Keith* and HMS *Boadicea*. *Boadicea* and *Keith* were both B-class destroyers built in 1930. HMS *Gipsy* was a G-class destroyer launched in 1935 and built in Govan in Scotland, and HMS *Griffin* was also a G-class destroyer, built in Newcastle and launched in

1935. The *Grom* was another British-built Polish Navy destroyer. HMS *Gipsy* was only just level with the fort at Harwich harbour entrance and inside the boom gate, when at 2123 there was a huge explosion. The stricken vessel crumpled. There was a desperate scramble to save the crew, but at least thirty were lost, including the captain, Lieutenant-Commander Crossley.

An He 115 buzzed the harbour at 1330 on the following day. Another visitor was Winston Churchill, furious that a vessel had been lost inside the harbour and that the anti-aircraft guns had not even fired at the German raider. Lieutenant-Colonel Ward, the garrison commander, was forced to resign. As a direct result the RAF put up barrage balloons around the harbour, and the following month saw similar ship-borne barrages across the mouth of the River Thames.

Until a solution was reached the convoys would be at enormous risk. It seems that the mines were predominantly sown by German surface and underwater vessels. Four German destroyers, under the command of Captain Bonte, supported by a light cruiser and torpedo-boats, had laid a number of magnetic mines around the Tongue lightship on the night of 12/13 November 1939. Three German destroyers, led by Commander Hartmann, had laid the minefields around Harwich on the night of 17/18 November. The *U15* had left mines off Lowestoft on 15 November, the *U19* off Orford Ness on 24 November, and the *U58* had sown additional mines off Lowestoft on 28 November. In addition to this, German floatplanes had dropped upwards of forty mines on 20 November. Further mines had been laid around the Humber approach, and it is believed that three German destroyers were involved, led by Commander Bey. It was one of their mines that claimed the Polish liner, *Pilsudski,* on 24 November 1939.

Desperate measures were needed to try and prevent another HMS *Gipsy*-style disaster. The Southend CSO, Captain A.S. May, mustered thirty-five sailors and issued them with nineteen Lewis guns. He positioned them around Southend pier and on motorboats. Sure enough German aircraft came over to drop new mines. They ran into a barrage of fire. Three miles away, at Shoeburyness, Captain Lloyd of the 518th Coast Artillery Regiment engaged the same German aircraft. One was shot down off Sheerness, and later Lloyd and his men found a mine buried in the mud at Shoeburyness.

This mine was examined by experts from the Royal Navy Torpedo and Mines Branch. They examined the mine in the darkness and took photographs. On the following day it was decided to try to defuse the mine. They discovered that it was an aluminium cylinder some 8 ft long and just over 2 ft in diameter. There was near-disaster when the mine started to tick, but this was a clockwork delay mechanism. It became clear that the mine was actually designed to sink to the seabed. It was triggered when a ship came close, and the clockwork delay mechanism meant that the mine would only explode when the ship was directly above it. This type of magnetic mine became known as the Type A.

On 23 November 1939 one of the mines blew up of its own accord to the south of Shoeburyness, in the entrance to the Thames Estuary. On 25 November two more German mines were accidentally triggered, one to the east of Gravesend and the other on Mucking Flats.

On 25 November, 23 Squadron sent out a number of Blenheims at dusk, hoping to pounce on German floatplanes laying mines. They found nothing, and consequently twelve Blenheims of 25 Squadron and 601 Squadron were dispatched from Bircham Newton on 28 November to attack the seaplane base in Germany, but little damage was done.

By the beginning of December the Germans had begun laying magnetic mines off Norfolk. One of them, believed to have been laid by the *U59* off Caister, sank the trawler *Washington* and the merchant ship *Marwick Head*. On 19 December a mine laid by the *U60*, commanded by Georg Schewe, sank the SS *City of Cobe*, a 4,373-ton steam merchant ship near Cross Sand Buoy, not far from Great Yarmouth. It is believed that the *U60* had laid the mine on 15 December. One crewman was lost, but the captain and twenty-nine crew members were picked up by HMS *Tumby* and the coasters *Corinia* and *Faxfleet*. The *U56* is believed to have been responsible for the loss of the freighters *Portelet* and *Onto*. The *Portelet* was hit, possibly by a torpedo, at 2040, and sank around a mile from the Smith's Knoll lightship. Two of the crew were lost but the captain and eight other crew members were picked up by the Finnish vessel, SS *Oscar Midling*, and landed at Immingham on 4 February 1940.

It was not all plain sailing for the Germans. On the evening of 5 December 1939 an He 115 was making its way towards the east coast of England. By mistake, largely due to poor weather, it crossed the coast close to Cromer, and at around 0300 it crashed into the sea, barely 70 m out. The body of the observer was discovered at 0500, but the other two crew members were never found. The British found the aircraft broken up into two parts, although both of the engines had sunk. They discovered that the aircraft's fuel tanks were protected by a rubberised material. On checking the wreckage it was also discovered that the aircraft was perfectly capable of carrying one of the dreaded magnetic mines. The racks proved that this was possible. However, the British had no idea what had happened to the mine that the aircraft had been carrying. It may have claimed the *Corea*, which was sunk to the north of Cromer light vessel on 8 December. On 12 December the *Marwick Head* was sunk close to Caister Buoy, and on the same day, four miles south-west of Happisburgh light vessel, the *King Egbert* was also lost. It is now strongly believed that both the *Corea* and the *King Egbert* were destroyed by mines that had been sown by a pair of German destroyers on 7 December. One of these two German destroyers, *Erich Giese,* had run into HMS *Jersey*, along with her sister ship, HMS *Juno*, on the night of 6/7 December. The two German vessels spotted the British destroyers at a range of 8,000 metres at 0255. Three torpedoes were fired at *Juno* and four at *Jersey. Jersey* was hit but managed to return home under tow from *Juno.* It would take until the end of September 1940 to repair her.

It was clear that the German mining operations were not only continuous, but also escalating. Consequently, on 12 December, Bomber Command decided to launch security patrols at night to intercept He 115s operating out of Borkum and Sylt. Initially, however, the security patrols were a failure; the Germans successfully launched fourteen missions on the night of 15 December alone. They were making sporadic attacks against British civilian shipping with their aircraft. A merchant ship was narrowly missed by a Ju 88 off Cromer on 6 December, and a number of German aircraft attacked three trawlers and a motorboat off the east coast on 17 December. The Germans were also trying to make deeper incursions into British airspace. A number of RAF aircraft were scrambled to try to intercept a Do 17 near Ely on 10 December. A similar aircraft was seen above Great Yarmouth on 27 December.

By this stage the RAF was beginning to operate up to fifteen miles out to sea, rather than its strict responsibility of five miles. Reconnaissance aircraft checked the seas, hoping to protect coastal shipping. A prime example took place on 9 January 1940 when a number of He 111s of *KG26*, operating out of Schleswig, attacked ten British ships and four Danish ships off the coast between Aberdeen and Lowestoft between 0930 and 1200. The SS *Delphinus* was machine-gunned and bombed, the SS *Oakgrove* was sunk by bombs fifteen miles south-east of Cromer Knoll light vessel, and the SS *Reculver*, the Trinity House tender, was attacked three times off Great Yarmouth and only just managed to get into harbour. A pair of He 111s attacked the SS *Upminster* around ten miles from the point where the SS *Reculver* had been attacked. She was badly damaged and went down with all hands.

Meanwhile, experiments were under way to try to deal with the mines that had already been laid. Experiments had taken place on the west coast of England, which involved dragging magnets along the seabed. This method was used off Grimsby and Harwich, and it was largely unsuccessful because the 6 ft bar magnets that were being dragged frequently became entangled. Another version, known as the skid, was also tried, this time off Canvey Island on 30 November 1939. A number of attempts were made both here and at Gravesend in December, but the skids, with their electromagnetic coils mounted on the raft, had so little magnetic pull that they had to pass very close to a mine to dislodge it. HMS *Borde*, a mine destructor ship was a converted merchantman with a massive electromagnet on her bow. This too was tried. Three Wellingtons were given magnetic loops in their fuselage. The officers, crew and scientific staff on board HMS *Vernon* became experts in mine countermeasures. A number of Lowestoft fishing drifters, including *Evening Primrose*, *John Alfred*, *Renascent*, *Sea Holly* and *Sweet Promise*, together with the tugs *Servitor*, *Shako*, *Slogan*, *Solitaire* and *Souvenir*, were fitted out with two pairs of electric cables, which were towed in parallel by floats. The cables gave out powerful pulses, generating a strong magnetic field. The first of the German magnetic mines was recovered and made safe on 24 November 1939. Several more drifters from Lowestoft, including *Achievable*, *Fisher Boy*, *Formidable*, *Lord Cavan*, *Ray of Hope*, *Scotch Thistle* and *Silver Dawn*, were fitted out to recover mines.

On 10 January 1940 part of the force assembled around north-east Spit Buoy, close to Margate. Disaster befell *Silver Dawn* at 1130 when a mine blew the drifter to pieces. More and more drifters were being requisitioned; Harwich requisitioned sixty-eight, although the majority of them were used as mine lookouts. Fifty more trawlers and drifters were used as mine lookouts off Great Yarmouth and Lowestoft. Some auxiliary minesweepers of First World War vintage were brought back into action in January, including *Dundalk*, *Dunoon*, *Elgin*, *Fitzroy*, *Kellett*, *Selkirk* and *Sutton*. Initially they were based at Great Yarmouth but were later transferred to Harwich.

Even older vessels, paddle minesweepers, which had been operating as pleasure boats on the Thames or on the Clyde, steamed into Harwich in February. These three vessels, *The Duchess of Fife*, *Marmion* and *Waverley* had all been built nearly forty years earlier. Additional paddle minesweepers, *Oriole*, *Queen Empress*, *Duchess of Rothesay* and *Princess Elizabeth* were also pressed into action.

The Royal Navy converted three more of the paddle steamers, *Crested Eagle*, *Golden Eagle* and *Royal Eagle* into anti-aircraft ships, copying what the Army had been using *The Thames Queen*, *Queen of Kent* and *Queen of Thanet* for in the Thames mouth since December 1939. All of these vessels had very primitive gun-laying radar to locate targets. Some of the ships had also been used to evacuate civilians from London to Margate, Clacton and other ports along the east coast.

Meanwhile, in the skies the RAF was still attempting to intercept incoming He 111s. At 0815 on 11 January 1940, Sergeant Cameron and Sergeant Stone, of 'A' Flight, 66 Squadron, flying Spitfires, were some twenty miles to the east of Cromer. They spotted an He 111 and gave pursuit. Stone's aircraft, running short of fuel, ditched near Happisburgh. It is believed that the He 111 crash-landed at Skaerbaek in south Jutland, and was set on fire by its crew after they had abandoned it.

British shipping came under attack on 13 January at 1620, around seven miles off Aldeburgh in Suffolk. The targets were some seventeen ships being escorted by three destroyers. No hits were achieved. At around midnight on 21 January a number of Ju 88s of *KG30* attacked nine ships to the east of the Thames Estuary. On 28 January a ship also came under attack to the north-east of Cromer.

The Germans launched a major operation on 30 January when some seventeen He 111s of *KG26* flew to within sixty-five miles of Cromer and then headed north to the Shetlands. They attacked around thirty ships and also attacked a pair of light vessels, one of which, *East Dudgeon*, was badly damaged. On the same day the SS *Royal Crown* was bombed some thirteen miles off Southwold while *en route* to America via Dover. At 1230 a 4,000-ton ship was bombed off Lowestoft, a Norwegian tanker was set on fire and later sank twenty-five miles off Cromer. On 1 February the *Voreda* was machine-gunned, and around twenty-four He 111s were seen off Southwold at 1109. In all, sixteen ships had been attacked that day; one was sunk, one abandoned and five damaged. Of the total, five of the vessels belonged to neutral countries.

Most of the German aircraft belonged to *KG26* and *KG30*, and it was now becoming clear precisely what the German tactics were in their anti-shipping attacks. Usually three aircraft, armed with 50 kg and 250 kg bombs, would attack each target. The first aircraft would buzz the target to see if it had any defensive armament. They would then attack at a height of around 50 ft, and drop bombs. They would then return and machine-gun the target.

Towards the end of February there were more night attacks. On 27 February three vessels were attacked for the loss of two He 111s. On 29 February the Italian-registered *Maria Rosa* was set on fire after an aircraft attack some fourteen miles north-east of Cross Light. Other ships were lost to mines, including the British *Triumph* on 13 February, *Clan Morrison* the following day and *Jevington Court* on 24 February.

The beginning of 1940 had also seen another major Royal Navy loss. HMS *Grenville* had been sent out on a patrol to check shipping along the Dutch coast on 19 January. On her way back from her mission she struck a mine some twenty-three miles east of the Kentish Knock light vessel. In near freezing conditions the crew took to their lifeboats, and the men's morale was kept up by Captain G.E. Creasy, leading a defiant sing-song. Seventy-seven of the crew were lost, and 118 men were recovered by the other five ships in the flotilla. It is believed that the mines had been laid by German destroyers.

Into March there were more enemy air attacks on British and neutral shipping. One ship was sunk on 1 March, two more on 2 March, ten He 111s operated between Aberdeen and Great Yarmouth on 16 March, attacking six ships and two lightships. At night the Germans attacked trawlers, and on the following day eleven trawlers were attacked around dusk. There were a number of mine casualties, including the *Chevy Chase* on 9 March and *Gardenia* on 12 March.

On 11 March 1940 the Germans had sown contact mines around Kentish Knock, South Falls and North Goodwin Sands. This was a dangerous area, as it was one of the major routes between the Thames Estuary and the Dover Strait. A Greek vessel, the *Niritos*, had already been lost in the region. The antiquated paddle minesweepers managed to clear the area, but not before four vessels had been lost.

The RAF was shuffling its squadrons. The new Boulton Paul Defiant came into service with 264 Squadron at Wittering on 22 March 1940, and meanwhile 229 Squadron's Hurricanes became operational on 26 March and 222 Squadron had been issued with

Spitfires. It is important to remember that at around this time the situation in Norway was taking precedence, but a German aircraft was shot down off Skegness on 29 March and aircraft from 504 Squadron shot down an He 115 on 2 April. The Germans had shifted most of their bombing effort to Scandinavia, but they still focused on minelaying along the east coast.

Probably the last surface minelaying expedition mounted by the Germans for some time took place on 2 April. The German motor coaster, *Ulm,* laid a field of contact mines around Smith's Knoll near the Norfolk coast. At the end of the month, on 30 April, one of these mines claimed the Great Yarmouth-based minesweeper, *Dunoon.* There was a determined effort to drop more mines along the east coast on 17 April. In fact some of the German floatplanes actually landed to deploy their mines.

One He 111 caused devastation over Clacton on the night of 30 April/1 May. The aircraft had two mines on board, and it crashed around 200 m from the seafront. The locals, hearing the noise, came out to investigate, and suddenly there was an enormous explosion. Three houses were flattened and another fifty damaged, two civilians were killed and 156 injured. Unbelievably, one of the mines remained intact. Experts from HMS *Vernon* arrived to find that recovery workers were actually sitting on the mine. This was a complete, intact, red or reversed-polarity mine. The explosion had created a crater 25 ft across and 5 ft deep.

The Germans lost another aircraft that night when at 0016 one of their aircraft was spotted near Mistley, heading towards the sea. Anti-aircraft guns engaged it at Landguard Point. The crews did not think that they had hit anything, but there were reports that a burning aircraft had crashed into the sea off Walton-on-the-Naze.

Undeterred, the Germans launched more minelaying missions on the night of 3/4 May, with at least one aircraft crossing into Norfolk. More German aircraft were seen in the late afternoon of 7 May, possibly engaged in reconnaissance missions around King's Lynn and Norwich. There was another reconnaissance mission on 9 May around Norwich. Each of these reconnaissance flights was probably undertaken by a Do 17 of *KG76*.

By the middle of May most of the German long-range bombers were engaged on mainland Europe and were raiding Holland. Soon the Germans would have more bases to operate from and could act more freely against the British east coast. It was becoming increasingly obvious that once the battle for western Europe had been won the real battle for the east coast would commence.

CHAPTER TWO

Escape and Invasion

Early April 1940 saw the war take its next inevitable twist as the Germans made a massive gamble in order to secure vital iron ore and mineral supplies needed for their war effort. The target was Norway, then a neutral country. The German plan was for their navy to land troops along the Norwegian coast from Oslo to Narvik in order to protect the coastal waterways. It was an extremely risky undertaking, considering the weakness of the German navy compared to the Royal Navy. They had the element of surprise, but there was still the danger that having landed the troops the Royal Navy would move to cut them off. The Germans' ace card was *Fliegerkorps X*, with around 400 aircraft that had been trained in anti-shipping warfare.

The British were alerted by major German fleet movements at the beginning of April. All of the destroyers in Nore Command, comprising the 5th and 7th Flotillas, and half of the 1st's, were bound for Scapa Flow. They were intended to escort a major minelaying operation in Norwegian waters to disrupt the German iron ore shipping. The British had begun to muster troops and put them on board naval vessels ready to be landed in Norway, but many of these were disembarked when the Royal Navy decided that it needed its vessels, not as troop transports but to engage the German fleet at sea.

The Germans struck on 9 April, invading Norway and Denmark. Initially the German plans went well, with one notable exception: the German cruiser *Blücher* was sunk by gunfire and torpedoes off Oslo. This was to delay the German occupation of the capital, and many members of the Norwegian government, along with the royal family, managed to escape. The German fleet suffered further casualties when the *Hipper* was rammed by HMS *Glowworm*. HMS

Truant, a British submarine, managed to sink the German light cruiser *Karlsruhe*, and her sister ship was damaged off Bergen by shore batteries. This ship, the *Königsberg*, was finished off by Royal Navy dive-bombers operating out of the Orkneys. Two further German destroyers were sunk in Narvik harbour, but by the beginning of May the German air force was beginning to dominate the area. German ground forces had established themselves, and ultimately the British troops that had been landed were being forced to retreat and face evacuation.

Northern Norway was still being held, and reinforcements were being brought into Narvik. The force consisted of British, French, Norwegians and Poles, backed up by Gladiators and Hurricanes. The Germans finally overwhelmed Narvik on 28 May. In the evacuation the British aircraft carrier HMS *Glorious* was lost when it was engaged by the *Scharnhorst* and *Gneisenau*. The *Scharnhorst*, however, was seriously damaged by HMS *Acasta*. Soon afterwards *Gneisenau* was torpedoed by the British submarine HMS *Clyde*. By the end of the Norwegian campaign the Germans only had three cruisers and four destroyers that were still operational.

The Royal Navy and the Allies had suffered casualties too: HMS *Effingham* had been badly damaged, the anti-aircraft cruiser HMS *Curlew* had been sunk near Narvik and the French had lost a cruiser and a destroyer. The Poles had also lost a destroyer and the British had lost seven more. As a direct result of the failure of the British to prevent German occupation of Norway, Neville Chamberlain resigned as Prime Minister, and this would open the door for Britain's greatest war leader, Winston Churchill, to assume that office.

Throughout the Norwegian campaign the east coast of England had played a vital role. Troops were being ferried backwards and forwards from the Humber, Aberdeen, Lerwick and other harbours along the coastline. There was a lucky escape by a Grimsby fisherman, Tom Higgins. He had been on board the naval trawler *Hammond*, and had approached Norway on 20 April. They slipped into a fiord and came under enemy aircraft attack. The *Hammond* tried to avoid the bombs but hit a reef and sank. Higgins and the other survivors joined up with some British artillerymen near Andalsnes, over 200 miles to the north-west of Oslo. They were ultimately taken on board HMS *Glasgow*, along with a number of other refugees, including the King of Norway. HMS *Glasgow* dropped the King off at Tromsø and then headed for Scotland, and Higgins, along with some 170 other survivors, was safely landed.

On the morning of 10 May 1940 it was not the inhabitants of eastern England who heard the terrifying drone of German aircraft above them; it was the Dutch, Belgians, French and Luxembourgers. No declaration of war was made. Between 0430 and 0500 German paratroopers landed around Dutch airfields and German aircraft attacked a broad range of Dutch targets. It quickly became clear that the Dutch could not hold out against these determined attacks and the massive German spearheads of ground troops pushing into Holland.

French and British troops began manoeuvring to protect Holland and Belgium, and elements of the Royal Navy along the east coast of England headed towards Dutch ports to lend as much help as they could. A destroyer out of Dover, for example, landed Royal Marines from Chatham at Flushing in Holland to act as an advance party for French troops moving up through Belgium. On the same day a Dutch ship was set alight by German aircraft, and it was towed into the Thames and to safety. Other British destroyers headed for the Dutch coast: HMS *Galatea* and HMS *Arethusa* left Sheerness to collect the Dutch gold reserves at Ijmuiden.

By 12 May Holland was on the verge of collapse. German armoured units were launching themselves to link up with the airborne troops, and by the following day the situation had become critical. The Dutch royal family and the Dutch government were evacuated on board HMS *Codrington*, HMS *Hereward* and HMS *Windsor*. HMS *Walpole* left Harwich for Ijmuiden on the night of 13 May with orders to drop off a British intelligence officer and two Dutch civilians. Their mission was to bring back industrial diamonds to prevent them from falling into the hands of the Germans, and their mission was a complete success.

There was enormous activity on 13 May, with many civilian vessels desperately attempting to escape the German attacks in Holland. On the morning of 14 May six destroyers from Harwich headed for the Hook of Holland with the mission to try and evacuate as many of the Dutch army as possible. As it was, HMS *Malcolm* and three other destroyers loaded on civilian refugees instead. The Dover-based HMS *Wild Swan* was also dispatched to the Hook of Holland, where it dropped off a four-man party that travelled to Rotterdam by pilot boat to collect twenty-six tons of gold. Unfortunately the pilot boat hit a mine.

Smaller vessels from Felixstowe were also involved; they were tasked to act as reconnaissance boats for the destroyers. They assisted the destroyers in evacuating British citizens from the Amsterdam Consulate and a Royal Navy landing-party. These motor torpedo boats were making their way back at 2000 when they were attacked by German seaplanes. On board Lieutenant Parkinson's MTB-24, Able Seaman Stanley Aldridge shot down an He 115, and a Do 18 was also damaged in the attack. Two more MTBs left Felixstowe at 1230 on 14 May, and one of them, commanded by Lieutenant Gould, managed to make it to the Hook of Holland early that evening. He waited for two hours for demolition parties to arrive, but they never did, so instead the MTB took away a Dutch family, a Dutch naval officer and five British soldiers.

British vessels were still in operation at midnight that day, and in fact nine Harwich-based destroyers were waiting to evacuate members of the Dutch army, but by this stage the Dutch had surrendered, and reluctantly, at dawn the following day, the British vessels headed home. Some of the Dutch fleet had managed to escape: *Sumatra* had reached the Humber, *Birkja*, a minesweeper, *Brinlo* and *Grumlo*, both gunboats, along with the tug *Zwarte Zee*, a coaster, three motor boats and four trawlers, had reached Harwich. Several other vessels, including merchant ships, made it into the Thames Estuary and a handful of Dutch seaplanes landed at Felixstowe. On 19 May HMS *Princess Victoria* hit a mine in the entrance to the Humber. She was a minelayer that had been operating off the Dutch coast. Four officers and thirty-two ratings were lost in this incident.

Nore Command's involvement in operations along the European mainland was not over. By 24 May the British Expeditionary Force and a considerable part of the French army was cut off. Vessels were sent to evacuate troops from Boulogne and Calais. At Zeebrugge ships were sent to try to block the port. The destroyer HMS *Vega* was sent with block-ships as part of Operation Lyster. The British also planned to block Ostend, but were too late. The focus of attention now turned to Dunkirk, the famed Operation Dynamo, the mass evacuation of British and other Allied troops which began on 27 May. In all, some 338,226 troops would be evacuated by a fleet of some 850 vessels. Every single available vessel was sent to the beaches to try to assist. Initially it was planned just to pluck what remained of the British Expeditionary Force from almost certain capture. On 29 May, 47,000 were rescued, 54,000 on 30 May, 64,000 on 1 June and 60,000 on 2 June. On the final day 26,000 French troops were saved.

Various craft from the east coast of England were used in the operation. Back on 14 May the Royal Navy, under the direction of Admiral Lionel Preston, had started the Small Vessels Pool. This involved registering every private motor boat in the Thames Estuary between 30 ft and 100 ft long. The idea was to use them for harbour duties and for patrols. By 26 May the progress was hastened and as many as possible were requisitioned. Over a hundred small craft from the Upper Thames area alone journeyed to Dunkirk, with officers from the Royal Navy Volunteer Reserve and civilian volunteers. A huge number of vessels began assembling at Sheerness; some of them had never braved the Channel before. Feverish activity aimed to make sure that they were seaworthy and had fuel. Rear Admiral A.H. Taylor arrived at Sheerness on 27 May, and he and his engineers would be responsible for making sure that the fleet of sundry vessels was up to the job. Commander Troup, his second-in-command, set himself up as the pier master on the west mole at Dunkirk and personally supervised the evacuation of around 10,000 French soldiers. One of the vessels involved was the Harwich-based anti-aircraft cruiser HMS *Calcutta*. On board was Malcolm Muggeridge.

On 30 May a number of destroyers, including HMS *Vega*, HMS *Vimy*, HMS *Windsor* and HMS *Wolfhound* all left Sheerness as part of the operation. Even the paddle steamers were involved, including *Crested Eagle*, but she was hit by bombs near Dunkirk harbour and was burned out. The *Medway Queen* and *Queen of the Channel* were also involved in the operation, the latter being sunk on 28 May. Armed yachts were also involved out of Sheerness, including *Amulree*, *Caleta*, *Christobel II* and *Glala*. Gunboats, the *Locust* and *Mosquito*, made it to the east mole at Dunkirk. The *Mosquito* was sunk and the *Locust* was towed back by the sloop *Bideford*.

Sterling work was also carried out by the *Monarda*, commanded by Lieutenant Lovelock of the Royal Naval Volunteer Reserve, who would receive a Distinguished Service Cross for his actions. The *Monarda* picked up 120 British soldiers, five French sailors and fifteen wounded men, trapped on a French trawler that was about to sink. Not content with this, they then pulled a Hurricane pilot, Squadron Leader McGregor, out of the sea, and then twenty-five other men and forty British sailors who had become trapped on a badly damaged naval cutter.

A number of Dutch-style, flat-bottomed sail-boats were requisitioned by the Royal Navy from Gravesend, Sheerness and

Tilbury on 26 May. Most of the crew members were men from the Royal Naval Barracks at Chatham. They made for Ramsgate and then on to Dunkirk. Some Thames sailing-barges were also used, but several were lost or abandoned, including *Lady Roseberry*, *Ena* and *Beatrice Maud*. Even the Southend lifeboat, *Greater London*, went to Dunkirk. She managed to tow a Royal Navy minesweeper, HMS *Kellett*, out of Dunkirk harbour, with some 200 French soldiers on board.

HMS *Kellett* had been in North Shields but had made the journey down to Chatham and then on to Dunkirk. She had anchored in Dunkirk harbour and positioned scrambling nets over the side and crammed as many men in as could possibly be managed. Men even sat on the coal in the ship's bunkers. The first trip was straightforward enough, but she had come under attack on her second visit to Dunkirk, and the bridge was badly shot up by German aircraft. None the less, she managed to get back and head to Dunkirk for a third time. On board this time she had 200 French stretcher cases and other wounded, but HMS *Kellett* ran aground and snagged one of her screws on an underwater obstacle. It was only the prompt action of the crew of the *Greater London* that saved her, and HMS *Kellett* would return to her minesweeping duties along the east coast of England.

The former Southend pleasure-boat, *The New Prince of Wales*, and two other pleasure-launches, *Southend Britannia* and *Shamrock*, also made an appearance at Dunkirk. A crew of Sea Scouts manned *Minotaur*, a pinnace, and Tommy Trinder, the captain and owner of *Chelmondeslegh*, also made it to Dunkirk and back. The elder brother of Lawrence Olivier, skippering the *Marsayru*, rescued around 400 French troops. Other smaller vessels, such as *Silver Queen*, took off a thousand men, and *Constant Nymph* took 900. The London-based fire-float *Massey Shaw* managed to take 700 men. From Burnham-on-Crouch in Essex the yacht *Ma Joie*, the motor barge *Viking*, the oyster dredger *Vanguard* and the fishing smack *Seasalter*, all manned by civilian crews, made their contribution. Other vessels from Brightlingsea, Clacton and Sheerness were all in attendance. Sailing-barges from Colchester, including *Queen*, *Unique* and *Ethel Everard*, all made the journey to the Dunkirk beach, although the *Ethel Everard* was unfortunately abandoned off the French coast.

The Walton and Frinton lifeboat *EMED* with a naval crew commanded by Lieutenant Mead of the Royal Naval Volunteer Reserve suffered a near-miss on 1 June when shrapnel killed Mead and it was believed that the lifeboat had been sunk. But she was discovered on 3 June and towed back to Dover, and then made another trip back to Dunkirk.

Sailing-barges from Harwich, including *Aldie, Barbara Jean, Cabby, Hilda* and *Spinaway* all took part in Operation Dynamo, as did *Mizpah* from Ipswich and the Woodbridge launch *Pelagia.* Harwich also sent the army launch *Vulture,* fourteen trawlers and drifters, eight more launches, five corvettes, three salvage craft, three tugs, six destroyers, two motor torpedo boats, a pair of motor anti-submarine boats and the anti-aircraft cruiser HMS *Calcutta.* Harwich also saw the arrival of two auxiliary minesweepers from North Shields and six vessels from Rosyth. One of the motor anti-submarine boats, MASB-6, actually brought back Lord Gort, the Commander-in-Chief of the British Expeditionary Force, to Dover.

The destroyers based at Harwich approached the French coast on 29 May and came under determined attack by German aircraft. HMS *Greyhound* was badly hit by a bomb and had to be towed off, HMS *Grafton* was sunk by a German E-boat and HMS *Gallant* was lost. Both HMS *Grenade* and HMS *Jaguar* were also hit by bombs, and *Jaguar* had to be towed back to Harwich by *Forde,* a salvage vessel. *Forde* would also save the ferryboat *Royal Daffodil* on 30 May. In all, the Harwich-based destroyers and minesweepers brought back 6,900 troops to the port. The minesweepers had been in action on the night of 28 May when HMS *Marmion* had picked up men in a lifeboat and had also plucked troops from the beach. HMS *Oriole* ran aground, and with great ingenuity she remained there to act as a bridge for troops to cross and board larger vessels. She was then refloated and escaped with 700 troops on board. HMS *Waverley* had worked tirelessly to save as many men as possible, and on 29 May she returned 600 men to Dover. Two days later, again off Dunkirk, she attracted the attention of a dozen He 111s. She suffered a direct hit and 360 men were lost when she sank.

Further north, along the east coast of England, other smaller vessels made their way to the Dunkirk waters. The *Abdy Beauclerck* and *Lucy Lawers,* lifeboats from Aldeburgh, and the Southwold boat *Mary Scott* made valuable contributions. From Lowestoft came the lifeboat *Michael Stephens* and the motor boat *Elvin.* Great Yarmouth sent the trawlers *Thomas Bartlett* and *Thuringia,* but both of these vessels were sunk. The Gorleston lifeboat, *Lewis Stephens,* along with motor boats or former lifeboats from Blakeney, Brancaster, Sheringham and Wells also aimed to make the trip, but most only managed to get as far as the Thames. The minesweepers HMS *Dundalk*, HMS *Fitzroy*, HMS *Salamander* and HMS *Sutton*, along with the Army launch *Pidgeon*, came from Grimsby.

A huge number of the evacuees were not only landed at Ramsgate, Dover and Folkestone, but also at Margate. Tragically a magnetic mine claimed the French minesweeper *Emile Deschamps* near North Foreland on 4 June, claiming 400 lives. Scattered groups of evacuees would continue to arrive over the next few weeks, even after the French surrender. Many would land at Clacton, Southend, Sheerness and other points along the east coast of England. In fact individuals escaping from occupied Europe would continue to arrive for many months. A prime example was two Dutch naval officers, who had escaped from Holland in a motor dinghy and arrived at Southwold on 2 May 1941. Just three days later four Dutch civilians took off in a pair of light aircraft and made for the English coast. One of the aircraft crash-landed at Cove Hithe in Suffolk and the other made it to Broadstairs in Kent.

There were other, even more incredible, escapes, including two Dutchmen who had paddled in a rubber kayak for twelve days. They were found clinging to Buoy 54B at the end of June 1941 by a Harwich trawler. By the end of the war literally dozens had made the perilous trip across the North Sea to the safety of British shores. Well over a hundred had landed at Great Yarmouth alone. Not all of the refugees were what they seemed, however. In April 1942 a number of Dutchmen were found and brought into Harwich. They were interrogated by Dutch intelligence and one of the men was proved to be a German spy. He was later hanged at Wandsworth Prison. There was another bizarre incident in November 1941 when a light aircraft landed at Scratby in Norfolk. The two men on board claimed to be Dutch, but in fact had forged identity cards. It transpired that they were German prisoners of war who had stolen an aircraft from Carlisle airport.

While the scramble to save military personnel from the chaos of the fall of France took place, the east coast was bracing itself for the inevitable attention of the German air force. By early May 1940 the RAF had been mounting defensive sorties along the length and breadth of the coastline, using Blenheims and Spitfires. The RAF was shuffling its squadrons around to give maximum coverage and protection. Terror had been instilled in the British population when they read stories of German aircraft machine-gunning Dutch civilians and attacking columns of refugees in France who were fleeing from the fighting. What remained of the British Expeditionary Force had to be rapidly re-equipped as best as possible, and plans set in motion for what seemed to be the certainty of a German invasion attempt. Possibly the most dangerous and brutal period of the war for Britain had now begun. Britain now stood alone against an occupied European mainland. The *Luftwaffe* now had access to French, Belgian and Dutch airfields.

The Germans had been mounting reconnaissance missions across the east coast of England throughout May. A pair of Do 17s had been seen over Norfolk on 15 May, but the first attack would come against Suffolk on 22 May. These were the first enemy bombs to land on the east coast of England. They fell at 0032, between Landguard Point and Felixstowe pier. There were five high-explosive bombs, and another eight landed shortly afterwards near the Cork lightship. At 0155 the first bomb to actually fall on the east coast was a single high-explosive device. It failed to explode when it buried itself in a 3 ft crater to the west of Butley Church, near Woodbridge, close to RAF Bentwaters. Another two fell at 0516 off Felixstowe, shattering several windows along Manor Terrace.

Heinkel 111s of *KG27* attacked West Raynham airfield at 0035 on 25 May, but no damage was caused. Another bomb landed near Harleston in Suffolk and yet another near Loddon at 0120, this one killing a cow. Two bungalows were damaged at Burgh St Peter, two bombs were dropped on Raveningham and another fell at Aylsham in Norfolk. Essex also suffered its first air attack when at 0145 on 25 May a number of houses were damaged by a 50 kg bomb when it landed at Wickford, close to Southend.

The first civilian injury was suffered at Strumpshaw in Norfolk at 0200 on 2 June. The Germans also tried to hit RAF Mildenhall. Three days later, on 5 June, the first full-scale German aircraft attack was under way, targeting a number of different locations across the whole of eastern England. Fifteen bombs were dropped close to Swanton Morley at 0026. Other bombs were dropped at Horsham St Faith and Bircham Newton. Eight bombs were dropped at North Tuddenham at 0122, parachute flares were dropped over Stoke Holy Cross and a bomb dropped on a road junction near Buxton at 0035.

The Germans also dropped their first incendiary bombs on Britain that night. They were aiming for Duxford, but instead they fell at 0011 in a field at Newton in Cambridgeshire.

There were no fewer than 170 incidents during the night of 6/7 June. A number of German aircraft skirted Great Yarmouth and tried to bomb RAF Feltwell, which was already by then the home of a Wellington squadron. Another raid attempted to hit RAF Marham; it too was a Wellington bomber base. Five more bombs were dropped near RAF Mildenhall, and a 250 kg bomb was dropped on Bedfield in Suffolk.

The Germans reappeared the following night, 7/8 June, and this time a raid was mounted on RAF Honington, six miles from Thetford. Further attacks were made on Bircham Newton and RAF Wittington, and five bombs were dropped on Peterborough. An He 115 was illuminated by a British searchlight and the dazzled pilot crashed into the grounds of the Old Rectory in Eyke, near Woodbridge, at 2331. The floatplane had been carrying mines. Over the next few days there were a number of reconnaissance flights, notably over the East Anglia region, but there was little doubt that the raiders would soon be back in force.

Major German operations got back under way on the night of 18/19 June. Involved were at least seventy-one aircraft; their primary targets were airfields and the railway network, and twenty-one of the aircraft were assigned to destroy the oil tanks at Thameshaven. This was a bright, cloudless night, ideal for interception. As the He 111s approached their targets the first to be scrambled to intercept was 29 Squadron at Debden. Squadron Leader McLean and the other Blenheim crews took off at 2250. Spitfires of 19 Squadron out of Duxford were scrambled at 2315, and bizarrely they would be facing He 111s from the airfield at Merville, when only a month earlier it had been a British airbase. The Germans passed over Clacton at 2300 and dropped bombs on Clacton and Holland-on-Sea. The bombers appeared to be making for Bury St Edmunds in Suffolk. More He 111s crossed at Sheringham and managed to shoot down a Blenheim of 23 Squadron. However, another Blenheim that lifted off from RAF Wittering at 2238 shot down an He 111 at 0015. It crashed in Blakeney Creek and the crew was taken prisoner. Bombs were dropping around Hargrave, six miles from Bury St Edmunds. The Germans had intended to target RAF Stradishall. More bombs dropped at Rede and others at Bressingham. The Germans had also targeted RAF Marham, but one of the He 111s dropped fourteen bombs near to King's Lynn and others were dropped at Narborough. An attack on RAF Mildenhall saw a number of bombs drop around Culford. By this stage the skies were becoming increasingly more perilous for the Germans, as no fewer than six fighter squadrons had been scrambled and were hunting for the invaders.

The air raid warnings sounded in Cambridge at 2330 on the same night; the Germans were targeting railway installations. Bombs fell around Vicarage Terrace, and a number were dropped around Ely between 2340 and 0140. Essex also received unwelcome attention that night when bombs fell at Wodensford, Great Canfield and at Little Henham. There was also minor damage to some houses in Bury St Edmunds. An He 111 was shot down and crash-landed in Springfield Road in Chelmsford, having been crippled by a Spitfire of 74 Squadron.

By this stage fighters of 19, 23, 29, 66, 74 and 604 Squadrons were in the air. Pilot Officer Barnwell of 29 Squadron out of Debden had already shot-up an He 111 and caused damage to its port engine. He then flew on and found another He 111 over Debden at 0100. The hydraulics on Barnwell's Blenheim had been damaged in the previous engagement but he shot-up this second German raider, although his aircraft received even more damage in the process. Precisely what happened to Barnwell after this has never been clearly explained, but his body was found on the shore at Walton-on-the-Naze. We must assume that he chased another German target and came to grief.

Meanwhile, four Spitfire pilots of 19 Squadron had scrambled. They were Flying Officer Petra, Flying Officer Bell, Flying Officer Lawson and Flight Lieutenant Clouston. Petra was over Newmarket at around 0120 when he spotted an He 111 heading towards RAF Honington. It was illuminated by searchlights and trying to take evasive action. Just as Petra was about to open fire a Blenheim arrived. The searchlight now illuminated Petra's Spitfire and the German gunners fired at him. One of the explosive bullets punctured the Spitfire's fuel tank. With terrible injuries from the fire, Petra managed to bale out, and his aircraft crashed near Whelnetham Railway Station. Petra had managed to riddle the He 111 with tracers and it too was crippled. The German crew jettisoned their bombs and baled out; one of the crew members had already died. The aircraft crashed at 0148 close to the A11 road.

Meanwhile Flying Officer Bell had attacked another He 111 over Newmarket, and Squadron Leader O'Brien, in a Blenheim of 23 Squadron, had shot-up another He 111. Unfortunately the Blenheim started to spin out of control, and the navigator, Pilot Officer King, was killed by the propeller when he baled out. O'Brien managed to escape, but the air gunner was killed when the aircraft crashed. It may well be that both Bell and O'Brien had attacked the same He 111.

Pilot Officer Kells of 29 Squadron shot down another He 111 off Felixstowe. Pilot Officer Humphries of the same squadron claimed another near Harwich, as did anti-aircraft gunners at Harwich when they engaged a raider at 0113. In all the British claimed that they had shot down eleven German planes, but in actual fact it was more like five definite and two probable.

The *Luftwaffe* resumed its attacks on the east coast of England on the night of 21/22 June. Ipswich's air raid sirens sounded at 2305, as He 111s dropped their bombs close to the town and then hit the Dale Hall Lane area. Three more bombs, known as oil bombs, were dropped on Rede in Suffolk and near Brigg in Lincolnshire. These oil bombs were designed to work as incendiaries. They carried a tarry liquid and had TNT, charcoal and magnesium to set them alight. During the night a number of other bombs were dropped at Hollesley, Branfield, Martlesham, Felixstowe, Bungay, Harwich and Brightlingsea. There were also German aircraft around Colchester, Harleston, Orford Ness and Winterton. A number of bombs were dropped at all of these locations.

The Germans switched targets to industrial ones on the night of 24/25 June, but there were also attacks against Bircham Newton, Coltishall, Debden, Duxford, Mildenhall and Wittering. Two bombs were dropped on Bradwell near Great Yarmouth, and four at Tattersett. Most of these bombs were incendiaries, although a high-explosive bomb was dropped at Steeple Bumpstead in Essex.

Further attacks took place around midnight on 25/26 June. Incendiaries were dropped at Stiffkey and at Rudham at around 0100, but the following night saw incendiaries dropped around Newmarket and bombs on March, Peterborough, St Neots and Winterton. Shortly after midnight flares were dropped over Saxmundham and bombs fell close to Alderton, Pelgrave and Snape. More bombs fell near Alderton at 0223 and a number of bombs and incendiaries were dropped around Clacton.

An He 111 was shot down by Pilot Officer Williams and Pilot Officer Atkinson of 23 Squadron on the night of 28/29 June, but the Germans managed to launch attacks on Coltishall, Harwich and Honington. A number of bombs and incendiaries were dropped on Dunwich in Suffolk; more were dropped on Surlingham in south Norfolk, just seven miles from the city of Norwich. More bombs and incendiaries fell the following night, this time around March in Cambridgeshire and Cardington in Bedfordshire.

While these early raids were both sporadic and, in comparison to what would come later, relatively ineffective, there was the ever-present threat that there would be a German invasion along the east coast of England. In fact there had been fears of this since Holland had been overrun in May 1940. Given the fact that the bulk of available British troops were either in Norway or in Belgium at this time, there was a reasonable fear that the Germans might attempt at least a limited landing using paratroopers and light naval vessels against the east of England. At this stage the bulk of the coast was unguarded. Even important ports like Harwich, Dover and Felixstowe were relatively unprotected. Harwich, for example, could barely muster around 900 soldiers and a single battery of artillery.

The Royal Navy was first to move on this problem by setting up what became known as anti-invasion striking forces. One was set up in Dover and others in Harwich, Humber and Sheerness. They were not particularly impressive forces: the Harwich force consisted of three motorised anti-submarine boats; the 1st Destroyer Flotilla; HMS *Calcutta*, an anti-aircraft cruiser; and some antiquated submarines.

Many coastal towns, including Felixstowe, Great Yarmouth, Harwich, Lowestoft, Sheerness and Southend, had taken in huge numbers of evacuees from London. But now there was the problem that these people might well be directly at threat should a German invasion go ahead. Many were re-evacuated, and in fact the civilian population by the late summer of 1940 in most of these towns had dropped to just sixty per cent of the 1939 population levels. This meant that large numbers of houses and streets were requisitioned as billets for servicemen.

There was also the problem of potential spies in the area. Many checkpoints had been set up, particularly around coastal towns that had naval bases or areas close to airfields. Most normal seaside businesses were closed down and any property facing the sea was requisitioned and sandbagged. By June 1940 the bulk of the beaches had been mined, and obstacles and barbed wire stretched across the beaches to prevent landing-craft from using them.

Once the campaigns in Norway and in France had been lost, there was a period of reorganisation in Britain. But there was still chaos. Harwich, for example, was supposed to have forty destroyers, but

prior to the end of June 1940 it had just four. By the end of June
more destroyers in the shape of the 16th and 18th Flotillas arrived.
These were reinforced by minelaying destroyers belonging to the
20th Flotilla in early July, and by this stage Harwich could muster
seventeen destroyers; there were also seven more either being
refitted or *en route* to Harwich. Harwich, however, had an enormous
amount of coast to cover; it had to mount patrols as far north as
Sheringham and Cromer.

By late August the 5th Flotilla had set up at Immingham, where
it was supported by HMS *Aurora* and HMS *Galatea*, both light
cruisers. Sheerness now had the 21st Flotilla, although it was
responsible for patrolling the area round Dover in conjunction with
destroyers based at Portsmouth. Sheerness also had HMS
Birmingham and HMS *Manchester*, both cruisers.

An entirely new fleet was being established just days after the
Dunkirk evacuation. The Royal Navy plundered the available
manpower from the Royal Naval Reserve and the Royal Naval
Volunteer Reserve, and also the crews of trawlers and drifters. A
new base was set up at the Sparrow's Nest in Lowestoft and was
dubbed HMS *Europa*. An enormous number of trawlers, drifters and
other small vessels were pressed into action. This meant that by the
spring of 1941 Nore Command had requisitioned no fewer than 746
light naval craft, most of which were former fishing vessels (around
half) and pleasure boats (a quarter). The bulk of these drifters and
trawlers had been based at Grimsby, Great Yarmouth, Lowestoft,
Hull and innumerable Scottish ports, as well as Fleetwood in
Lancashire. The trawlers would tend to be used for minesweeping
work and for convoy escort. Many of these men that would form
the crews had actually seen service in the First World War. Not all
of the vessels were British, and indeed there were a number of
Belgian, Dutch and French vessels that had escaped from the
continent.

Effectively they would all become Auxiliary Patrol Vessels and
would be given a bewildering array of different armament to protect
themselves. Some had deck guns, while others had machine-guns,
and the crews were often armed with cutlasses and a bewildering
array of firearms. To begin with most of the men wore their own
clothes, but slowly but surely the crews were whipped into shape
and a semblance of naval discipline was instilled in them. Typically,
one of these vessels would patrol an area of up to eight miles. She
would stay out to sea for three to six days and then return to her

home port for two or three days for leave and refitting. Some of the vessels were designated to search for smuggled goods and enemy personnel.

Further precautions were taken to protect the approaches to harbours, such as Lowestoft and Great Yarmouth. A number of torpedo heads from the First World War period were laid in the approaches. They were connected by an electric cable. Effectively, until the electric cable was turned on the torpedoes were dead, but by flicking on the electricity they became live. In other places, such as the River Crouch, chains, small yachts and other obstacles were left to prevent seaplane landings. The anti-submarine booms across the River Humber, Thames and the approaches to Harwich were improved. Around 400 men were involved in looking after the boom between Shoeburyness and the Isle of Sheppey, a six-mile-long obstacle.

At the beginning of July 1940 Nore Command was slightly reorganised. A new sub-commander was established at Great Yarmouth. This command would now be responsible for the whole of the Wash as far as Mablethorpe in Lincolnshire to Minsmere, between Dunwich and Leiston in Suffolk. Felixstowe would now come under the direct control of Harwich.

While the Royal Navy was reorganising itself and attempting to put in place measures to intercept possible German invasion vessels, the Army was also hard at work trying to improve its own defences. The first immediate action was to reoccupy many of the batteries that had lain dormant since the First World War. Specifically these were around the Thames, the Medway and Humber, as well as at Lowestoft, Great Yarmouth and Harwich. The vast majority of the so-called Coast Regiments were in fact manned by Territorials. They were armed with an enormous variety of different-calibre weapons. Huge improvements began in May 1940, with many of the guns now being placed in concrete and steel emplacements. Many of the new guns used to improve the defences were Royal Navy surplus, and initially they were manned by sailors, who then trained Army personnel to use them.

There were still problems in terms of manpower. Ideally, a two-gun coastal battery, while only needing eight men to work each gun, actually needed more than ten times that number for it to operate effectively. Men were needed as lookouts and range finders, to operate searchlights, to defend the battery itself, to man the magazine, the electric generator and the anti-aircraft guns, as well as providing a host of other necessary support services, such as food and shelter, and handling stores. In some cases the guns were positioned in old forts, such as a pair of guns that were put into Garrison Point Fort at Sheerness, or the anti-aircraft guns that were fixed into a Martello tower at Felixstowe. Some of the sea defences were actually positioned on very inappropriate ground, such as the sandstone cliffs at Cromer or Happisburgh. There were also mobile guns, and some of these were vintage howitzers from the First World War, some stationed up to five miles inland.

As far as infantry was concerned, these would be needed to repel any invader should they land along the coastline. Consequently, a handful of available, under-strength divisions were initially deployed along the east coast of England. These were first deployed in June 1940 and they had not seen action. They were woefully under strength, in terms of vehicles, ammunition, weapons and training. One division, the 55th, had to control the entire Suffolk coast with just three brigades of men. One of their first tasks was to build pillboxes and set up weapons pits. Wherever it was possible and available, they would use barbed wire, sometimes they would build speed bumps into the roads and they used all sorts of improvised defence works to make up for the lack of manpower. Most of their heavy armament was of course of First World War vintage, and in order to give some of their weapons mobility, smaller guns, such as the 6-pdr, were mounted on the backs of trucks. Around the naval bases and airfields were other units, usually at company or platoon strength, although the RAF and the Royal Navy organised their own local defences wherever possible.

On 25 May 1940 Winston Churchill launched the Local Defence Volunteers, or the Home Guard, and the following day hundreds of men turned up at public meetings to enrol. Over the next crucial months they would provide vital reinforcement as armed sentries and patrols, protecting gas works, railway stations, telephone exchanges and other strategic targets. They would keep lookout for enemy parachutists and downed enemy pilots, and they would routinely man road-blocks, direct traffic and carry out many other necessary duties.

The threat of invasion was very real; according to intelligence sources the Germans had mustered over 8,000 barges in Belgium and 18,000 in Holland. It was firmly believed that up to 5,000 of these barges would be used to invade the east of England and that the Germans would unleash ten divisions against the east coast.

There would also be constant rumours, particularly in August 1940, that an invasion could be launched from Norway. In fact on 13 August the entire Nore Command was given half an hour's notice that an invasion was in progress, but luckily it was a false alarm.

Another bizarre incident happened five days later when coastal vessels and those ground units protecting the coast were told to look out for unnatural fog. This was believed to be produced by the Germans to cover their invasion fleet. There were innumerable false alarms, but it was in fact just sea mist.

Nore Command, on 26 August, issued Operational Order P2, which warned that if any units received the signal 'Purge' they were to immediately engage enemy transport vessels. On 31 August Nore Command was once again put on alert; there were rumours that German transports were heading for the east coast from Holland. The 5th Destroyer Flotilla left the Humber, cruisers came down from Scotland and destroyers out of Harwich and Sheerness headed out to engage. There was, of course, no invasion, but there was a disaster.

The 20th Destroyer Flotilla, based at Immingham, headed for the Frisian Islands. Three of the destroyers, HMS *Express*, HMS *Esk* and HMS *Ivanhoe*, all hit mines at around 2300 in an uncharted minefield. HMS *Esk* went down with all but one of her crew, HMS *Express* suffered ninety killed or fatally wounded. HMS *Ivanhoe* was only slightly damaged, but as she tried to save the wounded from HMS *Express* she hit a second mine and began to sink. Vessels from the 5th Flotilla came to assist. Captain Mountbatten, on board HMS *Jupiter*, sped to help HMS *Express*, assisted by HMS *Garth* and HMS *Hambledon* of the 21st Flotilla. HMS *Javelin* tried to find what was left of HMS *Esk*, while other destroyers and minesweepers searched for survivors, protected by half a dozen Blenheims.

It took an enormous amount of time to save the men, and the vessels were still at risk on 1 September. Motor torpedo boats from Felixstowe arrived at dawn on 1 September to help take off the wounded from HMS *Ivanhoe*, and it took them three hours before they could get under way. In all some 300 men had been killed and over a hundred seriously wounded. This was Nore Command's worst day in terms of casualties since Dunkirk. As for the alert and the German invasion fleet, it was another false alarm.

It was still an extremely dangerous situation; there was firm evidence that the Germans had over 200 barges at Ostend. Some German spies had been captured in Kent and another had been picked up after he had parachuted into Northamptonshire. On 7 September the Germans made their first daylight raid on London; it now seemed that invasion was imminent, and consequently at 2100 the codeword 'Cromwell' was issued to all units. It meant that the invasion was imminent, not that an invasion was under way. None the less, there was confusion, and the skies, sea and land were scoured for the enemy, but all to no avail. By 10 September the invasion imminent alert had been reduced to one of just alert. There were rumours that the Germans had abandoned their invasion fleet and that the intended landings had been called off. This was also untrue, as the Germans had 1,600 barges ready and were still seriously considering their options.

Plans had been set in motion to launch Operation Lucid. This would involve towing two tankers that had been fitted at Sheerness and at Chatham into Calais and Dunkirk harbours and setting them alight to destroy the German invasion fleet. Three times the operation was due to get under way and three times it was called off.

Although there was no invasion in 1940, it was fully expected either in the spring or the summer of 1941. As far as the defenders of the east coast were concerned this would give them time. The garrisons at naval bases were doubled and they were given more artillery and inland defences were improved. Lincolnshire, Norfolk and Essex received more troops and field divisions were withdrawn so that they could train and become more mobile and respond to any possible invasion threat. However as the summer of 1940 continued, the *Luftwaffe* would return in ever greater numbers and cause even greater devastation.

CHAPTER THREE

Air Attack

A lthough it is now clear that the Germans never intended to
land anywhere north of Ramsgate, in other words at any
point along the east coast of England, this was not known
at the time. The British were also unaware of the fact that the failure
of the *Luftwaffe* to sweep the RAF from the skies had caused the
permanent cancellation of Operation Sealion. The naval, army and
air force defenders, coupled with the Home Guard and civilians,
were unaware that all of their fears of an invasion were unfounded.
What was more concrete, however, was the escalating scale of
Luftwaffe operations against Britain.

In order to view this with any kind of perspective we need to turn
the clock back to the beginning of July 1940 and examine how,
gradually, the *Luftwaffe* used its full strength and terror in order to
cause irreparable damage and harm along the whole of the east
coast of England. This was also at a time when the convoys moving
north to south and south to north along the east coast came under
increased attack. In fact we can typify the air war over the east coast
as being a three-fold operation. First the *Luftwaffe* was seeking
targets, both military and civilian infrastructure, on the east coast
mainland. Secondly it was striking at coastal targets, notably the
naval bases. Finally it was seeking to interdict and destroy as many
convoy vessels as possible that were using the east coast route. We
will first turn our attention to the *Luftwaffe* attacks from the summer
of 1940.

Even while the fighting in France was still continuing the Germans
made small-scale attacks against British airfields around the Wash
and the Humber. These took place on the nights of 24/25 May and
5/6 June 1940. The ports along the eastern coast were hit on the night
of 18 June. This time oil tanks seemed to be the main target, as

German aircraft struck Harwich, Sheerness and Chatham, Saltend, Killingholme and Thameshaven. At Thameshaven the Germans destroyed 12,000 gallons of oil. On that night the RAF claimed five He 111s, but lost two Blenheims of its own. The German aircraft were shot down near Sheringham, another at Margate, one close to Cambridge, another near Chelmsford and the fifth off Felixstowe.

The Germans appeared with even greater force on the night of 21/22 June. It has been estimated that around a hundred aircraft were involved, and the targets were oil depots close to the Thames Estuary, but they also struck Brightlingsea, Derby, Felixstowe, Grimsby, Harwich, Hull, Ipswich and Lowestoft. Although three civilians were killed in Ipswich the Germans achieved very little else from this raid.

On 1 July an He 111, flying out of Norway, again struck Saltend, targeting oil tanks. It was only the prompt action of civilians and firemen, who were later to be awarded George Medals, that saved the precious oil from being lost. As for the He 111, it was shot down over the North Sea by a Spitfire of 616 Squadron.

In broad daylight, at 1255 on 3 July, a Do 17 of *KG77* dropped nineteen bombs around Walberswick. More Dorniers attacked the coastline between Bawdsey and Harwich between 1600 and 1700. Shortly after 1600 another Dornier attacked Felixstowe; it was chased by four British fighters and it was forced to jettison its bombs about 20 m from the shore near Rede Pond. Frinton was also hit, as was Wrabness near Manningtree in Essex. Shortly before 1530 a German aircraft had dropped a stick of twenty 50 kg bombs on Ipswich, and one person was killed, with seventeen people injured, and many houses were damaged. Lowestoft also came under attack, this time a Do 17 dropped bombs around Clapham Road, killing three. However, one of the bombs hit the Co-op store, which burst into flames. The shop was also being used as a shelter, and had it not been for the prompt action of the fire brigade and others many more would have been killed. In total Lowestoft had suffered four killed, five seriously wounded and twenty other injuries.

Over the night of 3/4 July the German planes struck the Blythe area and several targets in Essex, and had in all targeted sixteen towns and villages in Essex and Suffolk, most of which were close to strategic targets. This suggests that many of the bombs landed on civilian targets in error. One bomb, dropped by a Ju 88, had struck Brooks flour mill in Manningtree, Essex, and the blaze took three days to get under control.

The daytime bombing on 7 July saw three bombs drop near West Raynham, and before 1000 hours the following day anti-aircraft guns engaged German aircraft *en route* to Ipswich. At around the same time an He 111 dropped bombs close to Clacton. It was chased out to sea by 17 Squadron Hurricanes, and they managed to shoot the Heinkel down. The attack on Ipswich began to develop at around 1025. Braving anti-aircraft fire, a Do 17 dropped ten bombs around the dock area. Amazingly none of the bombs exploded. An He 111 emerged three minutes later; it was immediately chased off by Hurricanes of 85 Squadron and it was shot down two minutes later, six miles out from Felixstowe. The final attack in daylight hours took place during the afternoon, as bombs were dropped on Horsey Island in Essex and Harwich. Later that night, at 2315, more German aircraft attempted to bomb Ipswich, but they were driven off by anti-aircraft fire. The Germans also made an attempt to bomb the airfield at Martlesham, but missed by a considerable distance.

Further north, on 8 July, a Ju 88 was shot down by 249 Squadron. It crashed at Aldbrough in East Yorkshire, inland to the west of Darlington. A farmer's wife took one of the crew prisoner and was later awarded the OBE. To the south, at Martlesham, Hurricanes of Nos 17 and 85 Squadrons now had responsibility to deal with daytime attacks. Spitfires of 66 Squadron were joined by Hurricanes of 242 Squadron at Coltishall. 242 Squadron became operational on 9 July and was commanded by Squadron Leader Douglas Bader. At Duxford and Fowlmere 19 Squadron had been established.

So far, the city of Norwich had rarely suffered from the raids, but this was all to change at 1700 on 9 July. The target was the riverside factory of Boulton & Paul. Around eleven bombs were dropped by Do 17s and Ju 88s, and some of them must have been incendiaries. Tragically, the incident coincided with the workers coming off their shift. Other reports suggest that at least twenty bombs had been dropped. Incredibly, in the main engineering shop, no one was killed or injured. Up to five bombs went through into the wire-weaving workshop, and ten were killed and almost seventy people were wounded. A couple of bombs also dropped on the railway lines at Thorpe Station. Just as the Boulton & Paul employees were coming off shift, so too were the Colman workers at the Carrow Road factory. A bomb burst in the air, maiming twenty people. More bombs fell on Barnard's ironworks at Mousehold, where two of their workers were killed and a strafing attack killed another woman. Spitfires of 66 Squadron chased the German planes but they managed to escape. A Heinkel He 111 was, however, shot down by 17 Squadron some distance off the Stour.

There were more German attacks that same night when bombs fell at Ringsfield and others near Blythburgh in Suffolk. West Raynham airfield was also targeted, and several Dorniers overflew Southwold at 0515, dropping their bombs close to Martlesham airfield. A few minutes earlier RAF Honington had also been attacked. There were more attacks across the whole of the day of 10 July; bombs and incendiaries were dropped on RAF Honington again and on Weybourne. A Do 17 was shot down off Winterton by 66 Squadron and an He 111 by 242 Squadron.

The first activity on 11 July saw incendiaries and high explosives dropping around Arkesden and Newport in Essex. There were also early incursions around Cromer and Lowestoft. One of these attacks was intercepted by three Hurricanes of 85 Squadron. A Do 17 shot-up the Hurricane flown by Squadron Leader Peter Townsend, and his aircraft crashed some distance into the sea off Harwich. Shortly after 0600 a Do 17 machine-gunned Cromer and then dropped fourteen bombs on the town. The first two bombs hit the beach station and a nearby house where one person was killed and two were injured. Another fell in Hans Place, and yet another killed a newsagent and his sister in Church Street. A further bomb came in straight through a toilet window at Brunswick House and failed to explode, but lodged itself in the basement of the house. A café on the eastern promenade was destroyed and the Do 17 shot-up the lifeboat and station. An hour later Wells was machine-gunned by another Do 17. Great Yarmouth was also targeted by another Do 17, and later in the day, after 2200, eighteen bombs fell around Ipswich docks. Although there were several injuries fortunately no one was killed.

At 0700 on 12 July it became clear that a number of He 111s and Do 17s were targeting a convoy moving north along the east coast of England. Shortly before 0900 a flight of 17 Squadron was sent up to intercept. They came across He 111s about to make dive-bomb attacks on the ships, which were now near Felixstowe. One of the He 111s was shot down and crash-landed off Orford Ness, and another He 111 was shot down and a second damaged by 85 Squadron's Hurricanes. One Hurricane was lost when it crashed into the sea off the coast of Felixstowe. The Do 17s were now engaged by 17 Squadron, and one was shot down at around 0905. Eleven Hurricanes of 115 Squadron out of North Weald now arrived. The Dorniers had assumed a tight defensive formation and managed to shoot down Flying Officer Allan, but Pilot Officer Halman managed to shoot down one of the Dorniers at around 0932. During all of this the German aircraft managed to sink one vessel, *Hornchurch*, just off Aldeburgh.

During the night of 14/15 July the Germans dropped a number of mines in the area from Flamborough Head to the Wash. Further mines were dropped in the early hours of 15 July between Orford Ness and North Foreland. The Medway towns were struck on 18 July and five were killed at Gillingham. The Germans, although they were concentrating their forces for a major assault on the south of England, continued to try to bomb convoys. Shortly after midnight on 18 July a German aircraft hit a barrage balloon cable over Harwich, but it is not known what happened to this aircraft. The Germans, however, pressed home attacks against shipping off Felixstowe; the town itself was hit, as was Colchester and Braintree.

The Germans continued to drop mines, primarily off Suffolk, in the early hours of 19 July. At around 0615 that morning a single German aircraft dropped high explosives on a number of Norwich streets, including Bull Close Road, Magdalen Street, Botolph Street, St George Street, Pitt Street and the Norwich Aero Club rooms. The following day a Ju 88 crashed at St Osyth in Essex and its four-man crew was taken prisoner.

A Ju 88 on weather reconnaissance duties was shot down in the afternoon of 23 July by Flight Lieutenant Powell-Sheddon of 242 Squadron. Another Ju 88 came in to bomb Harleston, but it too was chased off by aircraft of 242 Squadron. Shortly before 1700 that day a Do 17 dropped sixteen high explosives on the weapons store at RAF Pulham, some eighteen miles to the south of Norwich. RAF Pulham had originally been RNAS Pulham and had served as an airship station during the First World War. The Dornier had scored a spectacular hit, wrecking the former airship shed and a hangar annexe. But it was not just static targets that came under attack from the *Luftwaffe*. On 24 July, in the afternoon, German aircraft tried to destroy a pair of trains to the south-east of Colchester.

Shipping was targeted in the afternoon of 29 July by Do 17s and He 111s. Protecting the convoy, which was around forty-five miles to the east of Felixstowe, were Hurricanes of 85 Squadron. To its south was 17 Squadron, which managed to shoot down one of the attackers, and 66 Squadron was to the north. They also managed to shoot down an He 111 to the south-east of Lowestoft. Another raider was shot down near Hammond's Knoll, but the damage had been done; mines had been laid. *Clan Monroe* and *Moidart* were both lost on 29 July to the mines.

Norwich received unwelcome attention on 30 July. The raiders crossed the east coast at Great Yarmouth at around 0537. Bombs were dropped around Argyle Street, Compass Street, Surrey Street and Victoria Terrace. The printing department at Colman's Carrow Lane works was also hit. At Victoria Terrace ten people had been killed. The bombs were believed to have been dropped by a single bomber at around 0600, when it then fled home, crossing the coast at Kessingland.

The last day of July and the first day of August saw more bombing raids around Suffolk, and at around 1515 a Ju 88 dropped bombs that fell once more on Boulton & Paul's riverside works. These were the first incendiaries, and they all but gutted the joinery department and the office. The Ju 88 also machine-gunned the streets of Norwich. Three high-explosive bombs fell on Thorpe station, and this single attack by the Ju 88 caused the death of thirteen people, fifty-nine were badly injured and a further seventy-two were wounded.

The same day saw the Germans targeting another convoy along the east coast, this time off Norfolk. For an hour and a half, from 1800 hours, a number of Ju 88s and He 111s attacked the ships. Sergeant Richardson of 242 Squadron managed to shoot down one of the Ju 88s, and another crash-landed after it had been badly damaged by Flying Officer Christie. The Germans came back to try to attack the convoy again during the night, and as many as seventeen enemy aircraft were spotted this time.

There was a drop in activity over the next couple of days, although Freckenham, between Soham and Mildenhall, was bombed, as were Clare and Cosford. A Do 17 was shot down in the early morning of 6 August, and two days later an Army camp near Bawdsey was machine-gunned, and Southwold was bombed that night. Over the night of 9/10 August the Germans tried to shoot down barrage balloons around Harwich, and at around midnight Alwalton, Framlingham, Harleston, Southwold and Stowmarket were all bombed. This was the second time Southwold had been bombed in the same day; two bombs had demolished three houses in Lorne Road. During the day of 10 August bombs fell on Hethersett and three bombs narrowly missed Norwich City Football Club's ground. Under cover of darkness more German aircraft attacked the RAF airfields at Bircham Newton, Horsham St Faith and Watton.

The Germans were switching from raids on convoys to trying to knock out RAF airfields and radar stations. But before this switchover they tried to attack another convoy off Harwich on 11 August. This time Do 17s escorted by Me 110s made the attack. Spitfires of 74 Squadron engaged and Squadron Leader Mungo Park shot down an Me 110, and two other claims were made by other pilots from the squadron. Yet another Me 110 was lost to 17 Squadron's Hurricanes, and Squadron Leader Peter Townsend of 85 Squadron damaged another. Two Spitfires, however, were lost off Clacton.

Effectively the next phase was all part of the Battle of Britain, as 12 August 1940 was the prelude to *Adler Tag* ('Eagle Day'), the *Luftwaffe's* main offensive against Fighter Command. Manston airfield and Dunkirk were targeted, with at least a hundred bombs dropped by Me 110s on Manston alone. Eagle Day, officially 13 August, saw the Germans targeting RAF Detling, near Maidstone in Kent and RAF Eastchurch, on the Isle of Sheppey. In the two attacks twenty-three aircraft were destroyed on the ground and seventy RAF personnel were killed. What the Germans did not know was that these stations were Coastal Command bases and not Fighter Command.

On 14 August at least fourteen bombs were dropped on Felixstowe at around 1733. They fell across Station Road, Chaucer Road, Highfield Road, Leopold Road and Cobbold Road, but luckily only one person was injured. The following day there were major daylight raids on east coast airfields. The Germans began by bombing Dover and RAF Hawking at around 1100 hours. They then turned their attention to RAF bomber airfields in Yorkshire. Shortly after 1500 RAF Martlesham came under attack when nine Ju 87s dropped bombs, quickly followed by half a dozen Me 110s that dropped a number of bombs and incendiaries. The attack took the anti-aircraft gunners by complete surprise. These attacks were swiftly followed by a dozen more Me 110s, protected by some Me 109s. Three Hurricanes of 17 Squadron at Martlesham were scrambled just in time, but they could not stop the Me 110s from dropping eighteen bombs on the airfield, which effectively put it out of action for two days. The Hurricanes gave chase and over Felixstowe Flight Lieutenant Harper shot down an Me 109 before he too was shot down. Three other Hurricanes of 1 Squadron that had been sent up to assist were also lost.

Meanwhile, up to thirty Do 17s of *KG3* smashed the satellite fighter field at Rochester and did damage to Shorts' aircraft factory. Ju 88s operating out of Denmark destroyed ten Whitley bombers on the ground at Driffield airfield but six of the raiders were shot down over the North Sea. Elsewhere, north-west Essex was targeted when bombs were dropped at Elsenham and at Broxted.

The next day, 16 August, proved to be just as frantic. There was low cloud cover, which meant that it was almost impossible for the Germans to target fighter bases in Essex, and so they tried their luck on other targets. A large number of He 111s, having been foiled in their attempts to attack the fighter bases, hit Tilbury docks and Harwich instead. At Tilbury they badly damaged a cargo liner, *Clan Forbes*, and also hit a factory in Northfleet. Shotley naval barracks was hit; Harwich received attention, as did Felixstowe. It was a later raiding force that was engaged by Spitfires of 19 Squadron. The Spitfires were on their way back from Coltishall, bound for Duxford, and they were told to intercept an enemy force that was approaching Clacton. In fact they encountered a large number of He 111s, covered by around fifty Me 109s and Me 110s. The Spitfires focused on the Me 110s and two were shot down, one by Flight Sergeant Unwin and another by Sergeant Potter. In the ensuing struggle bombs and incendiaries were dropped on Harwich beach and on the town's Guild Hall, Manningtree station, Halstead and Saffron Walden.

There seems to have been little activity on 17 August, but on the following day, at 0400, Leiston was machine-gunned and bombs were dropped on Bedingfield and incendiaries on Harwich. In the afternoon of 18 August around a dozen Me 109s strafed RAF Manston, wrecking a pair of Spitfires on the ground. Later in the day fifty He 111s and twenty-five Me 110s acting as escorts were on their way to bomb North Weald. Due to the low cloud they could not see their target so they turned back and were intercepted by RAF fighters operating out of Debden, Foulness, Martlesham and North Weald. In the ensuing battle four German bombers and four fighters were shot down at the cost of five RAF fighters. Most of the German bombers dropped their bombs out to sea, but one landed on Shoeburyness, killing three people. One of the Hurricane pilots was saved by the crew of the Barrow Deep lightship, and another RAF pilot, having baled out, landed on Whitstable golf course. He was amazed to hear one of the members of the club moaning that the sound of aircraft above had put him off his game.

On 19 August the German operations were almost continuous; Clacton was hit at 0100 and again at 1715. Coltishall suffered four dead and twenty-five injured when it was dive-bombed at 1415, and the raider disappeared over the coast at Cromer. RAF Honington was bombed at 1615, and this time the He 111 was chased by Spitfires of 66 Squadron, but they lost it to the east of Cromer. No. 66 Squadron had already shot down an Me 110 off Aldeburgh earlier in the day. Do 17s of *KG2* were engaged by Spitfires of 19 Squadron off the Suffolk coast at 1820, and one of the raiders was shot down. Bombs fell on brickworks in Colchester, as well as a timber yard and a printing works. For most of the night the activity shifted west towards the Midlands, but East Anglia in particular suffered indiscriminate night-time bombing as German aircraft jettisoned their loads before returning home, leading to bombs dropping on Harleston, Honington, Stowmarket and Watton.

It was no quieter on 20 August: nine bombs were dropped on Southwold at around 1540 and they landed around Hotson Road, near the pier and on Reydon field. No sooner had the civilians and authorities begun to clear up after this attack than another raid developed, with thirteen bombs falling. No fewer than twelve different areas of East Anglia were attacked by single raiders on 20 August. There was an unconfirmed kill off Clacton when Pilot Officer Cappons of 257 Squadron claimed that he had seen a Do 17 with smoke coming out of its port engines after his attack. Another Do 17 of *KG2* was spotted off Southwold at 1800, and Flying Officer Mitchell of 257 Squadron intercepted, killing the rear gunner. The Dornier then disappeared into clouds. Yet another Do 17 dropped bombs on Great Yarmouth, and they hit High Road, Suffolk Road and the Ferry Hill electricity substation. In the attack Mr S. Wright of Gorleston was injured. One raid of around 190 aircraft managed to penetrate the Thames Estuary, but it was driven off. Shortly before 1500 there had also been an attack by twelve German aircraft against RAF Manston, and attacks were also made on Chelmsford and on Lowestoft, and a convoy to the east of Dunwich was also targeted. Norwich had also suffered early that morning when at around 0600 incendiary bombs had been dropped around the Guild Hall and in Magdalen Street.

Airfields across the east and down into the south coast of England were targeted by no fewer than 200 raids on 21 August. One of the first attacks took place at 0800 when bombs landed on RAF Bircham Newton. RAF Stradishall was also targeted, and a Do 17 was shot down to the west of Harleston shortly after noon by Sub-Lieutenant Gardner of 242 Squadron. Lowestoft was bombed for the third time at 1612: a single Do 17 dropped at least twelve bombs in the Belvedere Road area of the town. One fell directly on an air raid shelter in an engineering works, killing four people and wounding three others. Lowestoft's total casualties for the day were six killed and seven injured. The Germans also targeted shipping off Southwold, and this meant that Southwold once again received two bombs, which damaged a building in Lorne Road. Further inland Newmarket was hit, as were Weyland, Debden and Depwade. During the day a fighter of 66 Squadron damaged a Dornier off Great Yarmouth and a pilot of 611 Squadron shot down a Do 17, the body of one of the crew members being found after the aircraft had crashed into the sea off Brancaster Staithe. The crew of one Do 17, whose aircraft had been shot down by Flying Officer Brooker of 56 Squadron, faced a hostile welcome when their parachutes landed them in Ipswich.

A single Do 17 approached Duxford at 0913 on 23 August, and it was engaged by anti-aircraft guns. The Dornier was crippled and it jettisoned its bombs near Babraham before force-landing at Wickhambrook. The Germans also attempted to attack a convoy off Orford Ness but they fled, jettisoning their bombs. For three-quarters of an hour after 1900 a number of German bombers began to approach Dover, Deal and Manston. Fighters from six RAF squadrons were scrambled to intercept, and although the bombers only managed to drop a number of bombs on RAF Manston, it was sufficient to make it unserviceable.

During the day of 24 August there was little activity due to relatively poor weather conditions, but in the evening bombs were dropped near King's Lynn, Halesworth in Suffolk and at Gorleston. In the Gorleston raid around twenty bombs dropped in the Cliff Hill, Beach Road and Bells Marsh Road area. One person was killed and five were injured. In all, ten buildings were demolished and ten more were badly damaged. In the north Bridlington had been bombed at 0250, causing considerable damage. The German bombs had hit a café and several people had become trapped; ultimately four were killed, with one being injured. The night of the 24th saw Hull's first air raid take place. A single aircraft killed seven civilians in the Rustenburg Street area. The aircraft had been making for Immingham. Earlier in the morning there had been two small raids off East Anglia, and once again Gorleston was attacked. In the afternoon Spitfires had engaged around fifty Me 109s and Me 110s that were covering a bomber attack on North Weald. As a result bombs were dropped across many parts of central and southern Essex, including Hornchurch and Dunmow. The fighters from 19 Squadron claimed a number of kills; Squadron Leader Lane shot down an Me 110 and Sergeant Jennings did better, shooting down two. Shortly after 1600 an He 111 crashed, killing the crew, five miles from Colchester, at Layer, and an Me 109 crash-landed at Great Warley. During the day RAF Manston had been attacked once again, and this forced the RAF to evacuate. Ramsgate suffered bombing, causing damage to the gas works.

Once more there was little activity during 25 August, until the evening, when the Germans were now targeting airfields in the east and more distant targets in the Midlands. The airfields targeted included Bircham Newton, Bury St Edmunds, Duxford, Feltwell, Marham, Newmarket, Upwood, West Raynham and Wyton. Cambridge was also targeted. The Germans made for the instrument works on Arbury Road, and it was here that sights and periscopes for submarines were being made. The incendiaries actually fell on farmland.

In the early morning of 26 August an He 111 dropped a number of bombs around Royston and St Ives, where several buildings were damaged and a cow was killed. Another He 111 dropped bombs on railway installations near Cambridge, but most of these fell harmlessly into playing fields. At around 1422, upwards of 190 German aircraft crossed the British coast from the Blackwater Estuary to Lympne. It was clear that their objectives were RAF airfields. Part of the formation of Do 17s, protected by Me 110s, headed along the River Crouch towards Hornchurch. Hurricanes of No. 1 Squadron, Royal Canadian Air Force, intercepted them, claiming two Me 110s. Flying Officer Edwards was also lost. The Canadians pressed home their attacks, shooting down a Do 17, which crashed near Thaxted. There were unconfirmed reports of a second Dornier having been shot down; it may well have been the aircraft that had crash-landed at Whepstead in Suffolk. An attack then came in on Debden; the Germans were engaged by anti-aircraft fire, which managed to shoot one down that crashed at Cole End. At least twenty Me 110s dropped bombs and strafed the runway at Debden, where five were killed and fourteen injured. The Germans also indiscriminately bombed targets around Debden. Czech pilots of 310 Squadron now engaged the raiders, and the Dorniers and Me

110s fled for the coast. Any bombs that had not already been dropped were now jettisoned, hitting a number of targets across Essex. Squadron Leader Blackwood of 310 Squadron managed to engage a Dornier, but it fired back and he had to bale out over Wickham Bishop. Pilot Officer Fechtner claimed an Me 110, and an Me 109 fifteen miles out from Harwich shot-up Pilot Sergeant Prchal's Hurricane, but he managed to force-land close to Upminster. Pilot Officer Obergman was also forced to bale out over Southminster.

The Germans launched some reconnaissance flights the following day, and a Do 215, a light bomber often used as a reconnaissance aircraft, was shot down near Chelmsford. During the night there were a number of raids across East Anglia and the Germans also laid mines along the coast between the Wash and the Tees. Rochester, Chatham and Gillingham in Kent were all dive-bombed. The attacks were made shortly before 0200 on 28 August, and Gillingham seemed to have been the main objective, where twenty people were killed when bombs hit the bus depot. At around 1300 on 28 August about a hundred German aircraft crossed between Dungeness and North Foreland. Rochford received the bulk of the attention this time, and the raiders returned between 1550 and 1645, hitting a number of targets around the Thames Estuary and in Kent. There were more raids at 1900, again against Kent and the Thames Estuary.

From 2300 hours on 29 August a number of raids were launched against Debden and Duxford. In fact German bombs fell not only on these two towns, but also on Grantham and on Felixstowe. While a raid was broken up by 66 Squadron a Do 215 was shot down off Great Yarmouth, but at around 1100 on 30 August a hundred German aircraft passed over Dungeness and Dover. They were followed an hour later by another hundred. Their targets appeared to be across Kent and Surrey, but some attacked the Thames Estuary area. No fewer than 300 German aircraft were involved in a raid shortly before 1600, when they concentrated mainly on east Kent, but also hit targets at North Weald, Hornchurch and Debden. No fewer than thirteen RAF squadrons were involved that day, claiming nearly thirty kills.

The so-called 'Battle of Brightlingsea' took place on 31 August; it began with high-level reconnaissance flights over Norfolk, Suffolk and Essex, as well as the Thames Estuary. A mixed force of Do 17s and Me 110s reached the Blackwater at 0807 and turned inland, making for Debden and Duxford. Duxford anti-aircraft units began engaging them at around 0830; at least 120 high-explosive bombs landed around Meldreth, just ten miles from Cambridge, and incendiaries were dropped around Fowlmere. The Germans now headed for home and were engaged by Spitfires of 19 Squadron. Flight Lieutenant Clouston, Pilot Officer Burgoyne and Sergeant Cox all claimed a kill. However, the squadron lost Flying Officer Coward, Flying Officer Brinsden and Flying Officer Aerberhardt: the latter was killed. The area around Debden was bombed at 0839 and the Germans caused widespread damage. The Dorniers turned for home covered by around twenty Me 110s, but they ran into Flight Lieutenant Berisford and 257 Squadron. Berisford, along with Flying Officer Mitchell and Pilot Officer Cochrane, all claimed an Me 110, and Pilot Officer Henderson shot down two before he was shot down into the sea near Brightlingsea. Pilot Officer Gundry, chasing an Me 110 out to sea, ran straight into another German aircraft formation. In the running battle Pilot Officer Moffett was shot down. At least two Dorniers were claimed, one by 19 Squadron and another by 111 Squadron. The second was shot down off Felixstowe. Elsewhere, Spitfires of 66 Squadron chased and shot down a Do 215. They chased it all the way from Norwich to the south-east of Felixstowe before they finally caught and destroyed it.

The new month began with reduced levels of activity, but there were still a number of reconnaissance flights across the east coast, mainly between the Humber and Lowestoft, and later there were more reconnaissance flights in the Harwich and Cromer areas. The Germans seemed to be concentrating their attention further south. On 2 September, German daytime efforts concentrated on east Kent and the Thames Estuary again. Towards the end of the afternoon and into the early evening there were reconnaissance flights made over Norfolk, and three Spitfires of 66 Squadron managed to shoot down one He 111 some six miles to the north-east of Smith's Knoll light vessel.

There was a major engagement as the Germans once again tried to put Duxford out of action on 3 September. Czech Spitfire pilots of 310 Squadron engaged Do 17s making for Colchester; one Spitfire was lost but the Czechs claimed five Me 110s, two Do 17s and an unconfirmed further Me 110. No. 17 Squadron also engaged the same formation but lost three of its own aircraft: Flying Officer Hanson was killed, Squadron Leader Miller had to force-land and Sergeant Fopp baled out near Brentwood. No. 46 Squadron lost three Hurricanes and 257 Squadron lost at least another aircraft. He

111s dropped incendiaries on Felixstowe at around 2038, bombs and incendiaries were dropped on Harwich at 0100 on 4 September, and firemen who were dealing with the incident four and a half hours later were machine-gunned. Other incendiaries were dropped on Braintree and on targets in Bedfordshire, and during the night one He 111 crashed close to Rendlesham, near Woodbridge in Suffolk. During the day of 4 September there were some high-altitude reconnaissance flights launched by the Germans over Norfolk. They also hit targets around Hornchurch, North Weald, Debden, the Thames Estuary and Gravesend.

On 5 September one raid hit Newmarket, and later a single aircraft attacked the Harwich region. There were other sporadic raids from the Humber Estuary down to the Wash. Perhaps the greatest damage that was caused in the area on 5 September was that done to a pulp warehouse at Tilbury and a margarine factory at Purfleet. The oil refineries at Coryton, Shellhaven and Thameshaven were all hit, and in fact so bad were the fires at these refineries that they blazed for five nights. Naturally this attracted the *Luftwaffe*, which returned three times to inflict even more damage. This continued into 6 September, when additional fires were created due to bombing, and twenty-four people were killed at Dartford. There were smaller raids from Holland against Harwich, as well as minelaying along the east coast of England.

Many recognise 7 September as being the first real day of the London Blitz. The attacks began developing in the afternoon, with around 350 German aircraft aiming for targets across north and south London, east London, Kent and the Thames Estuary. There were other raids that hit Southwold, Skegness, Lincoln, Lowestoft, Purfleet and Rochford. By nightfall around 600 German aircraft had attacked the capital; there were hundreds of fires, and in fact it was so bad that 500 pumps were being used at Surrey Docks alone to try and put out fires in timber yards. Thirteen merchant ships had been sunk in the docks, entire wharfs had been gutted and it was said that the smoke, smell and glare of the fires could be seen as far as Suffolk.

The Germans would now focus on London until at least November 1940. The dockyards would be hit day and night. But while the main effort of the German air force concentrated on battering London into submission, other targets across the whole of the east coast still came under direct attack. The so-called 'Coastal Blitz' was still a priority for the Germans.

Coastal Blitz

Although there were no daylight attacks over East Anglia on 8 September 1940, there were a number of reconnaissance flights, notably around the Thames Estuary and the Wash. The enemy was still concentrating most of its aircraft on London, but this also meant that many of the Medway ports were bombed.

On 9 September there was increased minelaying activity off the east coast of England, and on the 10th not only was Colchester bombed, but so too was Great Yarmouth. This raid hit Harbord Crescent at around 1130, and a bomb also dropped in Admiralty Road, close to the Nelson monument. An Me 109 was badly damaged by Flight Lieutenant Mungo Park of 74 Squadron, a Ju 88 was intercepted to the north-east of Ipswich and an He 111 was engaged off the coast of Lowestoft. No. 74 Squadron's Pilot Officer Draper shot down a Ju 88 after it had bombed Great Yarmouth that afternoon. The bombs fell on Marine Parade and Nelson Gardens and damaged the windows of the Wellington Pier. The 11th saw air raid attacks on Cambridge that evening, and around 1,000 incendiary bombs were dropped over Brentwood.

This period saw a brief respite for the east coast, as the concentrated bombing took place around London and the south-east, but there were still lone daylight reconnaissance flights, launched by Do 215s and Ju 88s. By 14 September the sporadic air raids across the east coast had begun again, with Clacton, Ipswich, Southwold and Great Yarmouth all targets. At Great Yarmouth bombs fell around Queen's Road and Marine Parade. A kill was claimed when an He 111 was shot down near Bishop's Stortford, probably from anti-aircraft fire.

The next day, 15 September, is generally considered to have been the beginning of the Battle of Britain. There were enormous numbers of German aircraft operating against Kent and against London, but there was very little activity over East Anglia. However, later in the day there was widespread bombing, but it was largely inaccurate and ineffective.

By the middle of September the Germans had introduced the parachute mine. Unlike bombs, they exploded above the ground, rather than in the ground. They could devastate an area 100 ft in diameter, and some of these mines had a weight of up to 1,000 kg.

During the night of 18/19 September Norwich was once again bombed. One bomb fell on Theatre Street but did not explode, and it was not to be removed for five days; it had taken the best part of a day of digging before even the tail of the bomb could be spotted. It was also believed that a bomb had fallen straight into a well in the gardens of the Bishop's Palace. Bomb disposal experts excavated down to 30 ft before this proved not to be the case. Hurricanes of 17 Squadron engaged a Ju 88 on 19 September off Suffolk, and one Ju 88 was shot down and crash-landed on Oakington. It was claimed by both Spitfires and anti-aircraft gunners. A second Ju 88 crash-landed near Bury St Edmunds at 1100. It had been engaged by Flight Lieutenant Riley, Flight Lieutenant Jastrzebski and Flying Officer Kolowski of 302 Squadron. The Germans dropped bombs and incendiaries on Hartismere and more incendiaries on Saffron Walden. Of the bombs that were dropped on Chelmsford that day only one exploded, and anti-aircraft gunners claimed an He 111 that came down near Bishop's Stortford.

Major daytime raids were launched against the south-east and London on 20 September, although some of these raids meant that attacks took place against a broad range of targets, including Detling, the Isle of Sheppey, Deal and Hornchurch. After nightfall bombs fell around Duxford, Blakenham in Suffolk, and Stowmarket, and a mine fell at Bourn in Cambridgeshire. That night around a hundred parachute mines were dropped across the east coast region. At 0325 on the following morning a parachute mine partially detonated in the Cemetery Road area of Ipswich. Air raid wardens and bomb disposal experts worked feverishly to try to defuse what remained of the mine, which had already wrecked one house and damaged many others. In the end, the bomb disposal experts had no choice but to blow it up where it was, and in the resulting explosion seventy houses were levelled and 750 more damaged.

Just ten minutes after the parachute mine had landed on Ipswich another one fell at Rushmere St Andrew on the outskirts of Ipswich.

This time it fell on Camberley Road, causing a great deal of damage. A third one fell on Burnham in Essex, and several others, which did not explode, landed close to Chelmsford. This seemed to set the tone for the next period of the air war. Eight parachute mines landed across East Anglia alone on the night of 21/22 September; at 2140 on 22 September a parachute mine flattened a hundred houses in Ilford; and a mine that had landed near Saffron Walden exploded the following day. Elsewhere, Royston was attacked, Fowlmere airfield was bombed and there was intense activity from 2100. In fact there were three sets of raids on the night of the 22nd.

More mines landed on the east coast on the night of 23/24 September, four near Stradishall, one on North Witchford and the Isle of Ely in Cambridgeshire. Another fell in west Suffolk, at Clare; an ammunition dump was targeted at Bury St Edmunds in the early hours of the 24th; a parachute mine landed but did not explode on the Thetford–Ipswich railway line; and Bury St Edmunds was hit again shortly after 0400, with bombs dropping around the St Andrew's Street and Prospect Row area. No fewer than four parachute flares had been dropped over Bury St Edmunds, signalling the targets for the incendiaries; most of these fell in a cemetery near Bury Barracks. Another parachute mine dropped onto Queen's Road but did not explode. Cambridge received attacks at 0340, with oil bombs setting fire to crops near Cherry Hinton Hall. The Germans had also attempted to bomb Cambridge railway station, but all they achieved was to create a crater on a cricket field. Other bombs did fall on Gresham Road and Hill's Road. During daylight hours on 24 September, 74 Squadron chased off a Do 17 off Sheringham, but the main activity was again at night, with bombs and parachute mines dropping around Braintree, Downham Market, Saffron Walden, Dunmow and White Roding in Essex.

On 25 September the British received unconfirmed intelligence reports that Italian aircraft were being transferred from Italian airbases and would operate out of Belgium. This was in fact the case. The *Corpo Aereo Italiano* had come into existence on 10 September under Air Marshal Rino Corso Fougier. Many of the pilots had taken part in the attack on southern France. They would begin making their way from Italian airfields on 27 September, to establish themselves in their new airfields in Belgium in order to lend support to the *Luftwaffe* during the Battle of Britain. Mussolini was anxious to claim some credit in the crushing of Britain. The German High Command did not want the Italians to get involved in the air war against Britain, but it was seen as being politically expedient to accept their offer of assistance. We will return to the distinctly Italian attacks once we have investigated the remainder of the bombing activities of the German air force in 1940.

There was little activity on 25 September: two bombs were dropped on Cranfield airfield, and eight bombs hit RAF Henlow in the afternoon, killing three servicemen. At night parachute mines and oil bombs were dropped at Stradishall and Debden, another mine near Dunmow and incendiaries in the Cosford area. One mine failed to explode at Haveringham in Suffolk, but one did explode at Theberton and two mines fell near Peasenhall.

Lowestoft was bombed on 26 September: one hit the fish market, two hit the North Pier, four struck the herring basin and one fell in Beach Road. There was renewed activity the following day, with three major attacks taking place. Only the first two partially targeted the east coast, and there were a number of raids up and down the coast, but predominantly in Kent and Essex. Bombs and incendiaries were dropped in Cambridgeshire, and around Bury St Edmunds, Lowestoft and Duxford.

On 29 September it was relatively quiet, with reconnaissance missions being flown over the east coast and a convoy being attacked by a pair of enemy aircraft. At 1120 eighteen high explosives were dropped near the naval base at Lowestoft. The following day considerable damage was caused at Grantham at 2045 when high explosives were dropped, damaging utilities and a factory. Five were killed and eighteen were injured.

The first day of October saw incursions in the Humber and Harwich, with reconnaissance flights over RAF airfields. Kent bore the brunt of the attacks on the south-east, with no fewer than four between the hours of 0635 and 1608. On 1 October there was just one reported engagement, when an He 111 was spotted off Cromer between 1630 and 1730. A solitary Do 17 was shot down near Dunwich at 0840 on 2 October, and an He 111 was shot down near Skegness at 1830. Some raiders crept over the Norfolk coast in the early hours of 3 October, but the all-clear could be sounded by around 0230, as once again the Germans concentrated on London.

There were no fewer than nine individual reconnaissance missions launched against the east coast on 3 October. These took place between the Yorkshire coast and Harwich. Between 1300 and 1500 at least fifteen raids were launched on the east coast between Harwich and the Thames Estuary. Squadron Leader Stanford Tuck

German minelayer at work in the North Sea in 1939.

British troops being evacuated from Dunkirk in 1940 by a drifter.

Do17 being readied in the winter of 1940-1941.

Gorleston and Southtown Gas Works July 9 1941.

A downed Italian CR42 near Corton in Suffolk.

St Nicholas Church, Great Yarmouth June 25 1942.

Royal Naval Barracks, Great Yarmouth 24 July 1942.

Pleasure Beach, Great Yarmouth May 30 1942.

Albany Road, Great Yarmouth May 30 1942.

Victoria Road, Clacton.

Charles Henry Brown.

German seaplane base at Sylt, H59s and He115s are visible.

An Bf109 shot down by a Lewis gun in the Kent countryside.

ATS girls manning an identification telescope.

Heinkel crew.

The Marina area of Lowestoft January 1942.

A Do217 crash landed in a Cambridge allotment.

ading a 500kg bomb onto an He177.

sing a 500kg bomb to go into an He177.

Preparing a torpedo. (*Library of Congress*)

Assortment of German bombs.

8 reconnaissance aircraft.

rman mines ready for loading.

Loading mines onto a Ju88.

Do26 flying boat.

(257 Squadron) claimed a Ju 88 that went down ten miles to the east of Orford Ness. Great Yarmouth was once again bombed, as was Aldeburgh. Incendiaries and high explosives were dropped around Frinton and Walton, a Do 17 was shot down near Honington and another was shot down on 5 October by aircraft of 74 Squadron, off Harwich.

The worst damage was caused at Great Yarmouth when a pair of 500 kg high-explosive bombs exploded at 2335 on 5 October. They caused enormous craters, and most of the buildings within 500 metres of the Beach station were damaged. There were isolated bombing incidents in the early hours of 6 October. A Do 17 dropped high explosives on Framlingham, another dropped bombs to the south of Newmarket, and an attack on Debden failed when 17 Squadron shot down another Dornier. Also lost that day were the crew of a Ju 88, which crashed near Colmworth, in Cambridgeshire.

The night of 6/7 October saw the east coast targeted from 1900 to 0600 the following morning. By 0100 the targets were primarily airfields, but a number of bombs were dropped on south Cambridgeshire and on Stradishall. On the 8th, between 1300 and 1500, enemy aircraft flew reconnaissance missions over Harwich, Lowestoft and Great Yarmouth. A large number of incendiaries and high explosives were dropped into the countryside across the whole of Cambridgeshire that night, although there did not appear to be any obvious reason for this. The Germans made a determined attempt to put Duxford out of action on the night of 9/10 October. They also targeted Cardington, Henlow and Mildenhall.

There was a sense that the Germans were again building up for another major set of raids. But just a handful of bombs fell around Woodbridge on the night of 10 October, and Great Yarmouth was once again struck at 2055 when twelve bombs landed around the beach and North Drive. A Ju 88 crashed into the water to the south-west of Landguard Point on 12 October when it flew into a balloon cable. Essex was targeted on 13 October, principally with raids on Chelmsford. The mayor and the mayoress, along with their sons, two grandchildren and a maid, were all killed when a bomb hit their home. There were major attacks overnight between 13 and 14 October. Many of the 300 or more German aircraft targeted London, but on the 14th, between 1900 and 2105, a large number of the enemy aircraft crossed between Orford and Shoeburyness. Another large formation crossed between the Wash and Peterborough at 2300.

There were relatively small-scale attacks against the east coast throughout the following few days and nights. However, the crew of a Ju 88 crashed at Much Hadham in Hertfordshire and an He 111 went down into the sea off Shotley, across the river from Felixstowe. On 18 October Hurricanes of 242 Squadron just fail to prevent the Germans from bombing Lowestoft, and 242 Squadron lost Pilot Officer Campbell when he engaged a Do 17 over Great Yarmouth.

The Germans returned and bombed Shotley in the daylight hours of 19 October. The following day they dropped bombs around south Cambridgeshire. There was also a bizarre incident with a Do 17 that day: it had been sent on a reconnaissance mission over Liverpool, but it turned inland too soon. A magnetic storm wrecked the radio and then another strike disabled the compass. The crew were certain that they were over France, but instead they were over Salisbury. It was at this point that the crew, having run out of fuel, baled out. Incredibly, the Do 17 was discovered at 0800 hours seven miles to the south-east of Ipswich. It had crash-landed and was relatively intact. It was only after the crew had been interrogated that the whole story became known.

A relatively large number of bombs and incendiaries were dropped across the eastern region on 21 October, including at Duxford, Newmarket, Dunmow, Saffron Walden, Wivenhoe and Bishop's Stortford.

A Do 215 was at first intercepted by Hurricanes of No. 1 Squadron on the night of 24 October. It managed to escape but it then ran into three Hurricanes of 17 Squadron. Flying Officer Czernin, Pilot Officer Fajtl and Sergeant Hogg shot down the enemy aircraft, and it landed close to the A1 at Wyboston. The following day saw an Me 109 shot down by 72 Squadron to the north-east of Great Yarmouth shortly after 1400. The Germans dropped an enormous number of propaganda leaflets over Harwich on 27 October, and a Ju 88 attacked the trawler *Harvest Gleamer* just off Southwold at 1250. It sank in just under an hour. The Ipswich area was the principal target for the *Luftwaffe* on 27 October when over twenty Me 109s attacked Martlesham at 1640. Following this attack Do 17s and He 111s dropped high explosives on the airfield. In the general area and beyond, more attacks were made, including those on Newmarket Heath, Bury St Edmunds, Marham and West Raynham. Anti-aircraft guns at Coltishall took down an He 111, and another He 111 was lost at Saltfleet in Norfolk, but it was at Ipswich that the most concerning events took place.

It was around 1823 and a Do 17 was flying over southern Ipswich. At first those who saw what were falling from the aircraft believed them to be propaganda leaflets, but they were not; they were small, cylindrical bombs. Three police officers were injured, one of them later dying when they encountered one of the bombs. The bombs had actually fallen over a two-mile-long route, and instructions were quickly sent out that no one was to try to defuse or handle them. The bombs were no more than 9¼ in. long, and they became known as 'Butterfly Bombs'. The BBC said on the evening of 30 October:

> Reports have been received of enemy planes dropping small objects about the size of a Mills bomb or a fifty-cigarette tin with wire attached. The public are warned not to handle such objects, which should be reported to the police or wardens.

The weapons were clearly designed as anti-personnel weapons. From the Ipswich attack at least fifty-four of the weapons had been recovered. It was thought that around 200 had been dropped in total, some of which had burst in the air.

A Do 17 was shot down at Orford Ness at 0755 on 28 October. Another Dornier dropped three bombs on Bungay in Suffolk at 1124, where there was one fatality – a six-week-old baby. An He 111 crash-landed into the River Stour, a mile to the west of Parkeston Quay at 2320, the crew having been disorientated when they had been illuminated by a searchlight over Harwich. Conventional attacks were made on Newmarket, Mildenhall and other targets on 29 October. RAF Wattisham was also hit, and among the bombs dropped were more butterfly bombs. Three Dorniers had also attacked Newmarket. They had bombed and machine-gunned the town. Mildenhall came under attack from fourteen He 111s, Coltishall was attacked by a solitary Ju 88, but an He 111 that tried to attack the same target was shot down.

Twelve German aircraft attacked shipping off Harwich in the afternoon of 30 October, Clacton was attacked, as was Debden and East Dereham, and a number of villages to the south-west of Norwich came under machine-gun fire. A Ju 88 on a reconnaissance flight to Manchester was intercepted by aircraft of No. 1 Squadron over Skegness. The RAF aircraft shot-up the raider and the crew baled out, with the aircraft crashing near Ely.

Bassingbourn and Duxford were attacked on 31 October. Claydon was bombed at 1325 and Great Yarmouth was also bombed in the afternoon, with four bombs landing on North Drive, Middle Market Road, Regent Road and Nettle Hill; eight people were injured.

While Norwich suffered two incendiary bomb attacks in November, it was still the RAF airfields and strategic targets such as oil installations that were of primary interest to the *Luftwaffe*. On 3 November, for example, a pair of Ju 88s attacked Stradishall and another two attacked Wattisham. Small villages and market towns were not immune, as on the very same day the Germans strafed Stradbroke, Denington, Framlingham, Aldeburgh, Shotley and Rushmere. Ipswich also saw more anti-personnel bombs dropped across a council estate that night. Aldeburgh was again hit on 5 November, along with Halstead, Horsham St Faith and Newmarket. More bombs fell on Aldeburgh on 6 November, and a convoy off Clacton was targeted on 7 November.

There was a major engagement off the coast of East Anglia on 8 November when eight Hurricanes of 257 Squadron left to protect a convoy heading north at 1300. As they got airborne they could hear that 17 Squadron was already engaged in a running battle with the German raiders. The pilots of 17 Squadron had come onto the scene to see Ju 87s dive-bombing the ships. They were protected by about thirty German fighters. The pilots of 17 Squadron targeted the Stukas and in five minutes shot down fifteen and badly damaged another half a dozen. This was probably far more than were actually lost, but certainly the German casualties were high. Two of the ships were sunk, and Sergeant Page, in a Hurricane of 257 Squadron, was also shot down.

On the same day German aircraft bombed Colchester, Swaffham, Wymondham, Honington and Mildenhall, and destroyed a club in Southwold. An He 111 dropped bombs near Bury St Edmunds and then headed north and crossed the coast around the Humber. It then tried to machine-gun vessels off Mablethorpe. Content that its mission was complete, it now tried to escape across Norfolk, but it was intercepted eight miles off Great Yarmouth by 72 Squadron's Spitfires and shot down. A number of Do 17s had dropped bombs at Ely, Feltwell, Horsham St Faith, King's Lynn and Mildenhall in the afternoon. One of the raiders was damaged off Aldeburgh. Later in the day more attacks came, this time against Duxford and Debden. More bombs were dropped on Dunmow, and before the day was out the Germans had also targeted Bedford, Cambridge, Henlow, Norwich, Royston and Wittering. At 1656 a single bomb had been dropped on Admiralty Road in Great Yarmouth. The 500 lb of explosives went off in the grounds of the Royal Naval Hospital and two people were injured.

As we have already heard, the Italians began moving up aircraft to assist in the attacks on Britain in September 1940. The main force consisted of three *stormi*, each roughly the same size as an RAF wing. There was also a separate squadron, which would be used for reconnaissance. The Italian bombers left San Damanio di Piacenza and Cameri di Novara in the morning of 27 September. They headed in a north-easterly direction, crossing the Alps and refuelling on German airfields before making their way towards Belgium.

Some forty bombers of *43° Stormo* set off, but only thirty arrived at Chièvres, around four hours later. Up to three of them would never reach their destination, as they crash-landed or were lost. Thirty-seven bombers of *13° Stormo* set off, and again only thirty arrived at Melsbroek, the others suffering from engine problems. The fighters belonging to *56° Stormo* set off in three groups, each with fifteen Fiat G.50Bis and two Caproni 133s. Other aircraft would join them over the next few days and weeks.

By 22 October the Italians had established themselves in Belgium. They were now redesignated as *KG13, KG43, 18/JG56, 20/JG56* and *1(F) 172*. It was decided that they would operate between the Thames Estuary and Harwich. Operations began on 24 October, and by this stage the Italians could muster forty Fiat BR.20s, fifty Fiat CR.42 biplanes, forty-eight Fiat G.50s and a handful of Cant Z.1007Bis bombers.

The Italians launched their first night bombing raid on 24 October. The first group took off at 2035, followed by further aircraft at 2050. Around ten of the initial force managed to locate Harwich and drop their bombs. Of the sixteen or so aircraft involved, one crashed on take-off and two lost their way and were abandoned, and the bombing results were fairly poor.

There is some confusion as to the target of the Italians' second attack on 29 October. Some sources suggest that the target was Ramsgate, but according to Dover Command War Diary it was in fact Dover. All the raid managed to achieve was to drop bombs on Deal, where eight Royal Marines were killed.

The Italians targeted Harwich on 5 November, where they dropped a number of bombs in the sea. They desperately wanted to launch a spectacular attack on 11 November; all they had managed to achieve before this was to mount offensive patrols in the area around Dungeness, Folkestone, Canterbury and Margate.

The night of 11 November saw nine or ten BR.20s, escorted by forty or more CR.42s, approach Harwich at around 1440 hours. Hurricanes of 17, 46 and 257 Squadrons were scrambled to intercept. Thirty Hurricanes began to close in on the Italian formation. The Italians should have been part of a much larger operation, which should have included G.50s and Me 109s – another fifty aircraft – but now they were on their own. Flight Lieutenant Blatchford led the attack, shooting down two BR.20s and damaging two CR.42s. Two other pilots claimed a bomber each and two more pilots claimed one between them. Another two of his pilots, Pilot Officers Andrews and King, shot down two more bombers out to sea. It was beginning to be an absolute disaster for the Italians. Pilot Officer Mrazek, a Czech pilot of 46 Squadron, was suffering from engine problems with his Hurricane and had fallen behind. He then spotted an Italian formation:

> The Italians veered eastwards towards Southend, then making off on a slanting dive for Margate, the Straits and Calais. As they turned away I saw three BR.20s go down in flames followed by their crews in parachutes. At that moment I saw about thirty to forty unknown biplanes which I realised was a gaggle of CR.42s, supposedly protecting the bombers. As they crossed my path without seeing me, I gave the second a short burst at full deflexion – it went down like a fireball. The other turned to fight – due to its great manoeuvrability it kept getting on my tail, but after a series of successive bursts I saw it begin to smoke and flame.

Certainly one of these CR.42s crashed into the sea some four miles from Orford Ness, and the second around three miles from the same point. As it transpired, the authenticated totals were three bombers and three fighters. But it is also believed that ten of the Italian fighters were so badly damaged that they were in very poor shape when they landed back at base. The Italian fighters claimed nine kills: one of them, a Hurricane, was claimed by Giuseppe Ruzzin, although in actual fact only two Hurricanes were slightly damaged.

In a statement made by the Suffolk Police in 1971 more light can be shed on that day:

> At 1345 hours on November 11 1940 two formations of Italian bombers escorted by fighters were intercepted by the RAF off

the Suffolk coast. Approximately eight German and seven Italian aircraft were brought down in the sea, and three aircraft made forced landings in Suffolk, including a Fiat CR.42 biplane. The pilot was arrested and taken to force headquarters at Ipswich. There was an officer, *Tenente* P. Appian, in a very smart uniform and a number of men whose dress varied. The officer, who spoke English, had flown a bomber at 14,000 ft. He said that the effect of the lack of oxygen had made them partly lose their senses. The men were apprehensive of the treatment they were to get. They were told that their biplanes could manoeuvre while Hurricanes could not.

There was another ambitious attack on 17 November, when six BR.20s attacked Harwich. A number were launched against Norwich on 20 November, but the raid was called off due to bad weather. The next major attack took place the following day when twelve BR.20s took off between 2330 and 0045. The target this time was Harwich and Ipswich. On this occasion a night-fighter shot down one of the BR.20s.

The Italians launched a fighter sweep over the Margate, Eastchurch and Folkestone area on 23 November. Twenty-nine CR.42s and twenty-four G.50s were involved. No. 603 Squadron attacked the CR.42s, shooting down two of the enemy. The Italians fought well in their antiquated aircraft and claimed five kills, although the only Spitfire to have suffered any damage belonged to Pilot Officer Winskill.

There was an abortive attempt to bomb Eastchurch on 25 November, but on the night of 27/28 November six BR.20s bombed Ipswich and returned intact. An offensive patrol was launched on 28 November involving twenty-three G.50s and twenty-four CR.42s, but the RAF did not engage them.

The Italians launched an extremely ambitious quadruple raid on the night of 29 November. The targets were Great Yarmouth, Harwich, Ipswich and Lowestoft. Ten bombers took off between 1745 and 1830. A 100 kg bomb was dropped on the Co-op factory at Lowestoft at 1838. In all, across the four targets, the Italians dropped twenty 50 kg bombs and forty-one 100 kg bombs. Ipswich was again targeted by the Italians on the night of 5/6 December, this time with twelve BR.20s.

The next major attack took place on 21 December. Bombers raided Harwich at 1747, and additional bombs were dropped on other targets in Harwich that damaged fifteen buildings. Ipswich received its share that night, with high explosives and incendiaries dropping around Bixley Road, Princethorpe Road, Cheltenham Road and Cobblestone Road.

The last time that the Italians appeared over the east coast of England in 1940 was on the night of 22/23 December. Six BR.20s made attacks on a number of different targets in Harwich. The Italian involvement in the air war continued into 1941, but before that the Italians made one pitiful attempt to involve themselves in the London Blitz. A single BR.20 took off to bomb London at the end of 1940. The crew got lost and they baled out near Abbeville in northern France.

By 3 January 1941 only the G.50s remained in Belgium. The other aircraft were either all needed for operations against the Greeks or the Yugoslavs, or were desperately required in North Africa. The Italians would now focus on coastal patrols along the French, Belgian and Dutch coasts, and would remain in this role until 15 April 1941.

On 3 April 1941 a pilot and aircraft was lost when the G.50 crashed close to Desvres airfield. Another aircraft was lost on 13 April; this time the pilot had scrambled to intercept enemy aircraft over Belgium. There was some kind of problem and it crashed and killed the pilot. This was to be the last loss for the Italian air force in operations against Britain itself. On 16 April the remaining G.50s flew back to Italy or on to Libya. Bizarrely, in their last six months of operations, although the G.50s had flown over 660 sorties, they had never come into contact with any RAF aircraft; in fact they had only ever seen them twice.

Meanwhile the *Luftwaffe* was still in action, launching its own operations. A parachute mine was dropped on Royston Heath on 10 November 1940, and bombs were dropped on Mildenhall, Honington, West Raynham, Southwold, Norwich, Marham and Colchester on the 11th. There were more intruders the following day, mainly to the north of Cambridge and near Newmarket, although a convoy was attacked near Clacton.

The inhabitants of Cambridge could see long streams of German aircraft passing overhead on the night of 14/15 November. The intended target was Coventry. Throughout the remainder of November targets as widespread as Lowestoft and Great Yarmouth and Newmarket and Bury St Edmunds were all hit in East Anglia. But the main focus now appeared to be on the industrial Midlands, although this did not save much of the east coast from indiscriminate bombing and the jettisoning of weapons. Colchester, for example, was bombed on two occasions on the evening of 24 November, and one of the busiest nights of the month was 29/30 November, when upwards of 350 German aircraft were seen in the skies over the east coast of England.

Mercifully the weather in December was poor, giving the east coast much-needed respite from the widespread attacks and random bombings. None the less, Stowmarket and Great Yarmouth were bombed on 5 December, Martlesham was targeted on 9 December, several buildings were destroyed in Walton on 10 December, and during a raid on Birmingham on 12 December unlucky Ipswich, Debden and Great Abington, to the south of Cambridge, were all attacked.

The Germans still continued using their parachute mines, one exploding in Chelmsford on 13 December. Clacton was attacked on 16 December with conventional bombs, and once again with the target of Birmingham a huge number of German aircraft were over East Anglia on the night of 22/23 December. Most of the bombs fell in the south Cambridgeshire area. On the same night around thirty German aircraft dropped mines off Great Yarmouth and Withernsea. Even the festive period was not sacred: Chelmsford and Leiston were bombed on 27 December, and Lowestoft and Cromer on 29 December; a cider factory near Attleborough was damaged on 30 December.

If 1940 had been a particularly trying year for the British people, then 1941 would be far worse. There would be as much enemy activity in the skies and far more damage and casualties to endure.

CHAPTER FIVE

The Worst Year

January 1941 saw renewed action against the east coast of England, despite the fact that the weather was poor. Initially the *Luftwaffe* launched several weather-reporting sorties and reconnaissance sweeps. New Year's Day saw half a dozen Ju 88s drop bombs close to a hangar at RAF Wittering. At around 1920 seventy or more bombers belonging to *KG2*, *KG3* and *KG53* crossed the east coast between Dunwich and the Humber. They were heading for targets in the Midlands. There were strong winds on 2 January, but a mine exploded over Breydon Water, near Great Yarmouth, at 0055 on 3 January, and another at Harkstead at 0235. Earlier He 111s and Do 17s were in operation over Norfolk.

The Germans mounted daytime reconnaissance missions over the Blackwater Estuary, Lowestoft and Clacton on 3 January. On the 4th, combined incendiary and high-explosive bombs were dropped on Wherstead, to the south of Ipswich. They created several large craters. Shortly after 0800 on 4 January reconnaissance flights came in over Orford Ness and buzzed Harleston, Bungay and Southwold. A second shortly afterwards flew over Diss, Watton, Winterton, Norwich and Coltishall. In the afternoon a Ju 88 machine-gunned the High Street in Southwold. A number of He 111s crossed over the Norfolk and Suffolk coasts, but their target was Bristol.

The following day saw a number of daytime attacks around the Thames Estuary and along the east coast. Bishop's Stortford, Clacton, Norwich and Saxmundham were all bombed. At Norwich a number of bombs were dropped on the outskirts at around 1030. They fell on a golf course and playing fields before the raider machine-gunned the area around Unthank Road.

Swaffham was hit by a Do 17 on 6 January, and nine bombs were dropped on the railway station, which killed five soldiers and injured some civilians. A Royal Observer Corps post at Bircham Newton was machine-gunned and later the airfield itself was bombed by four Do 17s of *KG3*. Several He 111s flew up the Blackwater Estuary at 1515 and passed over Colchester, bombed Pitsea and disappeared off the coast at Clacton.

At least fifty bombers crossed between Harwich and the Thames Estuary at around midday on 7 January. A handful made for London while the rest hit targets across Essex, Norfolk and Suffolk. Bombs were dropped on Honington, Stradishall, Debden and Feltwell. A solitary He 111 dropped a pair of bombs on Ipswich and then machine-gunned the area around Rushmere, while another He 111 dropped a bomb into Holywell Park and then machine-gunned Wickham Market and Glemham. Even the small hamlet of Market Weston, near Diss, was attacked. Ten bombs were dropped, destroying a shop and damaging several other buildings.

A Do 17, unable to find any vessels to attack, made for Ipswich on 8 January. It dropped ten bombs and machine-gunned Rushmere yet again. Another, at around 1240, dropped its bombs over Happisburgh, but these fell into the sea. Halesworth in Suffolk was bombed in the afternoon, with a Do 17 dropping five bombs to the south of the market town.

Between 1735 and 0230 on the night of 9/10 January, the Germans launched 300 or more bombers between London and the Midlands. Most of these came in over the east coast, and consequently bombs were dropped on Clacton and mines on Frinton. At 2125 Great Yarmouth was targeted. It was the port's first air raid of the year, and fourteen bombs were dropped on South Denes and Riverside in Gorleston. An hour and a half later Clacton was bombed and a number of incendiaries started fires. The next few days saw very poor weather conditions, and the Germans were mainly restricted to reconnaissance flights.

There was much better weather on 15 January, and the air raids began shortly before 2000 and continued until 0800 the following day. The first set of targets was the Midlands, but then Harwich and the Thames Estuary were targeted. A Ju 88 dropped around 250 incendiaries in the Hyde Park Corner area of Cambridge; several buildings were set on fire. The Ju 88 returned and machine-gunned the fire brigade as they fought the blazes. Some of the buildings were still burning four or five hours later.

Airfields were targeted on 18 January – specifically Feltwell, West Raynham and Great Massingham. At Great Massingham a Do 17, avoiding anti-aircraft guns at Horsham St Faith, dropped sixteen bombs on the airfield. Shortly afterwards eight bombs were dropped around Halesworth railway station. Killed were the station master, Herbert Holland, his wife Hannah and their maid, Joan Clarke. Only a day or two earlier, four of the Sutherland brothers, living in Loampit Lane in Halesworth, had waved at a friendly pilot circling overhead. When their mother realised it was a German aircraft they were dragged inside. It is believed that the German attack had hoped to catch a munitions train passing through the station.

A Do 17 attacked five merchantmen and their Royal Navy escort some twenty miles off Lowestoft on 19 January. More bombs were also dropped on Clacton, and one of the high explosives killed four soldiers. There was another convoy attack off the Naze at 1320. The Germans returned the following day to try and find the convoy, but by now it had reached the Thames Estuary.

With the weather improving on 21 January, a raider crossed over Great Yarmouth and then headed south, bombing Hatfield and Cheshunt. There were other single aircraft sorties, and during one of these ten bombs were dropped near Swaffham railway station. During the day Aldeburgh had been attacked four times, each by single Do 17s, and Harwich, Frinton, Walton, Clacton and Swaffham had also been targeted.

Great Yarmouth was once again attacked at 1111 on 23 January; this time Caister Road received four high-explosive bombs, injuring one person. On 25 January, a single Do 17 crossed the River Yare and dropped bombs on either side of the water. It seems that the principal target was actually a convoy, which was just off Great Yarmouth at 1526. Part of the escort was the trawler, *Their Merit*, which was probably moored at South Quay at the time. Gary Brown of Gorleston recalled the incident relating to his uncle, Charles Henry Brown of Caister:

> Apparently the enemy aircraft were aiming at naval ships moored on the quayside near the Town Hall. Family legend has it that my uncle was firing the Bofors gun mounted on the deck when he died.

There were probably two attacks, possibly by different aircraft, within minutes of one another. Certainly two high explosives were dropped at the harbour's mouth at around 1435. The second attack came in at 1519 when a further ten bombs were dropped, some of which fell on the South Quay. Gary Brown's uncle was killed, along with another seaman on board the trawler.

Mildenhall, Bury St Edmunds and Royston bore the brunt of the attacks on 29 January, and on the following day there were a number of small raids across the east coast. Shortly after noon a Ju 88 barely escaped off Great Yarmouth when it was chased by Spitfires of 222 Squadron. Forty minutes later a number of bombs were dropped near Haughley, close to Stowmarket in Suffolk. A pair of parachute mines were dropped over Clacton; one exploded in Chilburn Road and the other landed without exploding. Shortly afterwards the Ju 88 crashed near St Osyth; it had been hit by flak guns. At 1315 a factory was targeted at Lakenheath and one person was killed and two injured. Bombs also fell on Mildenhall, Dunmow, Halstead and Melford. Later the same afternoon nine bombs were dropped on Cambridge, killing two. On 30 January bombs were dropped at Kentford, Barrow, Elmswell, Whepstead, Chevington and in the Cosford area.

Even worse was to come in February. Among the many raids, Great Yarmouth received at least twelve bombs, and there were other attacks on Honington, Mildenhall, Leiston and a second attack on Great Yarmouth, this time with twelve high explosives being dropped from Kitchener Road to Middle Market Road. One of the bombs of 1 February hit the five-storey Grout's Silk Factory in St Nicholas Road. There was a massive fire and it was incredibly fortunate that the bombs had dropped after noon; otherwise the factory would have been full of workers.

Initially 2 February started off quietly, with some solitary reconnaissance flights, but later in the day Newmarket, Mildenhall, Thetford and other places were targeted. The following day operations were mounted against Feltwell, Honington, Newmarket Heath and Mildenhall. There was also an attack against naval vessels off Harwich at 1330, but this was driven off by 242 Squadron's Hurricanes.

The convoys were targeted on 4 February, but there was another raid that seemed to be targeting Mildenhall. Two pilots of 257 Squadron, Pilot Officer Barnes and Sergeant Brejcha, were scrambled to intercept. The Do 17 veered off and headed towards Lowestoft. It dropped eighteen high explosives on the Herring Market, the harbour, Battery Garrison Road and St Peter's Street. Two were killed and nine were injured but it was too late for the raider: Hurricanes of 242 Squadron caught up with it and shot it down half a mile off Corton.

There were further German losses before noon. Fifty German aircraft were trying to intercept a convoy moving down the east coast of England, near Clacton. A pair of Hurricanes of 249 Squadron shot down two Me 110s. As darkness descended, about sixty German aircraft operating out of Holland crossed the east coast, making for London. There was mining activity by Ju 88s. Sergeant Bodian of 151 Squadron was on patrol to the west of Wittering at 2140 when he and his gunner blundered into a Do 17. The gunner fired at it and the Dornier exploded and fell to the ground. Lowestoft had been bombed during the evening, killing another three, and King's Lynn, Debden, Norwich, Frinton, Ely and Feltwell had also been attacked. In the attack on Lowestoft three naval ratings were killed when the NAAFI canteen was hit in Waveney Dock. It is probable that the aircraft that carried out this attack was the one that was eventually shot down by Bodian.

In the evening of 5 February parachute mines came down near Bradwell (now in Norfolk) and exploded near Gypsy Lane. Another parachute mine fell just to the west of Beccles Road. Great Yarmouth again received a terrible pasting when ten bombs dropped between Palgrave Road as far as the Regal cinema. Regent Road was hit and St Nicholas's church was hit by a bomb that did not explode. Casualties that night amounted to four killed and twenty-three injured. Mary Dove, now a resident of Bradwell but living in Gorleston in 1941, recalled the terrifying conditions under which they lived:

I lived with my mother and father in Nile Road, Gorleston, and a young school friend of mine who lived a few doors away was killed in a fashion shop that she worked in at Lowestoft. She was 18 years old and was to be married the next day. She was buried in her wedding dress. I was told this by neighbours who went to see her body. My parents would not let me go. She was called Lily and had the complexion of one, very fair and pale faced. She was hit by a boulder from the roof of the shop. It hit her across the chest. Another school friend was in the Anderson shelter in the garden of her house in Nelson Road, Gorleston. It also received a direct hit and I do remember seeing the funeral. You would expect to see three coffins – her mother, father and Muriel – but the remains of all of them filled a very small wooden box. I often thought at the time that my young life was wasted, and no doubt many more people did. There was nothing to do and nowhere to go, but looking back I am glad I experienced the people themselves. The only thing in our minds was to keep alive. If you saw a stranger in someone's house you could be very sure they were helping or comforting someone after a raid. I remember one small boy; he was born in Gorleston but after his father was called up into the forces he went to live in Yarmouth with his mother. Coming out of school one day he was thrown up against the wall by the blast of a bomb. It was almost instantaneous death, but he did first call for his mother. A young lady waiting at the school lay down on the ground and held him and said, 'Mum is here'. He died, but hopefully comforted by these few words.

On 7 February twenty high explosives and some incendiaries were dropped over the dock area at Lowestoft. They hit the railway station and the Customs' House, and the power house for the swing bridge was put out of action. Eight people were killed. The He 111 that carried out the attack was hit by anti-aircraft guns and it crashed into the sea off Zeebrugge.

Incendiaries caused an enormous blaze to the west of Thetford on the night of 9/10 February. Shortly after daylight Ju 88s attacked a shipping convoy off Happisburgh. Airfields around Bury St Edmunds were targeted that evening, with at least nineteen Do 17s involved. Poor weather now intervened until 13 February, when an He 111 machine-gunned North End in Great Yarmouth and then dropped a number of bombs around the town's harbour mouth.

The following day, 14 February, saw bombs fall around Breydon Bridge and Colman's Wharf in Great Yarmouth. Other bombs hit Blakeney harbour, Bircham Newton and Horsham St Faith. There was also an attempt to knock out RAF Marham, but bombs dropped on Swaffham, South Pickenham and Hilborough. Shortly before 2300 an aircraft circled RAF Debden. Incredibly, the He 111 landed. The duty pilot briefly spoke to the pilot of the German aircraft, who then got back into his aircraft and flew off. A German bomber, probably a Ju 88, was shot down off Lowestoft by Pilot Officer Klee of 222 Squadron on the same day.

In the early evening of 15 February, RAF Feltwell and Bircham Newton were attacked, as was Cambridge. But in the early hours of the morning of 16 February sixteen high explosives were dropped along Suffolk Road, Great Yarmouth, and some hit Gorleston North railway station. At the time Mary Dove was working at the railway station as a trainee booking clerk, at the age of 17:

> I and another young man in the office were called upon to do many things not in our line of duty, such as helping to unload trucks and load parcels onto the trains. We had a single-line track, so that trucks could be loaded and left on the track for storage. After the war ended we were told the trucks contained live ammunition. After a while we had an air raid shelter built for our use on the platform. This meant that when we wanted to use it we had to run down a long path from the office, onto the platform and then the same length to the shelter. We did not always arrive before the raid started. One day the young lad and myself came out of the dugout and back up to the path. He said, 'What have you done to your tin hat?' I discovered that a piece of shrapnel had hit the brim and twisted the metal to look like a rosebud – all the fashion in those days. I would have liked to have kept the hat to remind me I almost didn't make it.

About an hour later another twelve bombs fell on Southtown in Great Yarmouth, and twenty minutes after that more bombs fell on Regent Road and Queen's Place.

There was another strange incident with a German aircraft that night, involving a Ju 88. It had been involved in a bombing mission against Birmingham and it had become lost, was short of fuel and had put on its landing-lights. It came in to land at Steeple Morden, and in doing so the starboard undercarriage collapsed; the crew were taken prisoner.

The next day, 16 February, got off to a relatively slow start, but by midday the Germans had attacked Hunstanton, Cromer, Salthouse, Weybourne, Pulham, Buxton Heath and West Raynham. In the evening attacks were made against Lowestoft, Hemsby, Cromer and Haverhill, among others. There were also shipping attacks up and down the east coast, including attacks that would continue into the following day against vessels off the Yorkshire coast.

At around midday on 17 February a Do 17 narrowly avoided being shot down over Marham by aircraft of 222 Squadron. The squadron was successful a little later when it shot down a Ju 88 to the east of Cromer. There was a familiar ring about the rest of the operations that night: German aircraft were active over the east coast for two and a half hours from 0050, and in fact there were still enemy aircraft operational until at least 0600 on 18 February. One of the attacks came in once again against Great Yarmouth, which was fast becoming Britain's front-line port. For virtually a three-hour period bombs dropped around Fishwharf, Suffolk Road, Malthouse Lane, Admiralty Road, Southgate's Road and Cobholm Marshes, and then shortly before 0600 a high-explosive bomb penetrated the gas holder at the Great Yarmouth gas works.

Graham New's late father was in the police force in Great Yarmouth during the early years of the war. His father recalled the incident some years ago:

> We were also, as firemen, called on to fight a number of quite large fires. Twice we were involved with gasometers that were bombed by the Germans. Yarmouth gas works was hit one night and a gasometer caught fire, great flames were shooting up onto the supporting uprights and the danger was that they would buckle and the gasometer would explode. We spent a long time keeping uprights cool with jets of water while the area was evacuated. In time the gas burnt out and as the gasometer sank down it extinguished itself. The Gorleston gas works was also hit one night and set on fire, we managed to get all the flames out except one, a pipe right at the top of the building wouldn't stop, we tried filling the pipe with water but it was no good. I was inside the yard at the time when I saw the night stoker, a Mr Philpott, whom I knew from the time I was working in Gorleston; talking to him he told me that there was a valve high up in the wreckage which would turn the pipe off, he told me where it was but it was no good, and eventually he climbed up and turned the valve off on his own. Everyone was patting themselves on the back until I went and told them the stoker had turned the gas off. The fire chief told me I didn't know what I was talking about and told me to keep my mouth shut. I never did say anything about it, but if anyone deserved a medal Mr Philpott did.

No sooner had the fire been put out than the morning hit-and-run raids began. Five He 111s dropped high explosives near Attlebridge, and later an He 111 attacked a convoy to the south-east of Harwich.

Mildenhall was hit early that morning and a number of aircraft crossed between Clacton and Great Yarmouth in the afternoon. They targeted Honington, Feltwell, Aldeby and Southwold harbour. Newmarket was badly damaged when a Do 17 killed thirteen, and over a hundred were injured. The bombs had badly damaged nearly every building in the High Street.

There were further attacks over the next couple of days, but on 24 February, at 0945, a pair of Hurricanes of 257 Squadron were sent to find enemy aircraft believed to be in the Happisburgh area. Pilot Officer Atkins shot at the Dornier, badly damaging it, but in the attack his Hurricane was crippled. He was forced to bale out but his body was never found. The Dornier crashed into the sea. A Ju 88 had also been badly damaged, but it continued on its reconnaissance mission over the Wash and the Humber and actually managed to land near Brussels. Shortly after 1500 another Ju 88 attacked shipping off Great Yarmouth, but was chased off by a Coastal Command Blenheim. Twenty-seven German aircraft crossed the east coast over Southwold that evening. Attacks were then made on Brandon, Felixstowe, Norwich and Peterborough. Shortly after 2215 a pair of bombs were dropped on Ipswich, partially demolishing buildings in Bloomfield Road. It seemed, however, that Cambridge was the primary target that night, and bombs and incendiaries began falling at 2200. Most of the incendiaries dropped around the Cattle Market and near to the railway. There were a number of casualties.

It was Harwich and Felixstowe's turn on 24–26 February. Shortly after 2200 on the 24th, five houses and a shop were demolished and a hundred damaged at Harwich. Other bombs dropped at Wymondham, Cockley Cley and Mattishall, as well as close to Parkeston oil tanks during this period.

There were four attacks on Great Yarmouth on 27 February. Two 250 kg bombs were dropped at the junction of Euston Road and Nelson Road, demolishing a hotel. Three hours later the Royal Naval Hospital was machine-gunned, at 1240 another Do 17 shot-up the centre of the town and at 1413 at least thirteen bombs were dropped from Apsley Road to King Street. Two schools were damaged and several other buildings destroyed. Other bombs had dropped on Stowmarket, Swanton Morley, Feltwell, the sugar beet factory at Bury St Edmunds and Honington. Lowestoft had also received its share; two civilians were killed when four houses and shops were destroyed.

Things quietened down a little that afternoon. The Germans made four unsuccessful attacks against RAF Mildenhall, civilians in Saxted found themselves under machine-gun fire, Lowestoft again received four bombs, which killed four and demolished nine houses. A low-flying He 111 sped over Ipswich docks and dropped four 250 kg bombs at 1625, causing an enormous amount of damage.

A parachute mine was dropped by a Ju 88 at 1720 on 2 March, which fell on Birch Hall in Tendring, Essex. It was now clear that there were more German aircraft operating out of Holland, which gave them the range to reach as far as Northumberland. It was almost certainly these same aircraft that made attacks on merchant vessels off Lowestoft on 3 March.

The German raiders returned to Great Yarmouth over the night of 3/4 March, first dropping ten high explosives to the south-west of the town and then a large number of incendiaries around the Lowestoft Road and Marine Parade area of Gorleston. A number of Do 17s attempted to attack ships off Great Yarmouth on 4 March, and two days later, on the 6th, Sheringham was attacked at 1112, Feltwell was struck at 1245 and later in the day bombs were dropped in the River Yare and on Caister Road in Great Yarmouth. The Cromer Knoll light vessel was also attacked. In the early evening of 7 March bombs had also fallen on Lowestoft and Brightlingsea, and Rollesby and Martham had been machine-gunned. As the evening wore on, Ju 88s attacked shipping as far north as Scarborough and another attack was made on the vessels off Great Yarmouth.

The type of attack on Rollesby and Martham was recalled by Rosemary Hodgkin (née Whitehand), who now lives in Gorleston but at the time lived on the outskirts of Great Yarmouth, at Great Ormesby:

As far as I know we were the only house bombed in the village of Great Ormesby. I lived in a house called Meadowcroft House. It was a Saturday night and shortly after midnight. Caister Camp was full of soldiers and it was thought maybe they showed some lights and possibly it could have been a plane offloading after bombing the house before heading home. We were hit by two high-explosive bombs which fell around 20 ft from the house, completely destroying the back of the house. We were rescued from the upstairs of the house through the front windows by ladders. Many of the soldiers from the camp helped. I can remember the Ormesby policeman, PC Foster, made sure we were safe and said they had to try and find where all the other bombs had fallen, knowing there had been two explosions. It was not until daybreak they found they were literally side by side. I feel incredibly lucky to be able to tell you this story as I had played up this night, wanting to sleep in my sister's bedroom. She was eight years older than I and didn't want me in her room. Much to her annoyance my mum gave in to me, and this probably saved my life as my bedroom was blown to pieces.

Another attack that day on the convoy off Great Yarmouth saw the gun crews on board shoot down a Do 17. They were rescued from the sea and became prisoners of war and handed to the authorities at Great Yarmouth. Just after dark, a Ju 88 dropped flares around a convoy off Southwold to guide German E-boats in to attack. The attack on Lowestoft on the 6th had virtually destroyed the public library and much of Clapham Road. A trawler in the inner harbour, *Evesham*, had been damaged. The attack on Brightlingsea had damaged the Anchor Hotel. It now appeared to be the case that if German aircraft could not locate a convoy target then they would automatically seek other opportunities to drop their bombs on ports, airfields or factories.

Parachute mines were still a major threat, and on 5 March, for example, the tug *Silverstone* was towing a petrol barge around three miles from Rochester Bridge in the Medway area. A parachute mine had dropped on top of her and it sank both the *Silverstone* and the barge, and killed all of the seven crew members.

On 8 March 1941, after the RAF had failed to intercept a Do 17 over Norwich, the Germans concentrated on shipping off Great Yarmouth and also bombed Bircham Newton. As a Ju 88 dropped four bombs into the sea off Britannia Pier in Great Yarmouth at around 1033, Pilot Officer Clee of 222 Squadron came in to attack. He was supported by Sergeant Morland. Both of the Spitfires hit the Ju 88 and it turned and started to limp away to the east. Morland chased it and used up the rest of his ammunition, and then saw it crash into the sea off Gorleston. That night the Germans returned to attack Lowestoft once again. Four high-explosive bombs destroyed a house and damaged a number of others.

Before 0900 on 9 March a pair of Do 17s began hunting for shipping targets. Presumably they must have found some, as in the afternoon a number of German aircraft were seen over Great

Yarmouth and a vessel was attacked off Sheringham. Sheringham itself was targeted when at 1655 a bomb dropped on Cliff Road, destroying two houses there. Later in the evening three more Do 17s attacked a convoy off Happisburgh.

Upwards of twenty-five Do 17s operated over the Norfolk coast on 10 March. A Ju 88, operating over Lincolnshire, crashed near the Wash at Terrington. This was shortly before midnight. The Home Guard quickly rushed to the scene and took the crew prisoner. The Ju 88 had been specially adapted as a night intruder; it had been sprayed black and had more machine-guns than a standard Ju 88. It appears that these fighter-bombers also pretended to be RAF bombers coming in to land. This allowed them to get close to the runways before delivering their attack.

Over the next couple of days the Germans continued to concentrate on trying to seek out shipping targets. On the night of the 12th, however, a pair of 250 kg bombs were dropped on Ipswich, and at 0400 in the morning of 13 March ten bombs were dropped on a gelignite dump in King's Lynn. It was increasingly the case that the primary targets of the German attacks were shipping, but that other targets were chosen if the opportunity arose.

Thirty or more German aircraft operated over the coast on the night of 13/14 March. Beaufighters of 29 Squadron were continually on the hunt for the raiders at night. One of the Beaufighters found a Do 17 at 2145, which appeared to be heading toward the Humber. It was shot down, and the Germans also lost a second aircraft, a Ju 88, that night. Norwich had been hit by up to forty incendiaries that were dropped around the St Benedict's Street area, and one of the incendiaries melted the lead on the roof of St Swithin's church.

On 15 March both Lowestoft and Great Yarmouth were hit by Do 17s and Ju 88s. Great Yarmouth came off better, with four bombs and thirty incendiaries dropping around Southtown Road and an area stretching from Northgate Street to North River Road. Lowestoft came under attack for nearly an hour just before midnight. It is believed that up to twenty Do 17s were involved. Incendiaries dropped in an area stretching from Sycamore Avenue to Oulton Broad. Just before midnight seven bombs were dropped to the south of Notley Road, and more incendiaries fell on Beaconsfield Road and Salisbury Road. Fifteen fires blazed just after midnight over the north side of the town and bombs were dropped on Whapload Road and on Park Hill, Gorleston Road, Lowestoft. RAF Wittering had also been hit, with a single Ju 88 wrecking a hangar, two mess buildings, the station cinema and two of the barrack blocks.

When 17 March dawned, bombs were dropped on Great Yarmouth between Vauxhall Street and the River Bure, although most of these hit allotments. Pilot Officer Clee of 222 Squadron, this time operating with Lieutenant Van Mentz, ran into an He 111 of *KG53* to the east of Sheringham. Both of the Spitfires chased the raider, and the German aircraft dived low, but the Spitfires managed to finish it off. It crashed into the sea some twenty-five miles to the east of Sheringham. An attempt by a German aircraft on the night of 17/18 March to attack RAF Mildenhall was foiled when it was shot down.

On the following night, 18/19 March, Hull came under attack. So far, considering its importance, it had been relatively unscathed. This was now about to change when thirty German aircraft targeted the harbour. Over a hundred people were killed that night. It now appears that the Germans had actually sent over 200 aircraft to raze Hull to the ground, but most of them had missed their targets and had dropped bombs across Lincolnshire and Yorkshire, or out to sea.

At 0825 on 19 March Squadron Leader Stanford Tuck was flying just off Happisburgh when he saw a Do 17. He chased it and shot it down some four miles to the south of Cromer Knoll light vessel. A Ju 88, operating off Southwold that evening, barely got home after it was shot-up by Lieutenant Blatchford of 257 Squadron. On the night of 19/20 March, the Royal Navy's Victoria Dockyard, near Deptford, was plastered by high-explosive bombs and incendiaries. The Germans gutted thirty-three of the forty-three storage buildings, killing six people and injuring another six. The fire brigade dispatched fifty fire engines, but due to the London bombing it took them two hours to arrive. The Germans also sank *Helvellyn*, an anti-aircraft paddle ship in Surrey Docks. In Victoria Dock and at Shadwell two merchant ships, eight barges and a tug were damaged. In all, 750 people had been killed in the Greater London area that night. A number of delayed-action mines were dropped into the docks and into the Thames. Early in the morning of 20 March one of them detonated beside SS *Lindenhall*. In fact, a day later, off Barking Creek, another mine claimed the SS *Halo*, and a third mine was detonated by a skid being towed by the launch *Colette*. The other two mines lay undiscovered. The fourth mine claimed the SS *Grenaa* at Rotherhithe, killing seven. The explosion was so enormous that it also wrecked the sailing-barge, *Emma*. Luckily the fifth mine exploded in India Dock, causing no damage. As a result of this new development thirty-two mine-watching barges were positioned at every quarter of a mile along the River Thames, running from Dagenham to Gravesend. This number of barges was later increased to fifty. The vessels were manned by medically unfit naval ratings.

Meanwhile parachute mines were being dropped elsewhere. Two came down in fields near Wissett on 20 March and another two at Hollesley. On 21 March three Do 17s bombed Stoke Holy Cross and Aylsham, and on the following day Ju 88s dropped mines while He 111s hunted for shipping targets. At around 1730 an He 111 was shot at by a ship off the east coast. The aircraft was badly damaged and operating on just one engine. The crew managed to limp back to base and crash-landed at 1903. Meanwhile, at Harwich, a Do 26 flying boat dropped a pair of parachute mines into the harbour, and they exploded at around 1718.

During the early hours of 24 March, fifteen or more Ju 88s had been spotted over the east coast. Early that morning two Do 17s made a machine-gun attack on Shotley, and then, at 0618, they dropped bombs on Martlesham Heath. The Dorniers were chased by six Hurricanes of 605 Squadron. The Hurricanes ran into a pair of He 111s off Felixstowe. These two aircraft had dropped bombs near Ipswich airport. The German aircraft were too far out to sea for the chase to continue.

An Me 110 was shot up by two Hurricanes off Orford Ness in the afternoon of 25 March. Later that day, at 1950, two bombs were dropped on Lowestoft Road, Gorleston. The blast broke the windows of Gorleston police station and the nearby hospital. At 0906 on 26 March two Spitfires of 602 Squadron shot down a Do 17 to the east of Orford Ness. Gorleston was again targeted; shortly before 1600 six bombs narrowly missed the pier. Later that night, at 1942, eight bombs were dropped into Great Yarmouth's harbour mouth. The tiny seaside village of Walberswick in Suffolk was hit at 1300 on 27 March, when four bombs demolished a cottage and thirty other houses were badly damaged.

In the late afternoon of 1 April 1941, Hurricanes of 242 Squadron encountered Ju 88s and shot one of them down at 1715, over Worlingham in Suffolk. For the most part the Germans concentrated on targets out to sea that day, but a pair of bombs had been dropped in the sea off Gorleston shortly before 1400.

Norwich came under attack in the afternoon of 2 April. Bombs dropped around the Riverside area and a large bomb fragment smashed through the roof of the Shire Hall and fell into a packed court-room. Elsewhere there were German aircraft operating against a minesweeper lying off Walberswick: HMS *Lorna Doone* came under attack from three He 111s at 1230 off Lowestoft. Aldeburgh was bombed at 1435 and Norwich's Thorpe station received a direct hit from an Me 110.

It was far less busy on 3 April, but mines were dropped off the East Anglian coast, bombs were dropped on the railway linking Beccles and Bungay, two bombs were dropped on Upwood and an RAF Wellington of 115 Squadron was shot down to the north of King's Lynn.

There was a heavy raid against Great Yarmouth between 2100 and 2330 on 4 April. Two bombs were dropped into the harbour's mouth and upwards of 500 incendiary bombs were dropped from Newtown to Runham Vauxhall. In an official account, written shortly after the war, Charles Box, the Chief Constable and ARP Controller, recalled one of the incidents that night:

> Some indication of the zeal and enthusiasm with which the members of the public tackled the incendiary bombs is illustrated by the following episode. Without thought for himself or his own property, a man was busily engaged putting out incendiary bombs in the road in which he resided, and in neighbours' houses, with considerable success, but while relaxing to survey the results of his efforts, another neighbour remarked, 'What are you doing here? You are wanted at your own house.' Off he went, and, sure enough, an incendiary had penetrated the roof of his house. Without more ado he set about this and thus saved his own home.

In fact many of these small incendiaries were put out by local people, the police and the ARP. If 4 April had not been bad enough for Great Yarmouth and Gorleston, the night of 7/8 April would almost see the two towns obliterated. At one point there would be sixty major and 150 minor fires caused by just six aircraft dropping up to 4,000 incendiaries.

Richard Kerridge, of Bradwell, was a schoolboy in 1941 and well remembers the night:

I was ten years old and away at school in Bungay at the time, but I can clearly remember my father, who was living in Gorleston, telling me about that awful night. He was called out after 1 a.m. to go to Yarmouth because of the severity of the raid. He walked, I think, with his next door neighbour, a Mr Tunbridge, into Yarmouth, but they couldn't get along Southtown Road, which was completely blocked, so had to go via Suffolk Road and along the back road as it was then usually called. My father was one of the directors of A.E. Kerridge Ltd, a draper of 183 King Street, which was between Jarrold's bookshop and Rose's fashion store. When they finally arrived in Yarmouth, Regent Street was strewn with one mass of firemen's hoses over which they had to pick their way. My father was soon to discover that Kerridge's, Rose's and Marks and Spencer were all well alight and burning furiously. The whole area seemed to be enveloped in flames. My father told me that later in the night when he returned to the scene again everything was completely destroyed, and the office safes, which he could see, were still glowing red hot. I recall him telling me that they had had the foresight a few weeks before to take the safes down to the ground floor from the office on the first floor. When they were eventually able to get to the safes and prise them open, the ledgers and files in them were charred, but mostly still readable. This was thanks to the firemen, who had had the time to play their hoses on them. There was little else they could save. The office staff, I remember, worked in the front room of our Gorleston home for many weeks after the catastrophe – there being a horrible, lingering smell of charred paper whenever you went in there – a grim reminder of that horrific night. It has been imprinted in my mind ever since, for nearly every anniversary I seem to remember it. Boots the Chemist was destroyed, as was Marks and Spencer, Rose's, Hill's Restaurant and the upper floor of Jarrold's. I also remember that on the same night the Seagull garage in Queen's Road was hit – I believe by a land or parachute mine. One of the special constables killed there was Percy Smoulton. He used to be a teacher, but when the school was evacuated he remained in Yarmouth and ran a class in his front room in Nelson Road South for a few of the children who had stayed in Yarmouth with their parents.

Mary Dove recalls the perilous life of people living in the east coast towns. She had taken over working on the railway as a booking clerk from a man that had been called up:

> The young man whose place I was to fill finally went into the RAF, but before he went he and his family were bombed out of their home in Baliol Road, Gorleston. As there were empty houses in almost every road in Gorleston it was easy to be accommodated, and they moved to a house in Avenue Road in Gorleston, and were bombed out the same night. So with the exception of George they moved into the country. He went to live in the Anderson shelter in Baliol Road. It had been made very cosy so he was comfortable and people rallied round to help him with food and washing.

On that dreadful night German aircraft had been active between the Wash and the Humber. Some of the aircraft had made Glasgow their main target, but it was Great Yarmouth that received the lion's share of the damage that night. The raids began at around 0010, with incendiaries dropping around the west of the town, mainly into open ground. A pair of parachute mines then landed at 0032, and a number of buildings were badly damaged and two people were killed. Suddenly, at 0100 an enormous shower of incendiary bombs was dropped from the Market Place, across the Rows area and along South Quay to Gorleston. They ignited in seconds, and fires were being reported across the whole of southern Great Yarmouth and Gorleston. It was clear after an hour that the fire brigade was unable to cope. Additional fire engines began to arrive from Beccles and Lowestoft, and an hour later fire brigades in Norwich and in Cromer were begged to come to Yarmouth and Gorleston's aid.

The damage that had prevented Richard Kerridge's father from proceeding up Southtown Road had in fact been a pair of heavy 250 kg bombs. They had effectively cut Gorleston off from Great Yarmouth; the water mains were broken, but the fire crews, wardens, police and local inhabitants worked to control the blazes, and by 0500 many of the fires were getting under control.

Two more parachute mines were then dropped: one fell at the junction of Blackfriars Road and Queen's Road, and another fell in the Row area, near Middlegate Street, causing havoc and panic. The first blast killed five special constables and the one in the Rows levelled so many buildings and buried people that urgent requests for assistance were sent to as far afield as Norwich. Charles Box recalled:

> Human memory is short, but I shall never forget the appalling sight that Yarmouth presented that night, and with the additional fires that continually broke out, it seemed that nothing could prevent the destruction of the centre of the town and South Quay. But when day broke, owing to the untiring efforts of all concerned, all fires were under control and the situation, although bad, was saved from becoming any worse.

Throughout the night the German aircraft had also hit a plastics factory in Brantham, in east Suffolk. Bombs fell in Frinton shortly before midnight, which damaged twelve or more houses.

Not content with the damage that they had done to Great Yarmouth that night, the Germans returned. Four high-explosive bombs were dropped at 2130 on 8 April, and then another shower of incendiary bombs fell at 2307. Buildings along the River Yare were set alight and the Salt Union building was gutted, but most of the other fires were dealt with very quickly. Not content with this, the raiders returned at 0232 and bombs dropped along the beach and at the south end of the town. At 0244, more bombs fell, this time most of them falling into the river. The final attack came at 0307 when four bombs fell on Nelson Road and Upper Cliff Road in Gorleston. Ten houses were shattered and many more badly damaged; six were killed and five injured.

Twelve hours before, at midday on 8 April, the Castlegate Street area of Harwich had been bombed when eight high explosives were dropped. On the night of 8 April bombs had also been dropped on Parkeston, Harwich Quay and Felixstowe. A bomb that had fallen at Trinity Pier had sunk *Marmion*, a paddle minesweeper, and had also claimed *Darcy Cooper*, a drifter, and the Army launch *Falcon*. Nine soldiers and sailors had been killed. In fact so enormous was the explosion that a huge fragment from the drifter's boiler was hurled half a mile and landed at the Bathside gas works. The Germans had also targeted Essex oil refineries and had dropped a dozen parachute mines and bombs around Thameshaven. One of the mines exploded the next day under the tanker *Lunula*, killing thirty-seven crewmen. The tanker burned for four days before it sank.

Lowestoft had also been seriously damaged on the night of 9 April. At 2145 a single He 111 dropped 300 incendiary bombs in a line from St Paul's Street to Beresford Road. Five minutes later even more incendiaries were dropped. There were fires blazing out of control in Denmark Road, Commercial Road and the Palace cinema, and a wholesale grocery store was badly damaged. More German aircraft now droned overhead, dropping high explosives. Several houses were completely flattened in Clapham Road, Cathcart Street, Raglan Street and Gordon Road. At 2235 incendiaries dropped around Stradbroke Road and then ten high explosives were dropped shortly before 2300, one landing directly on an Anderson shelter in Rotterdam Road. It had been a devastating attack for such a relatively small community.

Ipswich had not escaped the bombers' attention. A large number of high explosives and incendiaries had been scattered across the docks and along the Orwell River. An engineering works, granary, shipyard, barges and other buildings had been destroyed or damaged.

There was no respite. At 0012 on 10 April bombs dropped around Nelson Road, Springfield Road and Lowestoft Road in Gorleston, killing two more people. At 0129 bombs hit the Royal Aquarium, Nelson Road Central and North Drive in Great Yarmouth.

Lowestoft was badly hit on the night of 10/11 April; around forty-five bombs and 900 incendiaries were dropped, killing twenty-two people. One of the bombs that had landed in Old Nelson Street failed to explode, but went off a week later when two bomb disposal experts from Colchester were attempting to defuse it.

Shortly before dawn on 11 April Cromer was bombed. The six bombs hit houses in Runton Road and Alfred Road, killing twelve soldiers in their billets.

Keith Farman's recollections of Hobland Hall in Bradwell probably relate to the night of 21 April, when a number of incendiaries and a high-explosive bomb were dropped close by. It created a crater 40 ft wide and 20 ft deep:

While we were at Hobland the war was at its worst. Only days after we had moved there three bombs were dropped in the fields coming towards us. We had a large dining-room table and we would get under it as soon as we heard the air raid warning. A friend of my parents used to come and stay at night. My mum used to laugh about him as he would only put his head under the table. Later we and the rest of the people in the other houses at Hobland would go into the cellars in the hall. There was one time that all the ladies were chatting in the midst of a really bad air raid and all the men had gone onto the roof to watch the action.

Lowestoft was also hit on the night of the 21st, at 2141. Incendiaries were dropped across Stradbroke Road, Pakefield Road and London Road South. A large store was alight, the thatched roof of Pakefield church was on fire, and a second clutch of incendiaries were then dropped across Lorne Park Road, Richmond Road, Claremont Road and Kirkley Cliff.

It was over this period that the Thames area had also been targeted. In the early hours of 20 April, Southend, Rochester and Dartford had all been bombed and fifty mines had been dropped on Essex. On 22 April it was Dagenham and Thameshaven's turn. On 23 April five Me 109s dive-bombed Harwich during the day. One of the raiders, flying back over the Ship Wash, had been shot down by the crew of the trawler *Bassett*.

RAF Marham was hit in the early hours of 26 April, and at 2146 on 27 April the Ferry Inn at Horning on the Norfolk Broads was struck by bombs, killing twenty-two people, including a number of servicemen. At 2118 on 29 April three Me 110s approached RAF Martlesham, and each of them dropped a 250 kg bomb. They had sneaked in just as a Hurricane had landed.

To some extent, May 1941 was a less fraught time for the east coast of England, as the *Luftwaffe* concentrated on major towns and cities. The month, however, did not pass without a number of tragic incidents. The airfields along the east coast were still a primary target, and the villages, towns and cities along the east coast would still present targets of opportunity for the German raiders.

On 2 May the RAF station at Waterbeach, five miles to the north of Cambridge, was rocked by six bombs and ten incendiaries at around 2305. A Ju 88 was probably responsible. Another of these aircraft, due to engine failure, crash-landed at Welney Wash in Cambridgeshire. It is also believed that the Ju 88 that had attacked Waterbeach shot down a Stirling of 7 Squadron, which crashed over Dry Drayton. Also on the night of 2 May, bombs and incendiaries were dropped across Lowestoft and Oulton. A Ju 88 returned the following morning, dropping fifteen bombs on Lowestoft before flying north of the Wash and close to Skegness, where it was attacked by a Defiant of 151 Squadron. The Defiant shot-up the raider's port engine and the German crew jettisoned their weapons and fled. It got as far as the coast and crash-landed on the shoreline at Sheringham. That evening a trawler was sunk off Cromer and there was considerable bombing around Harwich.

At around 2200, a Havoc of 85 Squadron, piloted by Flying Officer Hemmingway and Sergeant Bailey, engaged an He 111 close to Halesworth in Suffolk. They shot it down and it crashed into the sea some three miles off Dunwich. Bombs and mines were once again dropped on the port area of Lowestoft during the night of 3/4 May. One of the mines sank the trawler *Ben Gairn* and its sister ship, *Niblick*. The railway yard at Parkeston was wrecked and a house in Harwich was demolished, killing four people.

Over the night of 4/5 May a Defiant of 151 Squadron shot-up an He 111, which crashed near Holt at 0104. Earlier eighteen 250 kg bombs had fallen on Ipswich, and off Harwich the minesweeper HMS *Selkirk* and the patrol trawler *Franc Tireur* were damaged. The block-ship *Fidelia* was sunk in the harbour entrance at Lowestoft. Several other bombs fell across the town, one of which destroyed the Woolworth's store. In the early hours of 5 May Kitchener Road and Nelson Road in Great Yarmouth had received six bombs and 150 incendiaries. Clacton had been attacked, and one of the aircraft, a Ju 88, which had been bound for a bombing attack on Belfast, was forced to jettison its bombs and make a forced landing. It came down on sand dunes at Waxham in Norfolk. The aircraft was wrecked as it landed, and one of the crew was killed, and three injured.

Hull was attacked on two consecutive nights – 7/8 and 8/9 May. On the first night thirty enemy aircraft attacked, and on the second fifty. Collectively these were Hull's worst nights. Riverside Quay was burned out, a factory that made Brasso was destroyed, as was a flour mill, and Hammond's Department Store was gutted. The Seamen's Mission was destroyed, as was the Prudential Insurance building and two theatres. The main bus station was gutted and the Germans dropped dozens of mines across the city; one of them hit a public shelter in Hessle Road, killing several people. Nineteen barges and other vessels were sunk in the docks, along with the drifter *Justifier*. One of the mines claimed the trawler *Silicia*. Lieutenant-Commander Marson, who was on board, was thrown into the air and both of his legs were broken, and seven men on board were killed. Collectively around 200 people in Hull were killed over those two nights, and a mass funeral was held at North Cemetery. So widespread was the damage that 8,000 homeless people had to be evacuated. The bombing was so indiscriminate that many rural areas around Hull, including Holderness and Beverley, were badly damaged. Ultimately, around 30,000 people would leave the Hull area as a result of the bomb damage and ongoing threat.

Looking back on the night of 7/8 May, eight bombs fell on Fakenham and another eight on RAF Wittering. Stowmarket received three bombs and a hundred incendiaries, and Great Yarmouth was the unwilling recipient of twenty-two bombs that fell just after midnight on 8 May, running from Stafford Road to Southtown Common.

Attacks on Great Yarmouth resumed at 1231 and continued until 1351 on 9 May. Bombs dropped on Churchill Road, Mill Road in Cobholm and on the *Ethel Radcliffe*, a merchant ship that had been beached. Only one aircraft bombed Lowestoft that night, killing two people. The patrol drifter *Uberty* was sunk off Lowestoft, a beached shipwreck was hit off Shingle Street and more aircraft attacked Ipswich and Nacton. Six or seven German aircraft bombed Harwich and Felixstowe, where the railway station was damaged by incendiaries; luckily there were only a few injuries when bombs fell on the centre of the town.

It was London that was the main focus of attention on the night of 10/11 May. The Germans had mustered 350 aircraft against the British capital. But the east coast was not immune that night; at least a hundred aircraft crossed the coast between Flamboro Head and the Thames Estuary. A large number of Me 109s, with long-range tanks, made determined attacks against a wide range of targets, including Southend, Oulton Broad, Aldeburgh, Brightlingsea, Pakefield, Dunwich and Southwold. They attacked the *Queen Eagle*, an anti-aircraft ship, at Sheerness during the night of 11/12 May.

Shortly afterwards bombers began to appear. Six attacks were launched against Great Yarmouth alone between 1248 on 12 May and 0343 the following day. There were only two people injured, although nearly forty bombs had been dropped. The area was not so lucky nine hours later, when four bombs were dropped on Colomb Road and the High Street in Gorleston, killing three and injuring three more people.

This type of attack continued over the next few days, but German aircraft casualties continued to mount. In fact May had been a particularly bad month for the Germans, and a number of raiders had been destroyed. A prime example was the loss of two Ju 88s and possibly an He 111 on the night of 11/12 May alone. Such was the effect on the German squadrons that on that night 230 bombers had been identified. The following night, there were just sixty bombers. But regardless of the casualties, the attacks still continued.

In the afternoon of 14 May a vessel was sunk off Great Yarmouth and the town itself was bombed on two occasions. An He 111 was claimed by 25 Squadron, when Squadron Leader Pleasance had shot down the raider in his Beaufighter off Cromer.

Two truly enormous 2,500 kg bombs were dropped on Norwich at around 0100 on 17 May. Roofs and windows of around 400 houses were destroyed. In fact only four of these massive weapons were ever dropped on East Anglia; the other two came down on the Isle of Ely. Incredibly, Norwich would not suffer any more bombings, barring one incident, for nearly another year. Harwich had been hit that same night by a Type-G mine.

Events elsewhere would see a temporary lull in the German bomber offensive against Britain. Large numbers of German aircraft were being shifted to the East for the impending invasion of Russia. Aircraft were also badly needed in the Balkans and in North Africa. The Germans would still, however, use their fighters during the day, and their night-time intruder missions would continue.

While the Blitz against London subsided, this was not to be the case for Hull, Lowestoft and Great Yarmouth. They would still find themselves as principal targets of the *Luftwaffe*. In fact Great Yarmouth was struck on 5, 12, 15, 17, 23 and 24 June. The last two attacks were the heaviest, with twenty-two bombs and 200 incendiary bombs dropped in the last raid alone. On 23 June the Germans had fire-bombed the Smith's potato crisp factory.

Elsewhere, the block-ship *King Henry* was sunk in Lowestoft harbour on 13 June in an attack that also claimed the lives of fifteen soldiers billeted in Whapload Road. Earlier in the month shipping to the north of Cromer had been attacked over the night of 2/3 June, and the Germans returned for a second attempt the following night. There were bombers passing overhead *en route* to the Midlands on the night of 11 June when Diss was hit by nine bombs, and at King's Lynn sixteen were killed. In the early hours of 14 June a Ju 88 was shot down over the Wash. The Germans lost a second Ju 88 on the night of 21/22 June when it crashed at Deeping St James, near Peterborough in Cambridgeshire.

Many of the attacks during June were on shipping, and the *Luftwaffe* was also active in dropping mines. Two exploded at Holt on 17 June, convoy attacks took place on the night of 18/19 June off Norfolk, a ship was sunk off Cromer on the night of 20/21 June and a Ju 88 was shot down near Happisburgh on 29 June by a Hurricane belonging to 151 Squadron.

After a relative lull in the attacks on east coast targets during June, the Germans stepped up their offensive in July. Great Yarmouth was once again struck on a number of occasions. There had been sporadic attacks on 2 and 5 July, but between 0104 and 0259 on 7 July no fewer than four attacks were made on the port. Tragically four heavy high-explosive bombs fell on Anderson shelters in Frederick Road and Kitchener Road and seven people were killed. The bombs also demolished a pub, a shop and five houses. More bombs fell on Southgates Road, and then a large one fell on Row 127. It flattened eight houses and the Brett Foundry. To round off the attack another four bombs fell on Southtown Road; they wrecked a pub and several houses. The attacks had claimed twelve killed and a further six injured, but during that night a Ju 88 had been shot down by Squadron Leader Atcherley.

There was another major attack against Great Yarmouth two days later, on 9 July. This time the attacks came in between 0105 and 0345 when no fewer than twenty-one separate attacks were made by at least fifteen aircraft. Around eighty bombs were dropped, plus up to 1,000 incendiaries. The Germans also dropped a number of propaganda leaflets. There was extensive damage to shops, pubs, a chapel, a timber yard, a gas holder, railway installations, the quayside and houses. At Southtown railway station several carriages were overturned. One private surface shelter, which was protecting thirty people, narrowly missed a direct hit. At 0145 bombs dropped near to the Report Centre, but the staff inside carried on as usual, despite the fact that most of the windows had been blown out. Incredibly, just three were killed and twenty-nine injured. During the night a Hurricane of 257 Squadron managed to shoot down a Ju 88 off Happisburgh.

There were a number of attacks launched against Hull during July. Twenty-two people were killed over the night of the 10th and 11th; another twenty-five over the 14th and 15th, and 150 people in east Hull were killed on the night of 17/18 July. Over the course of the month sixty attacks had been made on RAF airfields. On 25 and 26 July alone there were eight such attacks.

August saw a definite drop in activity, and in fact the *Luftwaffe* only had around 120 aircraft available to them. None the less there was a major attack on RAF Marham over the night of 12/13 August. A Wellington, coming into RAF Feltwell early on 15 August was followed by German aircraft that then proceeded to bomb and machine-gun the base. Reinforcements arrived in the form of 604 Squadron at Coltishall on 22 August, and later that same day Wing Commander John Cunningham and Pilot Officer Rawnsley shot down an He 111 to the north-west of Coltishall. The German night-fighters still continued to plague airfields, dropping ten bombs on the landing-ground at Caxton Gibbet in south Cambridgeshire.

The Germans, however, were able to reinforce. Late in July, despite more aircraft leaving for the Russian front, *KG2* had arrived. Initially it was equipped with Do 17s, but it was soon to be re-equipped with Do 217s. They would become operational in August 1941.

Throughout August and into September 1941, the traditional German targets still remained very much the enemy's focus. Great Yarmouth was attacked on eleven occasions in August and three more times in September. Twenty-nine more people were killed at Hull during a raid on the night of 17/18 August, and another forty-one over the night of 31 August/1 September.

The Do 17s still ranged along the coast throughout August, trying to find targets of opportunity. For example, on the night of 3/4 August a convoy was attacked off Orford Ness. They ran into No. 71 Squadron, known as the American Eagle Squadron, and one of the German raiders was shot down. More attacks on convoys were made on 8 August, principally off Harwich and Happisburgh. Just as had been the case in the past when shipping did not present itself as a target, the ports in particular were vulnerable. On the night of 8/9 August, Cromer received ten bombs and Caister some more when German aircraft failed to find suitable seaborne targets.

On 19 August an He 111 was shot down twenty miles off Winterton at 2010 by 266 Squadron. Three days later 257 Squadron shot down another, again off Winterton, but this time at 0816. This aircraft had just sunk a ship lying off Great Yarmouth.

There was an even greater downturn of activity in September, with much of the effort falling on Ju 88s. On one occasion a single Ju 88 fired on a Beaufighter near Coltishall on 16 September and then, as it was heading home, dropped a number of incendiaries on Felixstowe. The Germans still mounted raids against shipping; on the night of 6/7 September a convoy was attacked off Great Yarmouth. A Ju 88 was shot down by anti-aircraft guns on 19 September, and four days earlier a Hurricane had shot another down off Happisburgh. As for Great Yarmouth, certainly East Anglia's most bombed target, it had been subjected to sixteen bombs and around fifty incendiaries, but for the first month in a considerable period of time no one had been killed in September. Bombing even further inland had also dropped off, although the airfield at Foulsham had been bombed on 9 September, and Colchester had had a bomb and incendiary attack on 13 September.

If anything, attacks along the east coast diminished even further in October. Great Yarmouth was bombed on seven occasions, evenly spread throughout the month, but once again there were no fatalities. Clacton had received two parachute mines at 1955 on 19 October; they destroyed two farmhouses. A week earlier anti-personnel bombs had been dropped on Colchester, but they only succeeded in breaking some windows in the Queen's Hotel. The busiest nights as far as raids on shipping were concerned were 2/3, 11/12 and 16/17 October. All of these took place off the Norfolk coast.

One of the first Do 217s came to grief when it crash-landed near Lydd in Kent at 0505 on 12 October. The crew believed that they were over France. They were low on fuel, having attacked Dorchester and then flown over Pembroke, heading for Tenby and Barnstaple. An examination of the aircraft showed that it could carry four 500 kg bombs and also be configured to carry a pair of 1000 kg bombs, with another 500 kg bomb under each wing. It could also carry mines and torpedoes.

Incredibly, there was a major switch in German tactics in October 1941. The *Luftwaffe*, on 13 October, was ordered to stop its intruder operations and to transfer the fighters to protect German air space against night-time attacks by the British. Consequently, as November and December passed, there were fewer and fewer attacks along the east coast. Colchester was bombed on 3 November, Harwich, which had seen very little activity since May, was dive-bombed on 6 November, King's Lynn was attacked at 0454 on 10 November and a 500 kg bomb bounced along the quay and exploded on a railway line. A second bomb wrecked a house and a transport building. The German aircraft then went on to drop 800 incendiaries, which fortunately caused very little damage. Great Yarmouth, of course, was not immune; it was attacked on five occasions in November. There was a direct hit on the railway line at Cobholm on 7 November, a vessel was sunk between Cromer and Southwold on the night of 17/18 November, and buildings had been demolished at Frinton, Walton and at Bradwell Village on the Blackwater Estuary. Three 250 kg bombs had been dropped on Lowestoft.

German minelayers were at work through December 1941 but very few German aircraft ventured inland. One did, however, at 1740 on 21 December, when it bombed targets slightly inland from Great Yarmouth. More bombs fell, this time on Holland-on-Sea over the night of 23/24 December, a most unwelcome Christmas gift for the inhabitants. A Spitfire pilot of 485 Squadron was shot down on 29 December by a pair of Me 109s protecting a Ju 88 hunting for a convoy.

Estimates as to the total number of casualties along the east coast is difficult. Around 65,000 people had been killed by the German air force during the course of 1941. As a reasonable guide, something in the region of 2,700 people died in locations along the east coast between Margate and Bridlington. It is important to appreciate that although it was not the most bombed target of the year, Hull suffered some forty per cent of all of these deaths. The German air force had dropped something in the region of 20,000 high-explosive bombs along the east coast alone.

CHAPTER SIX

Offensives and Convoys

For the most part we have focused on the German air attacks and the defensive moves by the British along the east coast of England. But the east coast also played another major role, as a series of bases and safe havens for British attacks on German shipping and other targets. During the First World War the east coast had played a vital role in policing and controlling the North Sea. Various points along the coast had served as submarine bases, such as Rosyth, Blythe and Harwich. Other ports had served as either bases or support bases for the home fleet, which effectively bottled up the German navy and prevented it from using the North Sea as a base of action against the British mainland.

As early as November 1939 the 3rd Submarine Flotilla was established at Harwich. Initially it had just six vessels; these were small compared to British submarines that had been built prior to 1933. They were S-class craft with six bow torpedoes, a 3-in. deck gun and a machine-gun. The flotilla's depot ship was *Cyclops* and she and the six submarines were based at Parkeston Quay. Initially it was decided that any major refits or repairs would have to be carried out at Sheerness, but this soon changed when civilian workers were enrolled to carry out these jobs at Parkeston itself. The 3rd Flotilla was responsible for patrolling the Heligoland Bight and parts of the French coast. Here it would keep watch for German warships and blockade runners. Sometimes it would remain on patrol for five days and only surface at night to recharge the batteries.

The first patrol was carried out by HMS *Salmon*. It was dispatched on 2 December 1939. On 4 December the German submarine *U-36* was spotted by HMS *Salmon* south-west of Kristiansand. HMS *Salmon* promptly sank her with a torpedo, and all forty of the German crew were lost.

HMS *Salmon* was equally successful eight days later. She spotted the German blockade runner *Bremen*. The *Bremen* was *en route* from New York, via Murmansk. Lieutenant Bickford, in command of HMS *Salmon*, surfaced near the liner and ordered her to stop. At precisely the wrong time a Do 18 flying boat appeared, and HMS *Salmon* had to submerge. But this was not the end of the patrol, as on 13 December she spotted the German light cruisers *Leipzig* and *Nürnberg*. They had just returned from minelaying operations off the Tyne. HMS *Salmon* hit each of them with a torpedo, then bravely surfaced to radio for assistance and came under immediate shell fire from the cruisers. Both of the enemy ships had been badly damaged and had to remain in dock undergoing repairs for several months. As a result of his exploits Bickford was awarded the Distinguished Service Order and promoted to lieutenant-commander.

Towards the end of February 1940 the 3rd Flotilla was told to make for the Baltic. There was feverish activity as the vessels prepared for the long and hazardous voyage. They were to be sent to assist Finland in her war against Russia, but at the last minute, on 13 March, due to an armistice, the order was cancelled. The flotilla was then joined by the French 10th Submarine Flotilla. The French were to take over the patrolling of the Dutch coast, while the 3rd Flotilla moved into Norwegian waters.

On 9 April 1940 the Germans invaded Norway and Denmark, which meant that the 3rd Flotilla would now be operating in the Skagerrak. On 12 April HMS *Snapper* sank a German petrol carrier, and three days later it sank two further ships. In this short campaign HMS *Sunfish* sank four vessels, but the British lost HMS *Sterlet*, which had been depth-charged by German trawlers and lost on 18 April. The French submarines left for Scotland to participate in the Norwegian campaign. The 3rd Flotilla was also involved in the operations around Narvik.

To replace the S-class submarines, five ex-training submarines were brought in from Portland and Portsmouth. They were H-class submarines, built towards the end of the First World War. In the first two weeks of June 1940 two more L-class submarines were brought in, and together they patrolled the Dutch coast. The H-31 sank a German anti-submarine boat on 18 July. The H-49 sank a large merchant vessel on 23 September, but on 18 October the H-49 was lost with all hands.

With the other submarines leaving for other bases, this just left the H-28. Harwich would no longer be a submarine base; it would now fall on the Royal Navy's motor torpedo boats and RAF Bomber and Coastal Command to carry out reconnaissance missions and raids along the Dutch coast.

As far as the RAF is concerned, at least initially its targets tended to be enemy vessels in the North Sea and against the ports in Holland, Belgium and northern France. Bomber Command launched attacks on the German fleet in the Heligoland Bight just hours after war had been declared. Further attacks on targets such as Wilhelmshaven on 18 December 1939 were not that successful, and of forty-four Wellingtons launched on that raid twelve were shot down.

Into 1940 the RAF's main targets were those of opportunity in the North Sea, along with the ports along the continent. Regular targets were Ostend, Antwerp, Boulogne, Calais and Dunkirk. None of the raids were particularly successful, yet the RAF was to play a vital role in helping to break up the concentrations of barges that were being amassed in these ports, as the Germans prepared for Operation Sealion, their intended invasion of Britain.

By 1941 there were fears that if the Russians collapsed then the Germans would resurrect their idea of invading Britain. This led to renewed attacks on the French and Belgian ports, and for the first time in early 1942 attacks on German sea ports, such as Emden. During 1943, for example, daylight raids were routinely launched against Ostend, Flushing, Ijmuiden, Rotterdam and Zeebrugge. It was not just ports that were now being targeted, but power stations, factories and military installations.

It was around this time that the US 8th Air Force began to lend its weight to this offensive. In fact for the last half of the Second World War many American bomber groups would forge a lifelong relationship with British villages, towns and cities up and down the east coast, such as 489th Bomb Group's enduring connections with Halesworth in Suffolk.

It was not just Bomber Command that was involved in activities along the east coast; obviously Fighter Command played an enormous role. They were not simply defensive; they were involved in attacks on enemy shipping all along the Dutch and Belgian coastline. By September 1941 the squadrons based at RAF Manston alone had made attacks on seventy-four ships, plus many hundreds of other, smaller craft. They had sunk in excess of 44,600 tons of enemy shipping and lost thirty-three of their own aircraft in doing so. The idea, of course, was to permanently close the English Channel and its approaches during daylight hours. This was a feat that was never entirely achieved.

Coastal Command also played a vital role. No. 16 Group operated initially from Bircham Newton, but later it would operate from Manston, North Coates and Langham. The North Coates airfield was just six miles from Grimsby, and primarily used by 22 Squadron, equipped with Beauforts. The squadron used it for its minelaying operations, and was operational from April 1940. Five of its aircraft bombed an airfield outside Rotterdam on 12 May 1940, just after it had been overrun by German paratroopers.

No. 22 Squadron was joined by Fleet Air Arm's 812 Squadron, equipped with Swordfish biplanes. On 15 September 1940 they sank a large vessel entering Ijmuiden, and on 19 September they launched torpedo attacks against German invasion craft on the Dutch coast. Beauforts from 22 Squadron were involved in attacks against the *Tirpitz* on 21 December 1940.

The Canadian 407 Squadron began operating from North Coates in mid-1941. They were not only involved in raids along the Dutch coast, but also had air-sea rescue duties.

It was not just conventional weapons being used in the early stages of the war from the east coast; other, more bizarre, enterprises were not just considered, but enormous enthusiasm was put behind them. The incredible story of Operation Outward dates back to the night of 16/17 September 1940. There were violent gales that night and many of the barrage balloons had been torn loose, and in fact Harwich only had one left that morning. Many of these barrage balloons' trailing cables caused havoc over Denmark, Sweden and Finland. They brought down phone lines and power cables and shorted electric railway lines by simply blundering into them. It was thought that if balloons were released from Great Yarmouth and the winds were blowing from the west then many of them would cross Germany. The idea was to destroy power lines and set fire to German forests. It was decided to put an incendiary sock around the trailing wires so that when they struck something they would set it on fire.

As it transpired, Felixstowe was decided to be a good place to launch the balloons, and the campaign got under way in March

1942. A report from the British Army's 54th Division on 29 March stated:

> The appearance of a number of strange-shaped balloons over Felixstowe, with trailing ropes to which were attached white metal canisters, caused great curiosity and some trepidation among the local population. The sight of the balloons caused two women to commence screaming hysterically that the invasion had commenced and Nazi parachutists were coming down. The uproar was promptly quelled by the local ARP warden.

There were other balloons stationed at Lowestoft and at Great Yarmouth. In fact they continued to cause alarm, and the RAF air-sea rescue unit based at Gorleston was often sent out on fools' errands when reports of parachutes landing in the sea had been passed on to them.

Incredibly, the British pressed on with the scheme, which ran from 1942 to around September 1944. In 1942 they released between 600 and 6,000 balloons each month, although this of course depended on the weather conditions. Intelligence reports suggest that the balloons caused up to ninety electricity failures a month in occupied Europe. Some of the balloons were seen as far away as Switzerland or Hungary. There were major German power cuts in 1942, some of which took place in East Prussia, over 900 miles from Felixstowe.

If the transfer of German aircraft to the East to take part in the invasion of Russia appeared to be a positive sign for Britain, it did not mean that the convoys passing up and down the east coast of England would be safer. There was a decline in activity, and coupled with that the British were beginning to organise a much better air defence and minesweeping policy, and to improve their convoy protection. In fact the drop-off in enemy activity had begun by around March 1941, but it would take a year before shipping losses actually began to decline in any significant way. As it transpired, when the Germans began shifting aircraft to the East this corresponded with an increased level of activity against shipping in the North Sea. In June 1941, of the ten vessels that were badly damaged by German aircraft, eight were sunk. This all happened in just seven days – from 21 to 28 June.

It was also clear that the German E-boats were working far more closely with the *Luftwaffe*. The Germans had the advantage of using

Ju 88s for reconnaissance. They prowled the east coast looking for targets to help guide in E-boats and bombers. The Germans had also sown a large acoustic minefield in the Thames Estuary on 1 July 1941. Some of these mines were also off the north Kent coast.

The numerous British motor minesweepers did sterling work up and down the east coast, trying to clear as many of the mines as possible. The first of these vessels, No. 39, was lost on 7 August 1941 close to Longsand Head. On 30 August minesweeping drifters *Monarda*, *Internos*, *Forerunner* and *Vernal*, with British LL magnetic equipment, which used an alternating electric current, pulsed through a cable towed behind the vessel in order to detonate the magnetic mines at a safe distance, got to work off Southend. In around an hour they blew up eleven acoustic mines and three magnetic mines. In fact when they triggered one of the acoustic mines five of them blew up at the same time, and when they blew up two of the magnetic mines another two acoustic mines were triggered. Unfortunately these brave little vessels took quite high casualties: *Forerunner* was lost in a collision in the Thames Estuary on 14 October 1941, and *Monarda* foundered in the Thames Estuary on 8 November 1941.

It was not all success: there was a major disaster at Harwich on 24 August 1941 when the Norwegian collier *Skagerrak* was making for Ipswich power station. It had come with a cargo of coke from Newcastle. It was proceeding up the River Orwell about a mile from Harwich when it struck two mines. The ship was literally cut in two and eighteen of the twenty-three crewmen were killed.

September 1941 saw more losses to mines, most of which had been dropped by minelaying aircraft. HMS *Corfield* was a mine-destructor ship and a former collier. She was lost off the Humber on 9 September. The tanker *Vancouver* was lost near Sunk Head Buoy. She was bound for Shellhaven and had voyaged all the way from Nova Scotia. Just three of the forty-eight crewmen were saved. Even smaller vessels were not immune from the mines. On 3 November the patrol yacht *Ouzel* with three soldiers and a crew of seven Royal Navy men was checking beach defence camouflage off Skegness and Mablethorpe. She struck a mine and everyone on board was killed.

The autumn of 1941 saw a determined attempt by the Germans to bomb shipping all along the east coast. This new offensive took place over a three-week period at the end of October to the middle of November. The merchantmen *Antiope* and *Friesland*, along with the trawler *Francolin*, were all lost off Cromer. Off Orford Ness the merchantmen *British Fortune* and *Nicholaos Piangos* were lost. Off the Humber the merchant ships *Marie Dawn* and *Brynmill* went down, as did the *Bovey Tracey* off Lowestoft and *Corhampton* off Withernsea. Another Norwegian collier, SS *Bestum*, also making the trip from the River Tyne to the power station at Ipswich, was sunk at Cork Spit on 22 November, but she was later salvaged.

Another major danger in 1941 was the arrival of more German E-boats along the east coast of England. Due to their size and speed they were incredibly difficult to catch or to intercept. They would remain a constant thorn in the side of the British and cause damage far in excess of their size and numbers. German E-boats were responsible for the sinking of the Polish freighter *Czestochowa* off Wells and the damaging of another vessel on 20 August. They were even more successful the following month, sinking *Teddington*, *Eikhaug* and *Duncarron*. All of these attacks were carried out by the 4th E-boat Flotilla. These vessels operated out of Ijmuiden, and each of the flotillas had its own tender or escort ship. They were relatively small but a highly successful force and at times were an enormous threat to British shipping.

The Germans had already deployed the 1st and 2nd Flotillas in 1940. The 1st Flotilla had shifted to Cherbourg and the 2nd and 3rd operated from Ostend and Rotterdam respectively. The 4th Flotilla had joined the force in July 1941, and its principal role was minelaying. It would operate across an enormous spread of the British south and east coast. The E-boats were not frightened to carry out conventional attacks on convoys, and this would eventually lead to the British having to deploy increasing numbers of motor gunboats to fend them off. One ruse used by the E-boats was to listen into radio traffic and then to try and contact one of the vessels, hoping that it would reply. This would assist the E-boat in working out the exact location of a vessel and then launching its attack.

The German 2nd E-boat Flotilla attacked a south-bound convoy on the night of 19/20 November 1941. The convoy was just to the north-east of Great Yarmouth. Two small colliers, *Aruba* and *Waldinge*, were both sunk. A third vessel was the oiler *War Mehtar*. This was the largest ship ever to be sunk by an E-boat on the east coast. The convoy that was heading south, known as FS50, had fifty-eight merchant ships and a very strong escort, consisting of HMS *Verdun*, HMS *Vesper* and HMS *Wolsey*, all destroyers based in Rosyth.

Also protecting the convoy were HMS *Campbell*, HMS *Garth* and HMS *Hambledon*, all destroyers out of Sheerness. Harwich supplied the destroyer HMS *Quorn*, a pair of corvettes, HMS *Kittiwake* and HMS *Widgeon*, and the trawler *Kingston Olivine*. Also present were a pair of motor launches and a motor minesweeper from Grimsby. Despite this strong escort the E-boats pressed home their attack and escaped to the north-east. Not content with this, the E-boats continued to attack over the next few days. They claimed the tanker *Virgilia*, the Dutch collier *Groenlo*, and three other vessels. In the attack on the *Virgilia* upwards of thirteen E-boats were involved.

The E-boats were very active until December 1941, when mines began to once again exact a heavy toll on British shipping. Fourteen vessels were lost that month to mines. The mines were laid by a combination of E-boats and German aircraft. The nights of 20 and 21 December saw the largest number of German aircraft dropping mines over the Thames Estuary for six months. A few days later thirty-five aircraft were located.

It was now apparent that the E-boats did not tend to operate around Sheerness or the Humber, primarily to avoid their own acoustic mines. By the middle of 1941 Nore Command had 199 minesweepers. They were responsible for sweeping enormous sections of the North Sea – in fact over 500 miles of Channel, half of which was the main convoy route.

The New Year, 1942, saw just as much activity: three ships were mined off Suffolk on 6 January alone. HMS *Vimiera* was lost on 9 January after she struck a mine in the Thames Estuary. She was in sight of Sheerness and leading a convoy south, and over seventy of the crew members were killed. There were more losses throughout January, including another collier, this time heading for Ipswich. She was approaching Harwich harbour, triggered a magnetic mine on 25 January and sank; her funnel remained above water for the remainder of the war. Another example of mine casualties was the Greek-owned *Atlanticos*, sunk on 21 February. She sank after HMS *Sheerwater* had plucked off her crew of thirty-three and tried to tow her into Great Yarmouth.

The mines and the E-boats were not the only hazard. German aircraft would routinely make anti-shipping attacks. Two prime examples were the minesweeping trawler *Irvana* out of Great Yarmouth that was bombed and sunk on 16 January 1942, and the Grimsby-based trawler, *Loch Alsh*, sunk in the Humber area on 30 January of the same year.

German aircraft were especially active in February 1942. On 2 February minesweepers and patrol trawlers out of Grimsby and Great Yarmouth were set upon by at least twenty enemy aircraft. This led to the loss of Great Yarmouth's *Cloughton Wyke* and *Cape Spartel* from Grimsby. On 18 February, close to where the *Loch Alsh* had sunk, the Grimsby-based patrol trawler *Warland* was also sunk.

It was difficult for the British to be absolutely sure how many claims of downed German aircraft were correct or mere flights of fantasy. In order to confirm the shooting-down of a German aircraft some kind of evidence had to be found, and this was not possible in many situations. What can be clear is that Grimsby trawlers shot down a Do 17 near the Humber light vessel, and the paddle ship *Balmoral* shot a German aircraft in the process of minelaying on 6 July 1941. The Ipswich-based patrol trawler *Norland* shot an He 111 down on 4 August, and off Withernsea the Grimsby-based minesweeping trawler *Wellsback* claimed a bomber on 9 August. On 15 September a Ju 88 was shot down by *Euclase*, a trawler from Lowestoft. Off Great Yarmouth on 12 November a Do 217 crashed after it hit the topmast of the trawler *Francolin*. The German aircraft was in the process of sinking the trawler. Although a Ju 88 managed to sink *Irvana* off Great Yarmouth on 30 January 1942, the vessel also crippled the German aircraft, which had to then ditch. On the same day the Lowestoft-based trawler *Fyldea* claimed another Ju 88.

After a period of absence the German E-boats returned in February 1942. There were four major engagements around Hearty Knoll, to the north-east of Great Yarmouth over the night of 19/20 February. There was a convoy heading south, with HMS *Holderness* on standing patrol, and the convoy was being escorted by HMS *Mendip* and HMS *Pytchley*, both escort destroyers of the 21st Flotilla at Sheerness. The two escort destroyers were made aware of the E-boats' approach by monitoring radio frequencies. They opened up with everything they had, from 20 mm to 4 in. guns. The salvoes probably sank two or three of the incoming E-boats. Meanwhile, HMS *Holderness* moved in to capture the crew of one of the wrecked E-boats. As Lieutenant Ditcham of the Royal Naval Reserve jumped on board, the captain of the E-boat set off a demolition charge, which took the top off the E-boat's wheelhouse. Undeterred, a boarding-party took eighteen prisoners. Lieutenant Ditcham was later to receive the Distinguished Service Cross for his actions.

In the first three months of 1942 E-boats only claimed two vessels along the east coast of England. The Rosyth-based destroyer HMS

Vortigern, which had been brought out of reserve and was of First World War vintage, was sunk off Cromer by E-boat *S-104*. This would be the heaviest loss of life of Royal Navy personnel in any one ship in the defence of an east coast convoy. Of the 110 men on board only fourteen survived. This was despite the fact that the corvette HMS *Guillemot*, based in Harwich, was in the vicinity. She had avoided picking up the survivors of the destroyer and concentrated on protecting the convoy.

On 12 April 1942 vessels of the 4th E-boat Flotilla, now based at Ostend, sank the Swedish merchant ship *Scotia* with mines near the Aldeburgh light float. On the night of 20/21 April, six of the E-boat flotilla vessels laid a contact minefield off Aldeburgh. In the area were HMS *Cotswold* and HMS *Quorn*, protecting a convoy heading south. They missed some of the mines that had drifted, and as a result the Belgian merchant ship *Vae Victis* and the merchantman *Plawsworth* were both sunk. HMS *Cotswold* was severely damaged when she hit a mine, and five of the crew were killed, with twenty-three being injured. HMS *Quorn* also ran into a mine. Felixstowe-based motor gunboats that were chasing the E-boats broke off their pursuit to assist the two stricken destroyers. Most of the crew of HMS *Cotswold* were evacuated, and four tugs from Harwich towed her towards Shotley, where they beached her. Meanwhile HMS *Quorn* was towed to safety by the corvette HMS *Shearwater*.

The following month saw only four British vessels sunk, and over the next eight months three ships were lost in the Sheerness region, another three in the Humber area and only four in the area around Harwich. There was only one shipping loss in August 1942. This was the SS *Kyloe*, which was mined off Great Yarmouth and later beached. One of the major reasons for the drop-off in losses was the more aggressive policy of the motor gunboats that were now based in Great Yarmouth, Felixstowe and Lowestoft. Each time the E-boats were spotted the motor gunboats set off in pursuit.

A new system was brought in during the middle of 1942, known as the 'Inner and Outer Z Line'. Effectively it was an anti-E-boat patrol system. A series of mooring buoys were set up every four miles from Harwich up to Wells. Each of the buoys was given the prefix Z and a number. Each night one in three of these buoys would have a motor gunboat, a motor torpedo boat, a rescue launch or a motor launch alongside it. In effect there were ten units, usually of two craft, on the outer Z line. More units were deployed along the inner Z line, ten miles closer to the coast. In addition to this, there were up to seven destroyer and corvette standing patrols. As an additional precautionary measure the convoy route buoys were now given new names.

Every six minutes the sub-command plot rooms would receive and send information to Chatham HQ. For example, Harwich and Great Yarmouth would be informed if convoy ships were *en route* either from the Dover Strait or from Sheerness. Great Yarmouth would inform the Humber sub-command, and it in turn would tell the Tyne sub-command. In this way everyone would know precisely where the ships were along the coast and who was responsible for their safety. This information would also be passed onto Coastal Command and Fighter Command. The ports would also be made aware, and everyone would then know the name of the vessel, its type, when it had left port, the route it was taking, its ultimate destination and its average speed.

Radar stations had been set up all along the coast, but they were not a great deal of help to the Royal Navy or to the convoy ships. The radar could usually only pick up larger vessels, and because the E-boats were so small and made of wood they were rarely picked up. Equally, the radar was not that effective in plotting incoming minelaying aircraft. The system had been improved by the end of 1941. Effectively it was a type of microwave radar; it could now pick up relatively small objects down to sea level at a range of fifteen miles. A number of stations were set up along the east coast.

Another valuable source of information was Y Service. It was designed to listen in to German radio traffic. Originally it had been set up in the middle of 1940 as part of the protection system in case the Germans decided to invade. At that stage the service had operated from mobile vehicles. By the middle of 1941 the service was now operating at Felixstowe, Southwold, Trimmingham, Winterton and Withernsea. Shortly afterwards there would be another at Sheringham, and a specialist RAF unit based at Gorleston that was responsible for trying to detect incoming minelaying aircraft. German messages were picked up by German-speaking WRNS, and the information sent on to Harwich and to Immingham. It was then disseminated to particular locations if it was of direct relevance to them.

As 1942 continued there were still victims along the east coast. On 27 May the Great Yarmouth-based minesweeper HMS *Fitzroy* was lost about forty miles east of the town. What is distinctly possible about this particular loss is that there is intense speculation that the mine was in fact British. On 9 July the boom trawler *Tunisian* based in Felixstowe went down after it struck a mine, killing twenty-nine crewmen. In the previous two months even tiny fishing-vessels fell victim to mines. *Little Express* was sunk on 4 May and *Maggie* on 17 June. The *Little Express* was working out of Tollesbury in Essex at the mouth of the River Blackwater, just nine miles from Maldon and twelve miles from Colchester. They had also lost *Thistle* in 1941 to a mine (not to be mistaken with the *Thistle* that was a naval examination drifter, which had been sunk by a mine off Lowestoft on the very same day in 1941).

The job of trying to recover and defuse mines was an unenviable task. One of the key places that this took place was on Corton beach, to the north of Lowestoft in Suffolk. On a number of occasions mines were brought in and successfully defused. These groups were often referred to as Rendering Mines Safe Parties. They would literally have to deal with almost any type of mine, German or British, which needed defusing. Upwards of 700 mines had been rendered safe by these groups along the Norfolk coast alone by the end of the war.

One of the major reasons for the lull in E-boat activity through the summer months of 1942 was the fact that they were focusing on the English Channel. The E-boats were redeployed back to Holland in the autumn, and they renewed their attacks along the east coast. On the night of 19/20 September 1942, HMS *Hambledon*, a Harwich-based destroyer, and the corvette HMS *Mallard* fought a running battle with E-boats off Great Yarmouth. On the night of 6/7 October 7 no fewer than twelve E-boats from the 2nd and 4th Flotillas came in close to Sheringham. They used torpedoes to sink the Harwich rescue tug *Caroline Moller*, Motor Launch 339 from Great Yarmouth and three merchant ships, *Ilse*, *Jessie Maersk* and *Sheafwater*. Just a week later, near Dudgeon Shoal to the north of Sheringham, the new 6th E-boat Flotilla sank the SS *George Balfour* and the Norwegian vessel *Lysand*. The 2nd Flotilla sank SS *Wandle* on 9 November, and on 12 December four ships heading north were sunk by the 4th Flotilla.

This pattern continued into 1943, but early on 18 February HMS *Garth*, a destroyer out of Sheerness, destroyed *S-71*, belonging to the 6th E-boat Flotilla off Lowestoft. The winter of 1942/3 claimed a number of vessels, most of which were relatively small. Twenty-one were sunk along the east coast, but all of these were sunk between Rochester and Hollesley Bay.

Compared to 1941, British shipping losses along the east coast had dropped by over sixty per cent, and by 1943 they had dropped in half again. Certainly one of the major reasons for the drop in ship losses was the fact that minesweeping was now being carried out by purpose-built vessels, rather than fishing vessels pressed into action.

By 1944 Nore Command had 288 vessels that were primarily dedicated to minesweeping operations. Thirty-three of them were fleet minesweepers and only 111 were minesweeping trawlers and drifters. The second key change was the stiffening of anti-aircraft defences, particularly around the ports and the Thames Estuary. It made it virtually suicidal for minelaying aircraft to try to drop their munitions, even at night. Radar had also improved, and it now pretty much covered the entire east coast. There were rotatable aerials covering every mile of sea along the east coast. All of these stations were directly linked by telephone to Nore Command and the plotting rooms. Anything that any of the stations picked up would immediately be transmitted and a response would be launched.

It took until 14 March 1943 for the first naval vessel to be lost off the east coast. This was the Lowestoft-based trawler *Moravia*. E-boats still made an occasional appearance; on 15 April the patrol trawler *Adonis* was sunk off Lowestoft by E-boats. On the night of 4/5 August at least seven German E-boats began laying a minefield to the east of Harwich. When the Ipswich-based patrol trawler *Red Gauntlet* appeared on the scene she was torpedoed, and sank with the loss of her entire crew.

No fewer than twenty-nine E-boats were involved in laying over a hundred mines around Harwich on the night of 24/25 September 1943. Their presence was discovered shortly before 0100 on 25 September. British vessels were immediately sent to investigate. First on the scene was *Carena*, an Ipswich-based patrol trawler, then another trawler from Ipswich, *Franc Tireur*, arrived, but was sunk by *S-96* with torpedoes. Another two trawlers, *Donna Nook* and *Stella Rigel*, collided with one another as they came in to investigate. HMS *Puffin*, a corvette from Harwich, and HMS *Pytchley*, a destroyer from Sheerness, approached from the north but were too slow to catch the E-boats, which were now beginning to move east. A pair of motor gunboats from Lowestoft and two motor launches from the same port closed in. The captain of ML150, Lieutenant J.O. Thomas, rammed the *S-96*, crippling her. Both of the motor launches managed to get back to Lowestoft.

An E-boat was lost on the night of 4/5 November, but they managed to torpedo two merchant ships off Cromer that night. Off Harwich on 13 November SS *Cormount* was sunk when she struck a mine laid by E-boats. Two weeks later *Morar* was lost in the same area. On 21 December *Norhawk*, a Norwegian merchant ship, was also lost to the same minefield. HMS *Worcester* out of Harwich and HMS *Holderness* out of Sheerness were both damaged by mines on 23 December.

Further north, around the Humber area, German aircraft dropped mines into the Humber approach. One of the aircraft crashed above Spurn Point on the night of 21/22 September.

Into 1944 just four vessels were lost along the east coast of England. On 13 February the 8th Flotilla sank the minesweeping trawler *Cap d'Antifer* from Grimsby, near Dudgeon. On 24 February E-boats from the 2nd and 8th Flotillas attacked a convoy at Hearty Knoll. They sank the merchant ship *Philipp M.* Mines accounted for the other two casualties; both were lost off Harwich on 20 May. One was the Dutch motor minesweeper 227 and the other the patrol trawler *Wyoming*.

When E-boats tried to lay mines in May 1944 they were spotted by a Swordfish of 819 Squadron, based at RAF Manston. The biplanes sank *S-87*.

There were some final offences against British shipping in 1945, which we will look at in Chapter Eight.

Unlike the First World War, where there were major fleet engagements in the North Sea, the German surface fleet only made one major and notable appearance in the Second World War. As it was, the operations would fall on the shoulders of the southern part of Nore Command.

The Germans had intended that their battle cruisers, *Scharnhorst* and *Gneisenau,* and their heavy cruiser *Prinz Eugen* would be used to attack British shipping in the Atlantic Ocean. By 1941 they were in the French port of Brest and under continual attack from British aircraft. Quite as to why the Germans chose to recall these vessels has been the subject of much speculation. In part it was the fact that the Germans thought that the Allies would consider trying to liberate Norway and it was an attempt to prevent the vessels suffering the same fate as the *Bismarck.* She had in fact left Germany with *Prinz Eugen* in May 1941, but she had not been so fortunate, and had been tracked down and destroyed by the British Home Fleet on 27 May 1941. The Germans had decided that rather than risk circumnavigating the British Isles and then heading into Icelandic waters and traversing the North Sea to get home, the vessels should make a dash through the English Channel and the Dover Strait, and skirt the southern part of the North Sea to get home.

The British had become aware of this possibility in early 1942. Two gaps had been swept in the British minefield and in the German minefield, so that Nore Command warships could assist in intercepting German vessels in the Dover Strait. Additional minesweepers and destroyers were shifted around, with a greater proportion of the force being stationed south of Nore Command. Experts studied the tides and looked for moonlit nights that would be possible dates on which the German vessels might attempt their dash.

At 0915 on 12 February 1942, under the command of Vice-Admiral Lyon, the Commander-in-Chief of Nore Command, six torpedo-equipped destroyers left Harwich. Four of them, HMS *Walpole*, HMS *Mackay*, HMS *Worcester* and HMS *Whitshed*, came from Captain Wright's 16th Flotilla, and two, HMS *Vivacious* and HMS *Campbell*, from the 21st Flotilla. The British did not know that *Scharnhorst* was already in the English Channel.

There had been little air cover that night as it was cloudy and moonless. Air cover resumed at dawn. In fact the German warships were not picked up on the radar until 1045, by which time they were closing in on Boulogne.

RAF Spitfires, on a sweeping mission, also spotted the German warships, but they did not choose to report what they had seen until they landed back at RAF Kenley. By the time the Royal Navy was informed it was 1137.

The RAF, meanwhile, had set aside 250 aircraft to make attacks should this type of incident happen. But it would take at least four hours before they would leave base. By this time the German vessels would be alongside the Dutch coast. Added to this, few of the crews of Bomber Command had any experience in attacking moving vessels. An additional concern was the fact that cloud cover was low, so the bombers would have to come in extremely low, and the worry was that their bombs would not pierce the armour of the warships.

As it was, the only aircraft that could make an immediate attack belonged to 825 Squadron of the Fleet Air Arm, based at RAF Manston. They had torpedoes fitted, and in three-quarters of an hour they were ready; fighters from 72, 121 and 401 Squadrons out of Hornchurch and Biggin Hill would fly as escorts.

The Swordfish got under way at 1220. They were soon joined by Spitfires of 72 Squadron. Leading the Swordfish attack was Lieutenant-Commander Esmonde. His leading aircraft was pounced on by Me 109s and Fw 190s. He peeled off and headed back towards the British coast, still being chased, but his aircraft crashed into the sea and he and his two crew members were killed. The other five Swordfish pressed the attack, and all of them were shot out of the sky by the anti-aircraft guns on the warships. It was simply suicidal.

The next attack came from motor torpedo boats operating out of Ramsgate and Dover. The Ramsgate vessels had been transferred from Felixstowe. They fired a number of torpedoes, but to no effect.

Meanwhile, the destroyers that had steamed out of Harwich arrived. The six vessels split into two groups. The captains and crew knew that they were hopelessly outgunned and that they were under threat, not only from the vast warships, but also from the German aircraft, E-boats and destroyers protecting the larger vessels. More Nore Command destroyers were now ordered out to sea. Three, HMS *Berkeley*, HMS *Fernie* and HMS *Garth*, were sent from Sheerness. Four more, HMS *Eglinton*, HMS *Hambledon*, HMS *Quorn* and HMS *Southdown*, were sent from Harwich. These steamed to a position some forty miles to the east of the Naze. Great Yarmouth sent eleven motor gunboats south, and rescue tugs left Harwich and Great Yarmouth. For safety's sake the RAF air-sea rescue launches operating out of Felixstowe and Gorleston also made an appearance.

By 1411 the responsibility for dealing with the Germans had fallen to Nore Command, as they were now out of Dover's area of operations. At 1507 HMS *Walpole* had to return to base due to engine problems, but at 1517 HMS *Campbell* picked up the distinct blips of German warships.

The Germans had actually split up into two groups. What they did not know was that *Scharnhorst* had hit a British mine and damaged her hull. At around this time some German Stukas (Ju 87s and some Ju 88s) attacked HMS *Mackay*.

At about 1531 the destroyers spotted *Gneisenau* and *Prinz Eugen*, and there were a number of escort aircraft and light vessels providing all-round protection. Undeterred by heavy shelling, the destroyers closed to within 2,500 yards and then fired their torpedoes. But they had no luck; not one of the destroyers hit a target.

Suddenly HMS *Worcester* was bracketed by eight hits in three minutes. Her mast and funnel were shot off and much of the superstructure wrecked. There were explosions up and down the ship. Almost immediately she began to list. Instead of finishing her off, the Germans, believing the destroyers to be cruisers, continued on their way. The action had taken just eleven minutes. HMS *Campbell* and HMS *Vivacious* pulled alongside HMS *Worcester* to help. At this point both of the vessels were torpedoed by a Beaufort of Coastal Command's 42 Squadron. Luckily the torpedoes missed.

The five destroyers came under a number of attacks from German aircraft, but there were no more hits. By this stage Bomber Command was now joining in, and thirty-nine of their aircraft tried to sink the ships. A small German trawler was sunk and a torpedo boat damaged. Bomber Command had launched over 200 aircraft, but the bulk of them could not find any targets.

As for HMS *Worcester,* she was about to be abandoned, as it seemed certain that she would sink. Incredibly she managed to get under way on her own, and she got back to base, having lost twenty-three dead and forty-five wounded. She was taken to Chatham to be repaired, and returned to active duty in May.

Although Nore Command had failed to destroy the German warships, all three of them had been damaged. They would be out of action for months. At least it would bring some respite to Allied merchant ships in the Atlantic and Arctic Oceans that they would not be on hand to assist the German U-boat attacks.

CHAPTER SEVEN

Baedeker and Beyond

O n 24 April 1942 the German propagandist, Baron Gustav Braun von Sturm, proclaimed, 'We shall go out and bomb every building in Britain marked with three stars in the Baedeker Guide.'

This was in response to a raid launched by RAF Bomber Command against the historic Baltic port of Lübeck on the night of 28 March 1942. Some 234 bombers had rained high-explosive bombs and incendiaries all across the old town part of Lübeck, largely comprising wooden buildings. The centre of the town had been destroyed and a thousand people had been killed. Hitler was determined to order reprisal attacks against British towns. They would strike against Exeter, Norwich, Canterbury, York and Bath.

The catalyst behind the Baedeker raids of 1942 was none other than Air Marshal Arthur Harris, the Commander-in-Chief of Bomber Command, who had been appointed to the post on 22 February. He believed that striking against cities rather than industrial targets would sap German morale and break their will to fight far quicker than strategic bombing. It was to bring devastation, not only to German cities but also to five historic towns in Britain, where upwards of 50,000 buildings would either be destroyed or badly damaged.

The so-called Baedeker raids are named after Karl Baedeker's international travel guides. The firm had been established in 1827 and the guides grew so popular that they were available in a number of international editions. Paradoxically, the Baedeker's company building by this stage in Leipzig was gutted in an air raid in December 1943. After the war, the company was revived and continues as an imprint, and is still available in translation across the world. It was on the basis of the Baedeker guide to Great Britain that the British cities were chosen for their historical importance as targets for bombing raids.

Since the Baedeker raids did not commence until April 1942, we must first look at the early months of that year and trace the progress of the air war over the east coast.

One of the main implications of the Germans introducing the Do 217 was that they could carry heavier bombs. This is amply illustrated by an incident that occurred at Lowestoft on 13 January 1942. At 1627 a Do 217 dropped four 500 kg bombs onto the centre of Lowestoft. Sixty-nine people were killed, one was classified as being missing and 114 were injured. The centre of the town's shopping area was virtually obliterated. The buildings were literally pulverised, and it was a nightmare for survivors and rescuers alike.

Four days later, in the *Lowestoft Journal* and *Mercury*, stories of enormous bravery and selflessness began to emerge:

> One of the acts of heroism revealed by the rescue work was that of the manager of a multiple tailor's shop. His body was found shielding his 17-year-old assistant, Beryl Bunn, who was rescued with injuries to her legs, which were not serious. 'The staff evidently had no time to bolt for safety,' said one of the rescue party, 'and he must have thrown himself on top of the girl as they fell to the floor. Mr Slater had been killed by the debris which fell on him.'

Edmund Penman was 20 in January 1942, and was working at a shipyard in Oulton Broad. He among many others was ordered to assist in the rescue attempts, as he recalled:

> There were so many people doing their best to release the buried casualties that the Incident Officer had to clear the site in order for the trained people to be able to work safely. I joined my party who were releasing casualties from the first layer of rubble, passing them to stretcher bearers, who were using the Odeon cinema foyer as a casualty clearing station. Our own rescue parties were joined by organised squads from the Royal Navy and the Army. There would be about 150 of us working on site. It was dark and floodlights were supplied by the harbour yard regardless of any further enemy action.

Kenny Bourn was just 15 at the time. He saw a Dornier come in low as he sat in an air raid shelter covered by an 8 ft square slab of 2-in. steel plate. The bombs dropped were so close that the plate lifted 8 inches and then fell back into place. He went on to describe what happened next:

> I rushed across to see if I could help once things had subsided a bit, and got into London Road North, where Wallers [a popular restaurant] was devastated. I came across a man who was injured but still alive. As he was trapped by an 8-inch by 10-inch wooden beam, I rushed back to the works [Kenny was working for a joiner] to get a saw and set about cutting through the obstruction. When I had cut through two-thirds of the beam, the saw struck a 6-inch wire nail, which blunted the teeth. So I went back for another saw and eventually we got this chappie free, but he died on us before we could get him away by ambulance.

Mrs Swaine worked in a grocer's shop. She was just about to leave the shop to buy some cakes when a number of bombs fell, and, in her own words:

> Within a flash thirteen shops were completely demolished – including the restaurant which I was about to visit. It was an extremely cold afternoon and snow was falling heavily. As I looked out, with all our windows smashed, the outside was as dark as night, for paving stones and earth were still floating about in the air.

The Germans were not finished with Lowestoft, and they returned on the evening of 19 January. This time two 250 kg bombs demolished a building in Denmark Street.

Close by Great Yarmouth feared the worst, but it was lucky in January, and just four bombs were dropped around Alpha Road at 1800 on the 21st.

Lowestoft's agony continued on 22 January; this time four 500 kg bombs shattered buildings in Till Road, Summer Road and Stanley Street. Other targets were not immune from attacks, although Lowestoft and Great Yarmouth seemed to be bearing the brunt. Four bombs fell around Horning school on the night of 10/11 January. At 1809 on 19 January two 500 kg bombs were dropped on

Sheringham. This had been the first attack since July 1941, and the weapons succeeded in killing four and flattening four houses. Five bombs were dropped on Southwold on 20 January, a mine was dropped off Felixstowe pier on 22 January and a Do 217, unable to find a shipping target, dropped four bombs around Lowestoft station. Reedham received four bombs on 31 January, and a second Ju 88 dropped bombs on Cromer.

It is important to bear in mind that this period had seen a heavy fall of snow. Conditions were not ideal for aerial activity; it was cloudy and the night-time temperatures dropped perilously low. Still the *Luftwaffe* pressed on in the worst of conditions. A pair of Dorniers dropped bombs on Southwold on 2 February, Do 217s braved icy conditions to drop four bombs to the south of Coltishall on 6 February. Three bombs were dropped on Mutford near Lowestoft on 17 February, and Great Yarmouth came under attack from sixteen German bombers on 18 February. They dropped four high-explosive 250 kg bombs, straddling Northgate Street. Eight people were killed and five were injured. The attack had come in at 1250 and had it been ten minutes later dozens would have been killed and hundreds injured as they made their way home for lunch. The RAF of 151 Squadron in their Defiants managed to shoot down a Do 217 that day, as they attempted to attack a convoy off Norfolk, and a heavy bomb was dropped close to Beccles.

Into March 1942 bombs dropped on Bradwell, Happisburgh, Winterton and Lowestoft. On 8 March night-fighters belonging to 406 Squadron shot down a German raider, probably an He 111. There was definitely a reduction in *Luftwaffe* activity, but the defenders could not let down their guard, as at any moment a major raid could be launched. Consequently, night-fighter defences were being improved, with the arrival of Mosquito squadrons at Wittering and Castle Camps in Cambridgeshire. The RAF was also being far more aggressive and actively seeking out intruders and striking against German airfields.

A prime example of the RAF's new striking ability took place on 3/4 March 1942. Over 220 bombers dropped flares, incendiaries and high explosives on a car factory near Paris. It was not only highly successful, but also the RAF suffered very few losses. Towards the end of the month, as we have seen, the RAF launched their assault on Lübeck. Up until this time no German city had been subjected to this kind of attack.

It took the Germans a little while to respond, but on 14 April Hitler warned of what was to come:

> When targets are being selected, preference is to be given to those where attacks are likely to have the greatest possible effect on civilian life. Beside raids on ports and industry, terror attacks of a retaliatory nature are to be carried out against towns other than London. Minelaying is to be scaled down in favour of these attacks.

All of the Baedeker raids were led by He 111 Pathfinder aircraft, and the bombers were guided into their target by radio location beams from Cherbourg and Boulogne. The Countermeasures Unit of 80 Wing was capable of jamming these, but there was another signal that the British knew nothing about: the location beams were very accurate; they were set by a map reference and the equipment aboard the He 111s would enable them to pick up the beams and then drop incendiaries and flares onto the target so that the other bombers could be guided in.

On the first raid against Norwich on the night of 27/28 April, the railway station seemed to be the central point. In fact the roof of the station was completely gutted. The centre of the target for the second raid was Orford Place in the centre of Norwich, and this again was completely wrecked. The air raid sirens began to wail at 2321. Searchlights hunted for the enemy raiders high above them. By way of a diversion, twenty Ju 88s had been dispatched to mine the area around Cromer and Southwold. The incoming raiders had been picked up as early as 2015. The first bombs began falling on Norwich at 2340; incendiaries fell all around the railway station. Straight afterwards low-flying German aircraft machine-gunned the streets. Then the main force of German bombers appeared.

Fighters were sent up, including nine Beaufighters of 68 Squadron out of Coltishall, ten Spitfires of 610 Squadron from Ludham and three Mosquitoes of 157 Squadron from Castle Camps. The first high-explosive bombs fell around Drayton Road, but others engulfed Shorncliffe Avenue and Valpy Avenue. More damage was done as bombs fell on Dereham Road and Hailsham Road. Bombs fell on the Clark's shoe factory, incendiaries around St Mary's Silk Mills, more incendiaries were dropped around the station, and soon the fire was out of control, extending to around 120 acres. There were fires in up to 180 different locations. The mixture of incendiaries and 500 kg high explosives shattered the centre of the city. Buildings in Elmgrove Lane, Earlham Road, St Giles Street and numerous other locations were shattered and the Co-op warehouse in Victoria goods station yard was gutted.

The bombing had reached such intensity by 0022 on 28 April that the telephone exchange was evacuated, effectively cutting off much of the city from the outside world. The Norwich Fire Service was operating 170 pumping points and nearly 8.4 million gallons of water were used over the next twenty-four hours. So much water was used that two reservoirs were emptied. There was danger from escaping gas and severed electricity cables.

The last of these bombs fell at around 0045. It has been estimated that two He 111s had operated as Pathfinders and that a mixed force of Do 17s, He 111s and Ju 88s were involved in this first raid. Certainly no more than around twenty-six bombers were involved. A total of 174 people were killed, of whom twenty-four were children.

In just ninety minutes this handful of bombers had caused irreparable damage to the city of Norwich. The authorities' reaction was swift. Enormous resources were poured into the city to help the injured, deal with the dead and cope with the homeless. Steps were also taken to try to prevent this from ever happening again. The area became a Gun Defender Area, with a battery of mobile guns of the 106th Regiment of the Royal Artillery (heavy anti-aircraft) being put in place. Their regimental HQ was at 221 Beccles Road, Gorleston. A rocket battery was also brought in, whose HQ was established in Unthank Road, Norwich.

Unfortunately Norwich's ordeal was not yet over. They returned for a second major raid on the night of 29/30 April. This time, seventy aircraft were involved, and in excess of 90 tons of bombs were dropped within the city area. The sirens sounded at 2310. It was a fine, cloudless, clear and moonlit night and the bombs started dropping on the city at 2325.

This time, having identified their targets with flares, they dropped 1 kg incendiary bombs and large high-explosive bombs. Once again the raid was led by He 111s, seven of them. They illuminated Norwich with flares and incendiaries. Following them were eleven Do 217s of *KG2* out of Soesterberg and eleven more from Schiphol. These were quickly followed by eight Do 217s flying out of Gilze Rijen, nine Do 17s of *KG55* and nine more of *KG40*. Following up the rear were five Do 217s of *KG4* and fifteen Ju 88s.

The centre of the bombing was around Orford Place and Rampant Horse Street. The inhabitants of Norwich were not even safe in their shelters from the massive 1,000 kg bombs. In Chapelfield a trench shelter received a direct hit and four people were killed. But there were some incredible escapes. In Miller's Lane five shelters were at the edge of a massive crater caused by a 1,000 kg bomb that had landed in that lane and in Nicholas Street. Twenty-seven people were sheltering in them, and just two people were killed.

One of the marked targets was certainly the city shopping centre, although Thorpe station and goods yard, the Bishop Bridge gas works and Boulton & Paul's factory were also secondary targets. The fact that the water works in Heigham Street had been put out of action in the previous raid caused enormous problems. This time the death toll amounted to sixty-nine, with eighty-nine more injured. It has been estimated that there were around 37,000 houses in Norwich in April 1942. The raids destroyed or damaged beyond repair nearly 1,500 of them, and another 19,500 were damaged but repairable. It would take weeks of work to make many of the buildings habitable again. The raids had destroyed three shoe factories, several engineering works, Caley's confectionery factory and a silk mill. It had thrown the city into chaos; emergency ration cards were needed and food was shipped as quickly as possible to the city to prevent additional privation. Several churches and other landmarks had been destroyed. Remarkably the Norfolk and Norwich Hospital, although partially damaged, had not received a direct hit. Mass funerals took place on 4, 5 and 7 May 1942. In some cases it had taken this long just to identify the bodies.

The biggest problem for Britain was to take positive steps to prevent the kind of devastation caused in Norwich from ever happening again. Fighter Command requested that barrage balloons be put in place around the city. By the beginning of May thirty-five of them were in place. On the night of 30 April/1 May, 68 Squadron claimed a Do 217 and two He 111s in the Wash area. At 0210 on 1 May bombs fell on Lowestoft. Meanwhile Norwich was bracing itself for yet another assault.

The raid started at 2345 on 8 May 1942 and continued to 0015 on 9 May. Seventy-six German aircraft had been dispatched. Of the hundred or more tons of bombs and incendiaries being carried, 1.5 tons fell on Norwich. The rest of the bombs fell in over twenty other locations across Norfolk, Suffolk, Kent, Hampshire and Sussex. The RAF launched thirty-seven sorties against the raiders. Compared to the two earlier raids there were very few casualties and far less damage.

It was not just Norwich that had suffered in the spring of 1942. On the night of 19/20 May Hull was attacked by at least twenty aircraft, while another seventy bombed targets in the Hull area. Incredibly just ten people were killed. On 30 May Hull was again the target, but little damage was done this time. But Great Yarmouth had not been so lucky, and four bombs had been dropped on Jewson's timber mill and on Albany Road, killing three and injuring three more.

Ipswich suffered a Baedeker-style raid all of its own on the night of 1/2 June, when thirty German aircraft were involved. It would have been another Norwich had the German aircraft not been decoyed by so-called Starfish Decoy Fires, lit by the British, which persuaded them to drop their bombs onto open heathland.

German losses actually began to mount over this period. On the night of 29/30 May a German aircraft had been shot down by anti-aircraft guns at Great Yarmouth. On the same night aircraft of 12 Group had shot down three Do 217s and a Ju 88, and in the early hours Great Yarmouth anti-aircraft gunners claimed a second kill.

A month later, 610 Squadron, flying Spitfires out of Ludham, shot down a Ju 88 that crashed into the sea at dawn off Yarmouth. This was the latest in a successful period for the squadron, which had claimed two Do 217s on 15 May.

King's Lynn was targeted on 12 June, when bombs fell around the Eagle Hotel and other buildings in the town centre and forty-two people were killed. Peterborough received a number of bombs and incendiaries in the early hours of 13 June. There was a great deal of damage caused by fire as the George Hotel, a nearby garage, a public house, a potato store and a clothing factory were all set ablaze. The same night saw Bedford bombed. Two 500 kg bombs dropped on Broad Avenue and Willow Road, and a thousand incendiary bombs were dropped from the four Dorniers across Cardington Road, Russell Avenue, Castle Road, Pembroke Road, South York Street, South Denmark Street, South Dudley Street, George Street and Greenshields Road.

The night of 24/25 June saw Great Yarmouth once again devastated, as high explosives and over 1,500 incendiaries were dropped on the town between 0130 and 0250. Bombs dropped across the whole of the centre of the town and gutted St Nicholas's parish church, Lacon's barrel stores and workshop and Brett's furniture store; and more bombs were dropped into the Rows area, between Row 107 and Row 128. Greyfriars Cloisters received additional damage, as did the library and the Toll House. Although the damage was widespread the casualties were remarkably low, with only three killed and nineteen injured.

Young Keith Farman watched the scene unfold from the roof of Hobland Hall that night:

> We could see in the distance that Yarmouth was alight, as this was the night that St Nicholas's church was hit. Many searchlights lit up the sky as they moved across, looking for German bombers. If they picked up one of the English fighter planes they would quickly move the lights. When they got one of the slower German bombers they would keep the lights on. As we watched I can remember the excitement when this happened and one of the RAF fighter pilots then chased a German plane that had two searchlights on it. We could see a yellow streak from our plane as the bullets left the guns on either wing, going straight into the German bomber. Our boy did his job well as he set alight the enemy bomber. As the plane burned it started to crash and we could see that some of the Germans had baled out and were coming down in their parachutes. 'That's one we got!' exclaimed Dad before he took me back to the safety of the cellar and my Mum.

On 4 July the Germans hit a target in the Newtown area of Great Yarmouth, which actually pleased many of the residents. A bomb scored a direct hit on the Corporation Refuse Destructor, which had an extremely tall chimney. Many of the locals were delighted when it was pulled down after being declared unsafe, as everyone thought that the German pilots used this as a landmark.

Incendiary bombs had been dropped near Peterborough, and high explosives near March, West Dereham and Bedford, on 3 July. A single Do 217 made an attempt to destroy the Lockheed hydraulics factory at Leamington Spa on 16 July. A similar attempt had been made on 13 June, but in this second attack four 500 kg bombs were dropped right on top of the factory. Luckily the damage was relatively slight. There had been another raid of a similar nature on 3 July, which had inflicted heavy casualties when a daylight attack by a Do 217 against the Rolls Royce factory in Derby had taken place. These specialised attacks also included one on 19 July, when buildings housing Marconi Radio and Hoffmann Ball Bearings were targeted in Chelmsford.

Great Yarmouth came under attack yet again on 12 July. The attack came in at 0145, and bombs fell on Wellington Road, where the Eastern Counties Omnibus Depot took a direct hit. There were four bombs dropped that night, killing two and injuring seven. Lowestoft was also bombed the same night; a high-explosive bomb hit the naval commander's office in Hamilton Dock and several workshops were damaged. One person was killed and five injured. In this attack the base commander's launch was sunk and two motor gunboats were wrecked.

There were a number of raids by Do 217s on the night of 21/22 July. A number of 500 kg bombs were dropped on Cromer at around 2337. Buildings were destroyed in Garden Street and Church Square, and eleven people were killed and fifteen injured. King's Lynn dock was also attacked, with incendiaries being dropped on St Anne's Street and North Street. More incendiaries fell on the Felixstowe dock area.

Eight different targets were struck late on 23 July, with nearly 500 incendiaries being dropped on King's Lynn dock by a pair of Do 217s. They came back an hour later and dropped high explosives. There was a dispute as to how many German aircraft were shot down that night; it was probably three, although at the time the British claimed seven.

There was one certainty however: a Ju 88 was shot down close to Smith Knoll light vessel on 25 July. Sheringham was attacked on the 27th, with nine people killed and two injured; and bombs also fell at Pulham, Aldeburgh and RAF Docking. Also on 27 July German aircraft penetrated as far as Cambridge the raid killing three and injuring eighteen people. Cambridge had been extremely lucky; a 1,000 kg bomb had dropped on an orchard, and although it had damaged a number of buildings no one was hurt.

The Germans tried their luck against Norwich again in the early hours of 28 July, attempting to drop incendiary bombs over the St Benedict's area of the city. A single Do 217 raided Great Yarmouth at 0856 on 29 July. At least four 500 kg bombs dropped from Royal Avenue to Palgrave Road and Alderson Road. Over forty houses were badly damaged, two shops were levelled, two people were killed and fifteen were injured. It is believed that the target was intended to be Vauxhall station.

On the night of 29/30 July, a number of German bombers, perhaps as many as a hundred, struck targets along the east coast, although many more flew further inland, aiming for Birmingham or even London. At 0142 five 250 kg bombs and some incendiaries fell on Bedford, killing four people. Between 0230 and 0330 there was enemy activity around RAF Feltwell, Honington and Newmarket. Cambridge also came under attack, but the Germans were not lucky enough to escape unscathed. A Ju 88 of *KG26* was shot by anti-aircraft guns near Cambridge and came down close to Peterborough. A second Ju 88 hit telephone wires in Norwich and was then hit by coastal anti-aircraft fire, and it came down into the sea. A Bofors gun, operating near Southwold, claimed an He 111 of *KG100*, a Do 217 of *KG2* was shot down by gunners in Lowestoft, and in fact in all six German aircraft were claimed that night, which was an unprecedented number.

A small number of raiders attacked Norwich again on the night of 1/2 August. Several fires were started in Exchange Street, St George Street, St Mary's Plain and Magdalen Street. During the course of the raid the rocket battery fired nearly 500 rounds, and the 3.7 in. guns 120 shells. None of the raiding aircraft were hit, but one Do 217 crashed into the sea off Norfolk when twelve of the aircraft attacked vessels.

In the late afternoon of 2 August eight Do 217s made a machine-gun attack on Watt's Naval School near the village of North Elmham, five miles north of East Dereham in Norfolk. Bombs were also dropped at Melton Constable, to the east of Fakenham.

At 0050 on 7 August flares were dropped on Cambridge. At around 0105, 360 incendiaries fell around Leys Road, Orchard Avenue and Arbury Road. High explosives then fell on a sewage farm and more incendiaries on Chesterton Road. Shortly afterwards more incendiaries fell on Newmarket Road and Ditton Walk. In all probability the primary target had been the Unicam works in Arbury Road, which made optical equipment for the military. By the time the raid ended at 0155 over a hundred homes had been badly damaged.

Peterborough's power station was targeted on 10 August. The first attack came in at 2351, quickly followed by another in which 250 incendiaries and three 500 kg bombs were dropped. None of them hit the power station but instead they fell on Oundle Road and around the Fengate pumping station. In the early hours of 11 August more incendiaries were dropped on Peterborough, in the

Loading parachute flares into a Ju88.

German bomb being prepared for a raid on Norwich.

Mines ready to be loaded onto a He 111.

German sea mine being winched onto a Ju88.

Do215B over the east coast.

nboard a Do17 bound for the east coast.

A flight of Do17s heading for the east coast.

Preparing a Do17 reconnaissance aircraft for take off.

He115 floatplane.

WRVNS billets, Queen's Road, Great Yarmouth, March 18 1943.

Watney, Combe and Reid's Maltings, March 18 1943.

Tail of a Me40 shot down near Shotley 23 August 1943.

Ju188 at Chartres in 1943.

...amage in Norwich during the Baedeker Raids.

RN vessel covering the Normandy landings in 1944

Aircrew safely aboard
an RAF ASR launch.

Naval help for
downed air crew.

V2.

3.7″ anti-aircraft gun and crew.

Caley's Chocolate Factory in Norwich after the second Baedeker Raid.

An Me410, a frequent visitor to the east coast in the latter stages of the war.

Derwent Road, causing a number of fires. High explosives were also dropped on Raeburn Road and Landseer Road.

So far, Colchester had not suffered a great deal from the raids, but this changed on 11 August, and it seems that the target was the Paxman factory. The works made engines for submarines and landing craft. A stray bomb hit a hospital for the mentally ill, killing thirty-eight of the patients.

At 2243 on 13 August sixteen or so German bombers approached Norwich. Now that the city was better defended, with anti-aircraft guns and the attention of RAF fighters, only five of the aircraft managed to unload their bombs onto the city. Around eighty incendiaries and three high explosives landed, shortly before 2300. A 250 kg bomb caused damage to Mousehold Avenue Infants School and fifty or so homes close by. The RAF would later claim that two Ju 88s were shot down that night.

There was an ineffective attack on Ipswich over the night of 14/15 August, and on the following night the Germans attempted to attack airfields, but were unsuccessful. Colchester was again raided on 16/17 August, when at least fifteen Dornier bombers were involved. The Germans failed in another attack on Norwich on the night of 18/19 August because they could not penetrate the defensive ring around the city. Instead they had to drop their bombs into the countryside.

Great Yarmouth's only attack in August 1942 took place on the night of the 22nd/23rd, when a single Dornier bomber dropped four 500 kg bombs. One of them hit a house in Baliol Road, but the others caused little or no damage, and only six people were injured. Also that night the Germans tried to hit the Unicam works once again. Four aircraft had been tasked to carry out the attack, but it was a disaster. One of the German bombers was shot down over Orford Ness by a Mosquito of 157 Squadron, and the others failed to find their targets.

A 500 kg bomb dropped straight onto an Anderson shelter in Moulton Road, Ipswich on the night of 25/26 August. It killed a mother and eight children sheltering inside. Luckier were the residents of a house in Harmony Square: a 500 kg bomb came straight through the roof but did not explode. Colchester was the target for twelve Ju 88s on 26 August, but they were decoyed and bombed nineteen miles to the west of their target. Anti-aircraft fire was able to claim one of the raiders.

A single Do 217 attacked Lowestoft on the evening of 28 August, and it dropped a number of incendiaries on Avondale Road. At least two Do 217s and a Ju 88 were shot down that night, mainly out to sea.

August 1942 had seen the introduction of the Me 210, and in fact one had been shot down off Great Yarmouth by Typhoons on 13 August. Another had actually been lost three days before that. This was a relatively new fighter reconnaissance bomber, and it had been moved for operations over Britain to begin at the start of August. The first sortie flown by *KG6* had taken place on 2 August against a convoy off the Yorkshire coast. Usually the Me 210s operated in pairs and it was one of these pairs that had been encountered on 13 August. A pair of them were tasked to bomb Norwich on 5 September. The air raid warning sirens went off at 1035; these aircraft were flying at 25,000 ft and they dropped four 250 kg bombs. Among the buildings that were hit were Frazer's Joinery Works at St Martin's Palace Plain and factories in Fishergate. In all, six people were killed and a number injured. Another two Me 210s were encountered by Spitfires of 610 Squadron to the south-east of Southwold that same day. Pilot Officer Creagh and Sergeant Gregory shot one of them up, and they saw it crash into the sea thirty miles to the east of Southend. The other Me 210 dropped bombs on Leigh-on-Sea and then headed home.

On 6 September another two Me 210s were spotted in the Middlesbrough area, and they were chased by Typhoons of 1 Squadron. Both of the raiders were shot down. Undeterred, these sorties continued, and six more were flown on 7 September. More of the sorties would be flown throughout the remainder of the month.

The Germans also deployed Ju 86 aircraft in 1942. It was a bomber and it had also been used as a civilian airliner. The Germans had converted these into high-altitude bombers. They began their operations in the middle of August. A pair of these bombers dropped 250 kg bombs on Cambridge on 25 August. At 0805 on 29 August a pair of Spitfires of 401 Squadron attempted to attack a Ju 86 that had been spotted over Horsham in Surrey. The problem was that it was flying so high, at around 40,000 ft, that they simply could not catch it. On the following day another Ju 86 targeted Chelmsford; this one was flying at 39,000 ft to the east of Ramsgate when it was spotted by Spitfires of 611 Squadron. Once again it was too high for the fighters, and the German bomber dropped its single 250 kg bomb on a warehouse in Baldon Road in Chelmsford.

The British realised that they had to respond to this new threat, and began to develop a Mosquito that was capable of catching the raiders. Spitfires had tried again on 5 September, when they had tried to engage one Ju 86 that had just bombed houses in Luton. The Spitfires got close but the bomber had managed to escape.

KG2 was now down to fifteen Do 217s instead of nearly thirty. It had lost the best part of half of its complement since mid-July 1942. None the less, four *KG2* aircraft and five others were launched against King's Lynn on the night of 17/18 September. They caused significant damage to the quay and the docks, and the railway line was also damaged. One of the Dorniers was lost to a Mosquito of 151 Squadron and the crew baled out near Docking. Eight civilians in Chapel Road, Colchester, were killed on 28 September when a low-flying Do 217 of *KG2* dropped four 500 kg bombs.

Certainly the intensity of German attacks was dropping off, as autumn gave way to winter in 1942. There were still some inland raids and activity against shipping along the east coast. But the British defensive systems had stiffened markedly; there were more aircraft in the skies by day and by night, and almost every target along the east coast bristled with anti-aircraft guns. Undeterred, sporadic attacks were still being launched. A prime example of the spread of attacks was on 19 October when German aircraft attacked Southend, Colchester, Little Oakley, Ipswich, Snape, Needham Market, Kessingland, Great Yarmouth, Cromer and Wainfleet. Most of these attacks were carried out by single Do 217s. Bombs were dropped at 0715 on the outskirts of Norwich, and just under two hours later more bombs fell on Pottergate and Westwick Street in the city centre. Incredibly one of the raiders, actually a Ju 88, was brought down by a Czech serviceman with a bren-gun at Oulton near Lowestoft. It was an expensive day as far as the Germans were concerned: near Cromer Knoll Flight Lieutenant Winward of 68 Squadron shot down a Ju 88, a Do 217 was lost without trace after it had bombed Norwich, and several other aircraft were badly damaged. It is believed that up to thirty-six German aircraft were involved in the attacks throughout the course of the day. Early-morning attacks were launched on 21, 22, 26 and 31 October; targets ranged from Walsingham to Orford and from North Walsham to Parham.

A solitary Do 217 set off just before dawn on 3 November to make a pin-point attack on a factory to the south of Thorpe station in Norwich. Poor weather and faulty navigation meant that the aircraft crossed just to the north of Great Yarmouth, rather than over Cromer as had been planned. As the aircraft approached Norwich there was a heavy rainstorm. At 0750 the air raid sirens began to wail. The aircraft came in, believing it was making straight for the factory. The first of the four 500 kg bombs fell on Surrey Street Bus Station, but it did not explode; it went straight through a single-decker bus. The three other bombs were then dropped onto the Cattle Market and All Saint's Green. None of them exploded. The Do 217 then headed for home, chased by a Beaufighter. It escaped, but the crew, although all were awarded the Iron Cross for their exploits, were to be shot down and killed on 2 January 1943.

There was more activity, this time by Me 109s and then by Do 217s, off Great Yarmouth and Happisburgh during the morning of 3 November. The Do 217 skirted around Norwich and then machine-gunned Southwold before it disappeared. On 6 November a solitary Do 217 bombed two shipyards and a malt house at Oulton Broad; one person was killed and a wrecked motor gunboat was destroyed. A month now passed before any other significant activity.

On 15 December 1942 a Do 217 used its machine-guns and then dropped four 500 kg bombs on the High Street at Aldeburgh. Eleven people were killed, including five members of the 5th Royal Berkshire Regiment, and twenty-nine other people were injured. One of the casualties was a 90-year-old man who had refused to leave his armchair.

Great Yarmouth was once again hit on 22 December. This time an enemy aircraft dropped a pair of bombs between Heigham Place and Albion Road. Also dropped were a number of phosphorus incendiary bombs. These new 50 kg incendiaries were being used for the first time on the east coast. The bombs caused significant damage to St Mary's Catholic School and started a number of fires. Eight people were killed and twenty-seven were injured in the attack. Anti-aircraft gunners around Great Yarmouth shot down the raider and it crashed into the sea.

By 1943 the frequency and severity of attacks along the east coast of England had seen a marked decline. There were still isolated anti-shipping and mine operations, and on a number of occasions when the German aircraft were unable to find suitable shipping targets they strayed inland to bomb ports and other targets.

Norwich received an unwanted New Year's Day gift when a Do 217 dropped nine 50 kg bombs around Russell Street. The bombs damaged St Barnabas's church and the Mission Hall. The raider then sped off and machine-gunned indiscriminately around Hellesdon, Salthouse and Neatishead.

Harwich was hit on 6 January by a Do 217, which shot-up Beacon Hill Fort, the Regal cinema and a saw mill. It then dropped four 500 kg bombs that landed on a farm at Ramsey Wash. Five days later, on 11 January, seven bombers were operating off Lowestoft. Two came in and dropped sticks of bombs on Lowestoft silk works. The second attacker dropped bombs across Kessingland and Oulton Broad. The following day four people were killed at Heybridge, close to Maldon in Essex.

Do 217s and Ju 88s attacked London on the night of 17 January. At least three were shot down by 85 Squadron and one was shot down into the sea off Bradwell, Essex. The Orford Ness Research Station was targeted at 1947 on 25 January. A parachute mine created an enormous crater at Gedgrave, and another bomb fell near Orford Quay.

On the morning of 9 February seven firepots were dropped on Southwold by a Do 217, and it also dropped a 500 kg bomb, which created a massive crater in Pier Avenue. Other Do 217s were active that day, with attacks being made at Huntingfield, Melton, Spexhall, Darsham and Metfield in Suffolk. On 17 February Fw 190s attacked Clacton. Each could carry a single 500 kg bomb. Their target was the Light Anti-Aircraft School at the Butlin's Camp. They killed one child in the attack.

Mines were dropped off Orford Ness at the beginning of March; these were new devices that were designed to anchor to the seabed and then rise at a predetermined time. There was a major German raid on the night of 3/4 March when upwards of a hundred Ju 88s and Do 217s crossed the Essex coast and bombed London, Chelmsford and a number of other targets. One attack killed two people when the Liverpool Street–Colchester train was derailed near Chelmsford. A number of bombs fell on Southend and Gravesend, and five were killed at Chatham Dock. This was the night when there was panic at Bethnal Green underground station and 178 people were trampled to death.

The Germans, however, did not escape without casualties; the Shoeburyness heavy anti-aircraft guns shot down a Ju 88 at Burnham-on-Crouch, and the Clacton guns claimed another. It is also possible that another Do 217, badly damaged, crashed near Antwerp.

At 0635 a Do 217 dropped seven high-explosive bombs along Queen's Road and Nelson Road South in Great Yarmouth on 18 March. One of the bombs fractured the gas and water mains, another hit Mason's Laundry, but one struck a large house at the junction of Queen's Road and Nelson Road South. It was occupied by WRNS girls as their quarters. Six of the women were killed and seven were listed as missing. Not content with this, later on in the day, at 2316, a pair of parachute mines were dropped towards the south end of Fish Wharf, and two more to the west of Caister Road. One of these mines damaged the Smith's potato crisp factory. There was also an incendiary raid on Gorleston High Street, and a parachute mine completely destroyed a malting in Southtown. Although a Mosquito of 410 Squadron shot down a Do 217 over the Wash and another Mosquito of 157 Squadron shot down a Ju 88, the Germans ranged far and wide that night, and Norwich was hit once again.

The attack came in at around 2230, with the first bombs dropping about twenty minutes later. Old Catton was hit first, then two parachute mines fell on Stoke Holy Cross. Bombs and incendiaries fell on Mulbarton and more on Raveningham. A pair of parachute mines fell at Oulton and incendiaries on Cringleford, Toft Monks and Halesworth. Bombs, mines and incendiaries damaged or destroyed buildings at Sutton, Swainsthorpe, Hemsby, Hainford, Bilney, Cawston, Beddingham, Colkirk, Runham, Heckingham, Colney, Kettlestone, East Raynham, Hempnall and Stratton Strawless.

The bombs landing directly on Norwich included high explosives and incendiaries, along with firepots. A large fire was started in St Andrew's Street; there were more fires in Pottergate. Bombs exploded in Cardigan Street, Devonshire Street, Russell Street, Old Palace Road and other locations. The telephone exchange was hit and in all there were thirty-nine incidents across the city.

Lowestoft also felt the brunt of the attack that night. Six or so German aircraft dropped high explosives and incendiaries along Oulton Road, Mill Road, North Quay, Princes Road, Water Lane and Rotterdam Road.

Aiming for Norwich once again, twenty Do 217s came in to attack on the night of 29/30 March. A combination of decoy fires, anti-aircraft guns and night-fighters meant that the Germans dropped bombs around Great Plumstead and Braberton. However, they also dropped phosphorus bombs and incendiaries on Hulver Street.

The oil refinery at Thameshaven was targeted by thirty enemy aircraft on 4 April. Four workers were killed. Other German aircraft mined the Thames Estuary, and this would later lead to the loss of SS *Josefina Thorden* and *Dynamo*. The anti-aircraft guns at Sunkhead Fort shot down two of the raiders and another anti-aircraft battery claimed a third.

Chelmsford was the target on the night of 14/15 April. The sirens went off at 0007, and at 0029 marker flares were dropped. But minutes later incendiaries started to fall, followed by phosphorus bombs and firepots. Most of the ordnance fell wide of the target, but two parachute mines landed near Victoria Road, some incendiaries fell on the prison, and other buildings around the town were also hit, including a department store, a suet factory and other premises. An explosive and chemical plant on Bramwell Island and a mine depot at Wrabness were also targeted, and bombs fell on Kelsale. The main target in Chelmsford had been the Hoffmann ball bearing factory: it was hit but not badly damaged. One of the Dorniers was shot down by 157 Squadron; three were claimed by Mosquitoes and two by anti-aircraft guns.

However, this was not the end of the Germans' ordeal; they still had to run the gauntlet of British aircraft that had been sent up to interdict them. Wing Commander Little of 418 Squadron shot down one of the Ju 88s at Beauvais in northern France. Squadron Leader Tomalin of 605 Squadron pounced on two Dorniers as they came in to land, but anti-aircraft fire saved them. Also over the night a number of Ju 88s laid more mines off Lowestoft and Harwich.

Another operation was planned against Norwich in the early hours of 5 May. The targets included Thorpe railway station, Boulton & Paul, the power station and other strategic targets. Bombs and high explosives began dropping between 0300 and 0400. As far as the city was concerned many of the bombs dropped around St Andrew's. Part of St Andrew's parish church tower was damaged, a shop in Bridewell Alley was destroyed and two premises in Queen Street were gutted. Other bombs fell around Larkman Lane, and Hellesdon, with a number of parachute mines dropping across East

Anglia. The Germans lost a Do 217 shortly after it had taken off from Eindhoven, and another crash-landed on its way home.

On 7 May there was another attack on Great Yarmouth, and this time seven Fw 190s attacked the port for the first time. They dropped a number of 500 kg bombs around Southtown railway station and Vauxhall station. One of the bombs was immediately defused by a naval bomb disposal officer who was waiting for a train. The German aircraft then machine-gunned the town, and thirteen people were killed, with fifty-one being injured in the attack. Virtually at the same time more Fw 190s dropped bombs and machine-gunned Caister, Hemsby and Winterton.

Four days later, on 11 May, at 0845, between eighteen and twenty Fw 190s dropped fourteen high-explosive bombs on the northern outskirts of Great Yarmouth. Three of the bombs fell into the marshland, but one hit an ATS billet, killing twenty-six girls. Charles Box, the Chief Constable and ARP Controller, later wrote:

> This and the previous raid on the 7th May, 1943, were part of the new technique adopted by the enemy, i.e. sweeping in very low at wave-top, and it seemed apparent that a balloon barrage would act as a deterrent. I made urgent representation to the Regional Commissioner, who visited this borough the same day, and within a few hours of his visit barrage balloons were flying. Whether or not it was due to this balloon barrage, no further attacks of this type were experienced; however, for a period the Civil Defence Service's duties were so arranged that these attacks were anticipated. These types of raids by their widespread and indiscriminate nature caused new problems but they were soon overcome. The housewives' service again rendered valuable assistance to the unfortunate householders. The casualties were 49 killed and 41 injured.

Eight Fw 190s screamed over Lowestoft at rooftop level the following morning. They killed six and wounded twelve. The primary target seemed to be the training trawlers *Strathgarry* and *Shova*. Seaman James Swann won the Distinguished Service Medal as he machine-gunned the raiders, despite the fact that four of his shipmates were lying wounded around him. Twenty Fw 190s came again at dusk. They dropped 500 kg bombs on the outer harbour, the High Street and the gas works. One of the bombs was dropped on Corton Road and it bounced 150 yards. Another thirty-three people were killed and fifty-five people wounded. One incredibly brave member of the Royal Naval Patrol Service, a stoker, sacrificed himself when he threw himself on top of a Wren in the High Street just as a pub collapsed on top of them.

Chelmsford was attacked by at least twenty-seven German aircraft at 0206 on 14 May. Bombs fell around the Hoffmann factory and the Marconi factory. One of the raiders dropped two mines; one hit the Marconi factory, flattening a testing shop and damaging an assembly shop. This was to halt production for almost a month. A 250 kg bomb hit the bus station in Duke Street and it also wrecked a number of buses and buildings. So intense was the fire that 250 tyres caught light.

At around dusk on 15 May Southwold and Felixstowe were attacked after the raiders had been frightened away from Harwich by the anti-aircraft guns and barrage balloons. Ten people were killed at Southwold and six were wounded at Felixstowe Ferry.

Frinton and Walton-on-the-Naze were attacked by Fw 190s on 30 May. At Frinton a bomb landed at the end of Connaught Avenue and another wedged itself in the girders of the water tower. The police station and Catholic church were destroyed at Walton-on-the-Naze, killing four people.

Margate was struck on 1 June, and ten people were killed when a church was destroyed at Manston. At dawn the following morning, again avoiding Harwich, bombers struck the dock area at Ipswich. They also bombed Felixstowe and Bawdsey. Incredibly, at Felixstowe, a gun emplacement was missed by literally yards, and at Brackenbury Beach a bomb bounced over a 60 ft cliff and landed on a road but did not explode. Although the raiders killed eleven people and wounded fifteen others at Ipswich, one of them came to grief when it hit a dock crane.

Although most of the activity seemed to be concentrated on the southern parts of the east coast, Grimsby had so far avoided much of the attention that Hull had received over the years. This changed on the night of 13/14 June, when incendiaries, anti-personnel mines and high explosives were dropped across Grimsby. In all, 332 fires were set and a huge number of unexploded anti-personnel bombs had to be dealt with. They had to be retrieved from gutters, tops of buses and trees. A number of people would be killed or injured over the coming days as a result. On the night of 22 June an Fw 190 crashed into the River Medway, near Rochester Bridge. Hull was attacked on the night of 23/24 June, but luckily there were few casualties. They were not so lucky on the night of 13/14 July, when twenty aircraft were involved. They caused sixty-nine fires around the town centre and station. Areas of Grimsby were also attacked, as was Cleethorpes. Some twenty-six people were killed in Hull alone.

The last major raids on East Anglian towns took place on the night of 23/24 October. Up to thirty Do 217s and Ju 88s launched a concentrated raid between 2258 and 2355. Great Yarmouth and Lowestoft were the principal targets. It has been estimated that 12,000 incendiary bombs and fifty high explosives were targeted at the towns. Most of the incendiary bombs fell in the south-west area of Gorleston at around 2330. Many also fell on Oulton Broad and others fell on Blundeston.

All in all, however, the raid was a complete failure, and this final raid of 1943 would be the last that Great Yarmouth would have to endure until 1 June 1944, when four high-explosive bombs would fall harmlessly onto the South Denes.

There was a dramatic drop-off in activity throughout November and December 1943. On 3 December there was a major attack on Ipswich, which developed around 1900. Bombs dropped at Rushmere St Andrew, Yoxford and Bramford, and Fison's chemical factory was set alight. The main force of bombers came in shortly afterwards, dropping bombs around Westerfield Road and Henley Road. More bombs dropped on Norwich Road, Leopold Road, Colchester Road, as well as Yarmouth Road and other targets. Around nineteen 500 kg bombs had been dropped, and over 1,000 incendiaries.

One of the last major attacks of 1943 was against Norwich. Two aircraft were involved, and they dropped incendiaries on Unthank Road and then high explosives around Bluebell Road.

The last recorded incident of 1943 took place on 10 December. Nine bombs were dropped at Wrabness and others across Essex, and four bombs fell on Colchester. On that night Flying Officer Schultz of 410 Canadian Squadron shot down three Do 217s off Clacton. They had been intending to attack Chelmsford.

When the raiders returned in 1944 new tactics would be needed and new types of aircraft would be deployed against the east coast. But never again would they be able to mount the kind of raids that they had launched in the previous years. The tide had certainly turned, and it would be Allied forces operating from the east coast that would bring death and destruction to German cities and the *Luftwaffe*.

CHAPTER EIGHT

Coastal Force Heroes

No account of the air war and operations along the east coast of England during the Second World War would be complete without looking at the exploits of those who manned the tiny minelayers, motor gunboats, motor torpedo boats and air-sea rescue craft.

One of the first arrivals was the 1st Motor Torpedo Boat Flotilla, which had arrived at Harwich in early 1940. It had just undertaken an epic voyage from the Mediterranean, passing through French canals and then across to Portsmouth. The boats were refitted at Parkeston, and they were allocated *Vulcan*, a trawler at Felixstowe quay, to serve as the HQ ship and depot for Lieutenant-Commander Donner's force. Donner had ten boats, and their first mission was when they saved the crew of a mined merchantman on 20 April 1940. In April and May 1940 two more motor boat flotillas arrived at Harwich – the 3rd, under Lieutenant Cole, and the 10th under Lieutenant Anderson. There were now sixteen vessels. HMS *Beehive* was established in July, and all of the torpedo boats were allocated part of Felixstowe dock. HMS *Beehive*, of course, was not a vessel but a shore base for the coastal forces. Eventually this would be the base for between 800 and 1,200 personnel.

Their role was not just patrols; they would be expected to mount raids. The vast majority of their work took place at night, so they were virtually nocturnal. The *Beehive*'s social centre was the Little Ship's Hotel. Officers frequently used the Ordnance Hotel, and others the Cavendish.

Three of the motor torpedo boats, along with a pair of destroyers from Harwich, were sent on a mission on 13 August 1940. It was not a great success, but it was to set the tone for many future missions. Three of the motor torpedo boats actually operating out of Dover had a marked success on 11 October. They sank two German trawlers off Calais. But this period had not been without losses; on 24 September MTB-15 was mined, and on 21 October a similar fate befell MTB-17. Towards the end of October a third, MTB-16, was also lost. Three more MTBs left on a mission in December 1940. They encountered a German merchant ship which they promptly torpedoed and sank.

As the months passed it would become clear that their principal enemies would be the German E-boats, armed trawlers and other escorts, such as minesweepers, steam torpedo boats, minelayers and destroyers.

Comparatively speaking, the motor torpedo boats were slow. The ideal adversary for the E-boats was the motor gunboat. The motor launches, which were even slower than the torpedo boats, were largely used to help protect convoys.

E-boats began operating against the east coast, primarily off Norfolk, in September 1940. As a direct response to this the 1st Motor Launch Flotilla was established at Great Yarmouth. Additional motor launch flotillas would be added, as would the 5th Motor Torpedo Boat Flotilla. Shortly afterwards another motor launch flotilla was established in Lowestoft. Ultimately, there would be motor launches operating out of Grimsby, Great Yarmouth, Lowestoft, Harwich and Sheerness. The motor launches based in Great Yarmouth and Lowestoft were responsible for convoy escorts between the Humber and Harwich. Even in these early months there were casualties. ML109 was sunk on 30 October 1940, and ML111 was lost on 25 November.

By the middle of 1942 there were six motor launch flotillas under Nore Command. Felixstowe and Grimsby had two each, and there was one at Great Yarmouth and another at Lowestoft. Sheerness was allocated harbour defence motor launches.

In March 1941, due to the absence of U-boats in the North Sea, a large number of motor anti-submarine boats were converted into motor gunboats to create the 5th and 6th Flotillas. Although these were not ideal for the job, the crews did their best to fend off E-boats and to help with the air-sea rescue effort. As we shall see, there were very few RAF air-sea rescue launches available, particularly high-speed ones. Slowly but surely, purpose-built motor gunboats began to arrive, which gave the flotillas a much better chance of intercepting the E-boats.

There was a major engagement between motor gunboats and E-boats on the night of 14/15 March 1942. Half of the 4th E-boat Flotilla left Ostend bound for the waters off Southwold. The 2nd Flotilla and the remainder of the 4th left Ijmuiden to raid Great Yarmouth and Cromer. The 2nd E-boat Flotilla sank SS *Horseferry* and the 4th Flotilla sank the escort destroyer HMS *Vortigern*. But unknown to the Germans, there were motor gunboats positioned off the Hook of Holland. They had been positioned there to stop attacks on minesweepers operating out of Harwich that were clearing a minefield that the Germans had recently laid. One group of these MGBs, from the 7th Flotilla based at Lowestoft, under Lieutenant J.B.R. Horne, was sent to intercept the German E-boats heading back for Ijmuiden. Great Yarmouth's 16th Flotilla was given similar instructions to intercept those heading back to Ostend.

What the British did not know was that all three groups of E-boats were heading back to Ijmuiden. The E-boat *S-111* had been damaged off Southwold and it was lagging behind. At daybreak on 15 March, Horne, on board MGB-88 and accompanied by MGB-87 and MGB-91, disabled *S-111* and boarded her.

They began to tow *S-111* home to Lowestoft, but as they got under way MGB-91 developed engine problems. Suddenly four E-boats emerged, looking for *S-111*. The MGBs put up a smoke screen and then disappeared into fog. They all arrived safely back in Lowestoft and nine prisoners were handed over. Just as Horne thought that MGB-91 had been lost, she limped into harbour with six wounded on board.

Covering this mission were fighters from 19, 137, 412 and 616 Squadrons. Wing Commander Hanks, at around midday, had attacked some E-boats and wrecked *S-38*.

By September 1942 there were upwards of thirty-seven motor gunboats belonging to four flotillas operating out of Lowestoft. They could now effectively try to trap E-boats as they returned from their missions off the east coast. In one such operation, on 30 September, motor torpedo boats sank the German motor ship *Thule* and a trawler. A few days later, on 3 October, MGB-78 failed to return from an offensive patrol.

The bulk of the motor gunboats had now been shifted to Felixstowe so that they could be more effective against E-boats. A major offensive was launched on 6 October 1942, which involved motor torpedo boats 29, 30, 69, 70 and 241. Also involved were motor gunboats 75 and 76. They were working on intelligence that the enemy commerce raider *Komet* was trying to get through the Dover Straits.

The British vessels encountered E-boats and R-boats, which were effectively German minelayers, off Blankenberge on the Belgian coast. Two of the motor torpedo boats, 29 and 30, collided, and all of the crew of MTB-29 were lost. MGB-75 was holed underwater and MGB-76's petrol tanks caught fire. The British claimed to have seen an E-boat catch fire and blow up, but what is certain is that the Germans lost four R-boats, probably to mines. As the British force limped back to Felixstowe MGB-76 burst into flames and then, after the crew had abandoned ship, blew up.

There was more action on 9 November when two motor gunboats torpedoed a German collier ship off Terschelling, an island in northern Holland. On 18 December, just off Ijmuiden, four motor torpedo boats operating with four motor gunboats out of Great Yarmouth (their base was known as HMS *Midge*) tried to attack a convoy, but in the poor weather MTB-30 hit a mine and was lost.

Early in 1943 five motor torpedo boats sank a German merchant ship and a V-boat trawler. On the night of 27/28 February motor torpedo boats attacked a German convoy as it entered Nieuwe Waterweg, a ship canal in Holland, and MGB-79 was sunk. On 5 March two German E-boats, *S-70* and *S-75*, were shot up by RAF fighter-bombers at dawn outside Ijmuiden.

The motor torpedo boats were now operating against German convoys around the Dutch islands. They were larger motor torpedo boats, with more fuel, more torpedo tubes and better guns. The Lowestoft-based (HQ known as HMS *Mantis*) MGB-20 found the remnants of E-boat *S-114* on 20 March 1943. She had collided with *S-119* and had to be abandoned and blown up. At the end of the month, on 29 March, a Great Yarmouth-based MGB rammed *S-29* and sank her.

Lieutenant-Commander Hichens accompanied Lieutenant Side-bottom on board MGB-112 on a mission on 12 April. Their role was to protect Lowestoft-based minelayers laying a field off Scheveningen on the Dutch coast, near The Hague. A cannon-burst hit the bridge of MGB-112, and Hichens was killed instantly and Sidebottom was badly wounded. This had been Hichens' fourteenth action and his 148th patrol.

The Felixstowe-based 11th MTB Flotilla, under the command of Lieutenant-Commander Trelawny, sank two German merchant ships off the Hook just a week after Hichens had been killed. On

13 May Lieutenant-Commander Dickens's 21st Flotilla sank two minesweepers in the same area. There was another major engagement on 24 July when seven motor torpedo boats were involved in an action off Ijmuiden and at least one German vessel was sunk.

These types of hit-and-run operation continued throughout the remainder of 1943 and into the first few months of 1944. Surprisingly, the British had never made any serious attempts to destroy the E-boat base at Ijmuiden. But all of this changed on 25 March 1944. A large number of RAF bombers plastered the port's anti-aircraft sites and the harbour entrance. This was a prelude to the main attack, which was launched by 373 Marauders of the US 9th Air Force. Their bombs plastered the area, but actually did little damage to the base itself. In the attack at least two E-boats, *S-93* and *S-192*, were destroyed.

By the spring of 1944 many of the motor torpedo boats based in Great Yarmouth and Lowestoft had been moved into the Channel. This meant that there was a major down-turn in the motor boat war in the North Sea. In fact the final reckoning would come in the period September 1944 to April 1945, when the coastal forces of Nore Command would fight their last battles against the Dutch-based E-boats.

Throughout the war the rescue and salvage of shipping and the picking-up of lifeboats and crews that had abandoned ship was a dangerous and vital role. There were already Royal National Lifeboat Institution stations along the east coast. These were based at Bridlington, Spurn Point, Skegness, Wells, Sheringham, Cromer, Caister, Gorleston, Lowestoft, initially Southwold, Aldeburgh, Walton, Clacton, Southend and Margate. Working in close conjunction with the RNLI were of course the vessels escorting the convoy ships, Royal Navy rescue launches, the RAF Air-Sea Rescue Service and the Coastguards. In the early stages of the war the coastguards and the lifeboat stations did not have radio or radar.

Perhaps one of the most famous lifeboat men of the war was the Cromer-based Henry Blogg. He had already won a number of medals during the First World War, but he now provided as vital a service in the Second World War. It is believed that over the course of the war he saved over 400 seamen. Shortly after the outbreak of the war the first rescue mission involved *Mount Ida*, a Greek merchant ship. Blogg and his crew brought twenty-four crewmen safely to shore. He also saved thirty Italian crewmen from *Traviata* on 4 January 1940. For this and many other exploits Blogg was awarded the British Empire Medal. On 27 October 1941 he plucked forty-four men from the *English Trader*, which ultimately won him the George Cross. It is worth bearing in mind that Blogg at this stage was in his 70s.

Another less-well-known but equally distinguished individual was Robert Cross, who was based at Spurn Head. Cross was in his late 60s, and among many other missions he saved nine men from the trawler *Garth* on 12 February 1940.

Up and down the coast the lifeboats all saved hundreds of lives. At Aldeburgh *Abdy Beauclerk* rescued seventy-four men in one operation on 10 September 1939. At Frinton *EMED* rescued a number of barges in October 1939, and in November of that year saved Japanese sailors from the *Terukuni Maru*. At Clacton the *Edward Z. Dresden*, temporarily working out of Brightlingsea, saved seven crewmen from a coaster in November 1940. On sixty-six occasions the Southend lifeboat, *Greater London*, launched and saved over 300 men throughout the war. The Harwich-based anti-submarine trawler *Kingston Olivine* saved over a hundred men from three different wrecks between March and April 1942. All along the east coast sailors owed their lives to innumerable small boats, both professionally and amateur crewed.

Navy rescue tugs were responsible for the ships themselves. Usually a ship would be towed into harbour or onto a sandbank, where she could ultimately be repaired. Most of the salvage bases were staffed by civilians. Many of the rescue tugs were also manned by civilians and operated under the direction, but not direct command, of the Royal Navy. The tugs were vital in clearing blocked channels and salvaging vital vessels and their loads. Unsalvageable and dangerous wrecks were usually dealt with by explosives.

The salvage bases were established up and down the east coast. The Hull salvage base also had a section based at Great Yarmouth, and between 1940 and 1944 they took part in 214 operations. Harwich was a major salvage-and-rescue tug base. They were based at the Alexandra Hotel, Dovercourt, ultimately moving to Church Street, Harwich, and then into the Great Eastern Railway Hotel on Harwich Quay. They had three large salvage vessels, each with cranes. They were assisted by small motor boats and converted trawlers. It was not until January 1945 that purpose-built fleet tugs were deployed. Up until that point antiquated tugs were used, and even captured French ones.

Working out to sea, trying to salvage vessels, was a hazardous task. One of the Harwich-based rescue tugs, *Muria*, was bombed and sank with the loss of the complete crew near North Foreland on 7 November 1940. Another rescue tug, *Caroline Moller*, was sunk close to Sheringham by a torpedo fired by an E-boat on 7 October 1942, and over half of her thirty-man crew was lost. Throughout the war the Harwich salvage vessels were involved in a hundred major and over 150 minor operations.

Where possible, even if the ship itself was not salvageable, everything was stripped off it. Condensers were taken out so that the copper could be reused, and engine parts, shafts, propellers and any other removable object was salvaged. On many occasions deck guns were also salvaged, and if it was possible the vessels were patched up enough to tow them home to be broken up, so that the steel could be recycled. Operations such as this continued through 1942 and 1943, but by mid-1944 the scale of operations had much diminished. On 5 February 1944 rescue tugs based in Harwich saved the escort aircraft carrier HMS *Slinger*, which had been mined off Lowestoft.

When the Second World War broke out in 1939 there was just one air-sea rescue base on the whole of the east coast. This was at Felixstowe. Grimsby would also be given a rescue launch, but for the first year of the war the majority of air-sea rescue operations had to be mounted by civilian lifeboats or the Royal Navy. The RAF had already set up a system by which aircraft that had come down in the North Sea could be located. These fixer stations were based at Wix near Harwich, Debden, Duxford, Stowupland near Stowmarket, Shropham near Attleborough, and Barton Bendish near Downham Market. The responsibility during the Battle of Britain for air-sea rescue fell on the shoulders of the Royal Navy. Auxiliary patrol vessels and motor torpedo boats would be used. Also, the Royal Navy had its own air-sea rescue boats. By the autumn of 1940 it was also using motor yachts and speedboats crewed by members of the Royal Naval Patrol Service. These vessels operated along the whole of the east coast, from Ramsgate to Grimsby.

Early in 1941 the RAF set up its Air-Sea Rescue Directorate. Initially it was focused on rescue training and the acquisition of equipment necessary for crews to survive in the hostile North Sea environment. By August 1941 not only had Lysander aircraft been based at Martlesham Heath to help find downed aircraft, but it had been agreed that Coastal Command would now be primarily responsible for air-sea rescue operations. This meant that high-speed launches, air-sea rescue boats, spotter planes and other assets would now fall under one command.

One of the major issues was trying to find where an aircraft had gone down. Towards the end of 1941 Walruses were being used and Lysanders were still in operation. They would not only spot British and later American downed crews, but also German and Italian crewmen. Hudsons were used for longer-range air-sea rescue searches, and they would also drop airborne lifeboats and ration packs.

It has been estimated that over the course of the war and within the Nore Command area 1,500 aircraft went down in the sea. There were some 7,000 airmen aboard. Around a third of them were saved.

At the northern end of Nore Command was RAF 21 Marine Craft Unit. It launched its first rescue missions in December 1940. At Grimsby Royal Dock was RAF 22 Marine Craft Unit; initially it had just one high-speed launch but later would have half a dozen. One of the most spectacular rescues took place on 21 January 1944 when thirty-nine aircraft were involved in searching for a Halifax of 578 Squadron, which had gone down forty-four miles to the east of Flamborough Head. Four men were saved in appalling conditions.

RAF 23 Marine Craft Unit was based at Wells from 1942 to 1944, but the most active air-sea rescue base along the east coast was at Gorleston. The 24 Marine Craft Unit operated out of the River Yare and also ran a launch out of Lowestoft. The Gorleston launches covered an enormous distance, as far as the Heligoland Bight. At its peak the unit had sixteen high-speed launches and four more at Lowestoft, plus other aircraft. It has been estimated that this base alone saved 800 crewmen. Unsurprisingly, the Gorleston base was the one that lost the most rescue launches. HSL108 was captured by the Germans off the coast of Holland on 1 July 1941. The crewmen would spend the rest of the war as prisoners in Silesia. On 3 March 1944 a friendly-fire incident took place. HSL2706 was shot up by American aircraft and only three men survived. A second HSL, 2679, arrived on the scene to pick up the survivors. Finally, on 29 June 1944, HSL2551 was just off Ijmuiden when she was attacked by German aircraft. The HSL had just picked up a number of survivors from a Flying Fortress. Three other HSLs came to assist, although a number of the crew and the Americans were killed or wounded.

Felixstowe, covered by 26 Marine Craft Unit, was equally busy. On one occasion they saved two Spitfire pilots who had collided on 18 May 1942. Another time, in the early hours of 5 June 1942, HSL125 went into the River Mass to pick up six bomber crew. The Felixstowe air-sea rescue unit was also instrumental in saving large numbers of merchant seamen, such as the eleven they brought home after their ship, SS *Linwood*, hit a mine on 15 November 1942. In 1943 new, faster high-speed launches arrived at Felixstowe. This improved their ability to respond. It has been estimated that over the course of the war the unit was involved in fifty-six air crew rescues, picking up 260 men. Among this total were a large number of American crewmen and Germans. The unit was also actively involved between 17 and 21 September 1944 with rescues directly related to Operation Market Garden. The Felixstowe-based unit picked up sixty-two airmen and soldiers in this period alone.

Brightlingsea carried out around eighteen rescues, picking up twenty-eight airmen and a large number of sailors, primarily from barges that had come to grief along that stretch of the east coast. Their most famous exploit took place on 21 June 1941 when they had been involved in the rescue of Stanford Tuck, the commander of 257 Squadron out of Coltishall. He had tangled with three Me 109s over the Belgian coast. He shot two of them down, but the third got him and he baled out off Clacton. The Brightlingsea unit retrieved Tuck from a Gravesend coal barge. The barge's crew had believed him to be German.

Air-sea rescue boats initially operated out of Sheerness, but in May 1942 it became RAF 31 Marine Craft Unit. This was involved in a large number of rescues and was particularly busy from 1943 onwards, when it saved a large number of US pilots and crew.

In the Brightlingsea area Amy Johnson, who worked as an air transport auxiliary pilot, crashed near East Knock John Buoy, about twelve miles off Foulness on 5 January 1941. The balloon vessel HMS *Haslemere* attempted to save her, but she kept going under the crashing waves. Lieutenant-Commander W. Fletcher, Royal Naval Reserve and the captain of the ship, had jumped in to attempt to rescue her, but was unsuccessful. He was pulled out of the water and later died as the result of immersion hypothermia in a hospital in Sheerness. There has been much speculation as to the death of Amy Johnson, and many believe that she was on a secret intelligence mission and the Germans had targeted her and shot her down. Her body was never washed ashore. Wreckage of her aircraft was picked up by the drifter *Young Jacob*.

The smallest of Nore Command's air-sea rescue bases was at Herne Bay on the north Kent coast. It had a single air-sea rescue boat, *Dandy*. It was ideally placed, as it was close to the Reculver bombing range. Margate also had its own lifeboat and by virtue of its position was involved in a large number of rescues. On 28 August 1940 the lifeboat and two small vessels saved four German bomber crewmen. A few days later, on 3 September, they picked up Flight Lieutenant Richard Hillary. He was badly burned and would later endure three months of painful surgery to repair the damage to his hands and face.

Although Ramsgate was in Dover Command, it did carry out a number of rescues at the very edge of Nore Command. In 1942 it had three high-speed launches and other vessels. On 1 June 1942 they saved Pilot Officer Richards of 65 Squadron, who had been shot down by an Fw 190. On another occasion, on 17 August 1943, they picked up nine crewmen of the US 8th Air Force, who had been involved in the raid against the ball-bearing factory at Schweinfurt. The following morning they went out again in HSL127 and towed in a Walrus and seven more Americans from the same unit.

Without these coastal force heroes, operating on a shoestring and in the most extreme conditions, many more airmen and sailors would have perished in the North Sea over the six years of conflict.

CHAPTER NINE

The Baby Blitz

By January 1944, even prior to the Allied landings in Normandy, the war had definitely turned, and it was not a question of whether the Allies would win, but when. Throughout the days and nights the population of the east coast could look up into the skies and see aircraft. These were not the raiders that had driven them into air raid shelters, shattered their homes, destroyed their places of work and killed their relations and neighbours. Instead the skies were full of British and American aircraft, pounding occupied Europe and preparing the ground for the inevitable liberation of the occupied countries.

None the less, the German aircraft were still active, albeit on a far reduced level. They had introduced new types of bomber, such as the Ju 188. This was a high-performance medium bomber, which after a number of teething problems with prototypes had entered service in 1943. It was essentially an upgraded version of the Ju 88, and although a large number of the aircraft would be produced by the Germans, it appeared too late to create any significant impact on the course of the war. In fact from the summer of 1944 not only was Allied air supremacy virtually complete, but the Germans were finding it increasingly difficult to produce fuel for these aircraft.

The other new arrival was the He 177, a long-range bomber and essentially the only heavy bomber that was ever produced by the Germans. Once again its production had been dogged by problems, particularly with the engine. Ultimately around a thousand of these aircraft would be built. Again, it entered service in 1943, and it would play a minor role in the last major German bombing campaign over Britain.

Unknown to the British a Ju 188 was shot down by Squadron Leader Maguire and Flight Officer Jones in a Mosquito of 85

Squadron on 15 October 1943. The bomber, having been abandoned by its crew, landed on soft marshland beside Kirton Creek, near Hemley on the River Debden, close to the Suffolk coast. Two of the crew were picked up at Hemley, but the aircraft itself, including its bombs, was not recovered until 1988.

On 21 January 1944 air raid warnings began to sound at 2100. A total of 115 German bombers and twenty-one fighter-bombers had begun taking off at 2000 from airfields in Belgium, France, Germany and Holland. Ninety bombers and fifteen Fw 190s crossed just to the north of Southend. Leading them were He 177s, and their primary target was south-east London. The bombers had a mixed pay-load of phosphorus bombs, incendiaries and high explosives. The raiders were flying at a height of 13,000 ft and they commenced their attack at around 2202.

Some of the bombers had strayed further north, and a number of 2,500 kg bombs were dropped to the south of March. They were dropping *Düppel*, effectively small pieces of aluminium or plastic that operated as a radar countermeasure. This aimed to confuse the British and send them off target when aircraft flew in to intercept.

A second attack came in at around 0500 on 22 January. Around forty bombers crossed the coast, again heading towards London. After they had dropped their bombs many of them exited close to Southwold or Lowestoft. Many of the bombers had also struck various targets along the east coast, including Dunmow, Braintree, Melford and Newmarket.

Not only was this the first widespread use of the *Düppel*, but the Germans were beginning to copy RAF bomber tactics by using a pathfinder force to mark the target and then to indicate the approach route for the main bomber force. The Germans had mounted a number of night training operations over Britain in December 1943. In many cases they had gone hopelessly wrong. One of the attacks against Chelmsford on the night of 10/11 December 1943 had got so out of control that most of the bombs had landed twenty-five miles from the intended target.

This marked the beginning of the so-called Baby Blitz; effectively the *Luftwaffe*'s last major fling and attempt to retaliate against the widespread bombing of German towns and cities.

A second raid was launched on the night of 28/29 January. This time it involved fifteen Me 410s, some Do 217s and fifteen Fw 190s. The Me 410 was essentially a heavy fighter, very much in the mould of the Me 110, but with greater power and the ability to operate as a light bomber. It was also designed so that it could carry torpedoes. This raid crossed over the East Anglian coast, as well as the south-east, and various targets were bombed as only one of them managed to penetrate as far as London.

A larger operation was launched on the night of 29/30 January, with over a hundred bombers involved. A Ju 88 passed over Lowestoft at approximately 2027, and it was engaged by a Beaufighter of 68 Squadron, flown by Flight Sergeant Neal. The Ju 88 jettisoned its incendiaries and crashed to the north-west of Ipswich, at Barham. In all, six German aircraft were shot down that night. The other five crashed out to sea. Bombs were dropped around Halstead, Clare, Brightlingsea and Stansfield.

Sixty or more German aircraft were involved in a raid over the night of 3/4 February. One of the aircraft dropped flares over Cambridge. Most of the German aircraft crossed around Aldeburgh and Orford Ness. They dropped *Düppel* and headed inland, passing Aldeburgh at 0420. Others followed, crossing at various points between Deal and Lowestoft. Fifteen of the aircraft managed to penetrate London's defences. Some of the raiders crossed close to Great Yarmouth and came under anti-aircraft fire. Now the British fighters closed in to try and intercept them. A Ju 188 was shot down off Southwold; however, bombs and incendiaries fell near Woodbridge, at Halstead, Melford, Wainford, Samford, Lothingland, Lowestoft, Southwold, Clacton, Tendring and Lexden, near Colchester in Essex.

On the night of 13/14 February, thirty or more aircraft attempted to foil the radar around the Thames Estuary by dropping *Düppel*. Eight of the aircraft turned back with engine problems, and only four were able to deliver their bombs on target.

The second major attack saw nearly a hundred aircraft cross over the east coast between Deal and Lowestoft. Fifteen of them managed to make it as far as London, but most of them dropped their bombs on Suffolk and Essex. Six hundred fell on the Dovercourt holiday camp, others fell around Felixstowe, Samford, Frinton, Walton-on-the-Naze and Brightlingsea. Clacton was badly hit, with bombs and incendiaries covering the area from Pier Avenue to Station Road. Several shops and homes were gutted with fire, and the Butlin's holiday camp was set alight. Bombs also fell around St Osyth. The attacks that night also saw bombs dropped on Martlesham and Elsenham.

Essex was the target on the night of 18/19 February, when around forty-five aircraft passed over Felixstowe; these were followed by around 120 more that crossed the coast between Winterton and the Thames Estuary. Some of the aircraft bombed King's Lynn, others targeted Luton, and bombs dropped on Mitford, Clacton, Dunmow, Braintree, the outskirts of Cambridge and Saffron Walden.

Sixty bombers crossed the Dutch coast at 2100 on the night of 20/21 February. The majority of them crossed the coast between Harwich and Hythe. Mosquitoes belonging to 25 Squadron shot down a Do 217 and a Ju 188. Again the target was London, but bombs fell on Chelmsford, Dunmow and Clacton.

The night of 22/23 February saw just fourteen He 177s launched against Britain. The leading aircraft passed over Harwich at 2355 and the others crossed at various points between North Foreland and Great Yarmouth. A Mosquito of 25 Squadron shot a Do 217 down over Norfolk, and another Mosquito of 410 Squadron hit a Ju 88 at Earl's Colne. During the night, primarily between 0020 and 0100, a large number of incendiaries were dropped over Pakefield, Claydon, Kirton, Falkenham and Orford. Incendiaries and high explosives fell on Dedham, Yoxford, Dovercourt, Dunmow and other locations.

A single bomber approached Colchester shortly before midnight on 22 February and dropped phosphorus bombs and incendiaries. An enormous area of the town was engulfed in flames, including clothing factories and a furniture store. A number of shops and houses were burnt out. To put out the fires around two million gallons of water were used. At one stage there were 130 separate fires, but there was only one casualty.

The Isle of Dogs was the target on the night of 23/24 February. There was a mixed force of Do 217s, Ju 88s, Ju 188s and He 177s. Incredibly, a Do 217 was shot-up over Ealing. There was damage to the engine, wing and cockpit, and the crew baled out over Acton. The aircraft, however, continued on its way, heading north-east and slowly losing height. At 2230 air raid sirens went off around Cambridge. The inhabitants expected the worst, but instead it was the crewless Dornier, which then landed on allotments close to St George's church in Chesterton.

February had been an expensive month for the *Luftwaffe*. It had lost at least seventeen aircraft, and these were casualties that it was increasingly unable to replace. Throughout the remainder of the month the raids continued on a smaller scale. But as March dawned the raids tailed off considerably, and the next major operation was launched on the night of 14/15 March.

A large number of German aircraft from a variety of squadrons began crossing the east coast between Clacton and Cromer at 2211. The vast majority crossed between Southwold and Great Yarmouth and then headed for London. Around thirty of them managed to penetrate London's defences. That night the Germans lost seven aircraft when anti-aircraft gunners claimed four; a Ju 188 was shot down by a Mosquito of 488 Squadron. Mosquitoes of the same squadron also took down another Ju 188 over the coast.

Hull was the target on the night of 19/20 March. Three enemy bombers, a Ju 188, an He 177 and a Do 217, were shot down by 25 Squadron. None the less, the raiders dropped a number of incendiaries close to Walsingham and on Aylsham and Horsham St Faith.

A major assault on London was launched on the night of 21/22 March. Most of the ninety or so bombers operating out of Holland crossed over at Southwold from around 0025. They were to turn to the south-east of Cambridge. Simultaneously another force of Me 410s and Fw 190s headed for London from the south. Around sixty of the aircraft in all managed to bomb London. The Germans had launched a diversionary group of aircraft, which had come in across the coast between Great Yarmouth and Felixstowe. On that night a number of targets along the east coast were hit, including Lothingland, Dunmow, Saffron Walden, Mitford, Wainford, Southwold, Colchester and Long Melford. A Mosquito of 488 Squadron shot down a Ju 88 and it crash-landed at Glemsford. The squadron also claimed a second kill when a Ju 88 crashed on Earl's Colne airfield. A third was shot down by a Mosquito over Chelmsford and it crashed near Latchingdon. The following night a Mosquito of 25 Squadron shot down a Ju 188 some forty-five miles off Lowestoft.

By April it was clear that the Baby Blitz was over and that the Germans were once again concentrating their efforts against airfields. This did not, of course, mean that the raids against London were over, but rather that they were less frequent.

Twelve or so Me 410s were active over Cambridgeshire, Norfolk and Lincolnshire on the night of 11/12 April 1944. There had been a number of 50 kg bombs dropped around the Loddon area. The next major attack took place on the night of 18/19 April when around ninety enemy aircraft struck against London. They hit the North Middlesex Hospital and there were fires across Romford.

Meanwhile, ten or more Me 410s were launched against airfields in East Anglia. A Mosquito of 410 Squadron shot down an He 177 at 0103 near Little Waldon airfield in Essex. The Heinkel's target was intended to be Tower Bridge. This was one of five aircraft that had taken off shortly after 2300 and had crossed the Dutch coast and then the east coast of England at Orford Ness. The aircraft had then made for their turning point, to the east of Newmarket. This particular aircraft had been bounced by a Mosquito just to the south of Orford Ness. After three attacks by the Mosquito the crew were unable to jettison their bombs, so they decided to bale out; four of the crew were taken prisoner. That same night an Me 410 had followed in a pair of Lancasters of 115 Squadron. They were returning from a bombing raid on Rouen, and the Me 410 shot them both down. Elsewhere that night a number of houses were damaged at Westleton in Suffolk and farm buildings near Sheringham, and other bombs were dropped on Hockwood in Norfolk, Earl Soham, Mickfield and Stonham. Incendiaries were also dropped around Leiston and Hollesley. Certainly a second German aircraft was lost that night – a Ju 88. It had been shot-up by anti-aircraft guns and it crash-landed in Bradwell Bay.

A total of 130 German aircraft were launched against Hull on the night of 20/21 April, but not a single one of them found the city. Some of this force, and diversionary aircraft, bombed other targets, primarily in East Anglia. Six 500 kg bombs were dropped close to Lowestoft, some falling on Oulton Broad. At around 0425 the airfield at Horsham was hit, as was the airfield at Shipdham, near Thetford in Norfolk. Lakenheath was also attacked, with at least eight 50 kg bombs falling across the airfield. Bombs also fell on Benacre and other targets in Lothingland.

The Germans launched six Me 410s to pounce on American B17s and B24s landing at airfields in Norfolk and Suffolk. Coming in that night were 125 American bombers, and this new tactic against the Americans proved to be extremely effective. This attack took place on the night of 22 April. The Germans claimed five B24s over Norfolk and two more as they came in to land at Rackheath. Friendly fire from anti-aircraft guns around Norwich took down another B24, and the Me 410s claimed yet another, making the total for the night nine lost. They also managed to destroy a pair of Liberators on the ground. One of the Me 410s was claimed in response. A B24 of the 448th Bomb Group shot down the intruder, which crashed at around 2210 at Ashby St Mary, between Loddon and Norwich. In all, twenty B24s were so badly damaged by this operation that they were unfit to fly. Also during that night, a number of German bombers laid mines along the coast, but a single Ju 88 dropped a number of 50 kg bombs on Rackheath airfield.

What is particularly amazing is that this type of operation was never mounted by the Germans again. Had they persisted with this tactic it would have seriously blunted the American bombing effort against occupied Europe.

As the Allies made their final preparations for Operation Overlord, the long-awaited liberation of enemy-occupied Europe, the Germans continued to bomb the east coast, albeit on a much reduced scale. A number of bombs were dropped on RAF Bourn, near Cambridge, and against RAF Great Ashfield, near Bury St Edmunds, which was being used by American bombers, primarily flying B17s. The 385th Bombardment Group flew nearly 300 missions between the middle of July 1943 and April 1945, in the process of which they lost 129 aircraft. More bombs fell on Forhoe and Aylsham in Norfolk on 23 May 1944. Just over a week earlier, on 15 May, an Me 109 pilot wrecked his aircraft when he attempted a landing at Herringfleet, near Lowestoft. The aircraft had not been shot down; instead, the pilot was deserting.

There were continued attacks, even more sporadic than before. On the night of 24/25 May, bombs fell near Tuddenham, on 29 May they narrowly missed a hangar at Oakington, and the same day a Mosquito of 25 Squadron shot down an Me 410. A Ju 188 was shot down on the night of 5/6 June, and on the night of 7/8 June a B24 was shot down and parachute bombs, with air-burst fuses, fell on Wickham Market and Framlingham.

Even after the Normandy landings the attacks still continued. A pair of Ju 88s dropped bombs on Wattisfield and Cley on the night of 12/13 June, the same night that an Me 410 crash-landed near Barking. Over the night of 14/15 June bombs fell on Rattlesden, and there were more heavy explosives at Little Tey, close to Colchester, on 21 June. A handful of bombs dropped at Bawdsey and Felixstowe on the night of 23 June, and in the early hours of 26 June there was limited bombing against Peasenhall in Suffolk, and at Boreham, near Chelmsford in Essex. The last bombing of this phase took place on 27/28 June, and this effectively ended the bombing offensive of the east coast, at least in conventional terms; Bungay, Seething and Debden all received high-explosive bombs that night.

What was about to happen was the stuff of nightmares. Although the majority of the new types of weapon that had been developed by the Germans would fall on the south of England and on London, the east coast would not be immune. Initially, people would hear something sounding like a motorcycle engine. Suddenly the engine would cut out. They then knew the true horror, as seconds later an enormous explosion would erupt as the flying object crashed into the ground. These were the infamous German V-1 flying-bombs. They were launched virtually blind, primarily at London. So unreliable were they that they could undershoot or overshoot their target and land literally anywhere. But worse was to come – the V2 rocket.

CHAPTER TEN

Last Raids and Rocket Attacks

It was dawn on 13 June 1944. Mosquitoes were landing at Gravesend when suddenly they heard a strange engine drone overhead. The engine cut and they saw an object gliding toward the Thames at Swanscombe. It was quickly followed by a large explosion. This was the first-ever sighting of a German V-1 flying-bomb.

Many of them would find their way to the east coast, despite the fact that this was not their primary target. They would be launched from the Pas de Calais area, crossing over the British coast around Dover, with the primary target of London. Several would fall around Essex and Suffolk.

The Doodle Bugs, or Divers, as they were known by the Allies, were relatively primitive devices. They used aero-engines, and when the fuel was exhausted the weapon would literally glide down to indiscriminately strike the ground. Development had begun as early as the 1920s, strangely enough by the British. The Germans had a working model ready in November 1939, but this primitive, pilotless, winged bomb was given greater priority by 1942, primarily as a terror weapon against British towns and cities.

Production began in September 1943. It was hoped that they would be ready for the Baby Blitz, but it was not until the beginning of December 1943 that the launch sites were ready and the crews had been sufficiently trained to handle, maintain and fire these weapons.

The Allies were perfectly well aware of the development of this weapon, and likewise the Germans knew that the secret was out.

Hence they began to replace the fixed launch sites with smaller launch ramps. V-1, or *Vergeltungswaffe-1*, is literally 'Vengeance Weapon One'. In the period 7–16 June 1944 around eighty sites were ready to launch a massive salvo against the British Isles. By 12 June over fifty of the sites declared themselves ready for operations, but many of the sites had not even practised the launch sequence.

None the less, the order was given that the rockets should begin to descend on London at 2340 on 12 June. The firing would continue until 0445, by which time it was hoped that 500 of the weapons would have been fired. There were inevitable delays; none of the sites were ready to fire by 2300. The first ten were not fired until 0330; five of them crashed, one fell into the Channel and four made their way to the British coast. They fell at Bethnal Green, Gravesend, Sevenoaks and another in Sussex.

By noon on 16 June the Germans had succeeded in firing 244 of the weapons towards London. Another fifty had been fired at Southampton, an important embarkation and supply port for the fighting going on in Normandy. So far only eleven had landed on London. Anti-aircraft gunners had shot down several of them, as had fighters, but most had either crashed or landed in uninhabited areas.

The weapon was extremely unpredictable. Just after 0028 on 16 June one of the weapons exploded over Lodge Farm, near Peasenhall in Suffolk. Ten hours later, at 1019, another fell near Cold Norton, close to Bradwell Bay in Essex. At 1614 a third crashed into a field at Woolverstone in Suffolk.

The weapons were not designed to travel as far as they were apparently able to achieve. In fact by 30 June seventeen had reached the East Anglian region. So far the damage to Essex, Suffolk and Cambridgeshire was relatively slight. Amazingly, a V-1 made its way to Lowestoft on 1 July. It was destroyed by an aircraft of 316 Squadron five miles off the coast.

Into July and August the Germans were managing to fire off at least a hundred V-1s every day. The fighters protecting the coast were able to deal with around thirty per cent of them, but many of the others fell across the south coast and around London. In July eighteen penetrated East Anglian air space and thirteen in August. The V-1 offensive was relatively short lived, and by September the Allies had broken through the German front in northern France and were surging along the French coast, overrunning the launch sites around Calais. The Germans decided to shift their launch sites and concentrate on European mainland targets, principally the French ports that were rapidly falling into Allied hands.

The V-1 offensive, however, was not quite over. A bizarre and terrifying new twist came on 5 September 1944. Nine V-1s approached the east coast of England between 0500 and 0600. They had been air launched. The Germans had been feverishly working to adapt He 111s to air launch the weapons, not only giving them greater range but, they hoped, greater accuracy. Between the end of the first week of July and 31 August the Germans had been using this technique further south. Ninety of the air-launched weapons had been fired at Southampton; twenty were fired at Gloucester and a staggering 300 against London.

Four of the air-launched weapons fired against the east coast on 5 September landed in the region, one of which fell as far inland as Eyeworth in Bedfordshire. This was an ominous sign, as providing the He 111s could penetrate British air space any target was now achievable. As a temporary defence the British set up balloon barrages to protect the south-east of London. But there were simply not enough barrage balloons to protect every new potential target.

There was far worse to come. Hundreds of anti-aircraft weapons had already been shifted to coastal areas in order to deal with the V-1 threat. In effect all the way from Great Yarmouth down to north Kent was an anti-aircraft free-fire zone. Allied aircraft would have to fly around this anti-aircraft gun shield. At its height, there were around ten anti-aircraft guns to the mile. Gun operation rooms, already set up at Great Yarmouth, Felixstowe and Vange, near Tilbury, along with Chatham, had new gun-operating rooms set up at Burnham-on-Crouch, Thorpe-le-Soken, Southend, Orford, Theberton and Saxmundham. They were all linked to radar stations and other anti-aircraft batteries. It was now hoped that the anti-aircraft guns could put up a barrier of fire and deal with any V-1, or German aircraft about to launch a V-1.

In many cases, when the V-1s landed into soft ground or mud, they would fail to go off. This certainly saved a number of lives, as these weapons landed around areas such as Thorpeness, Woodbridge or Bawdsey. As the V-1s continued to be fired there had been relatively few casualties along the east coast. But this had certainly put Harwich and the naval towns along the Medway back into the front line. On 8 November 1944 eight civilians were killed at Rochester by a V-1, on 10 November one fell on a playing-field, one near the old shipyard and another in the harbour mouth at

Harwich. Five civilians were killed when two V-1s fell on Ipswich. Incredibly, on Christmas Eve 1944, sixty He 111s flew towards the Humber. They fired sixty V-1s directed at Manchester.

As the V-1 threat began to recede it was replaced by an even greater threat, the V-2. Effectively this was a prototype intercontinental ballistic missile. It carried a warhead of some 980 kg; it was 14 m long with a diameter of 1.65 m, had a wingspan of 3.56 m and theoretically had an operational range of 200 miles (320 km). It was fuelled by a mix of ethanol, water and liquid oxygen, and had gyroscopes for altitude control. The prototype rockets had originally been successfully launched in 1934. Development had continued, and by September 1943 much of the preliminary work had been completed. It was still not ready for launch until the middle of 1944, but by this stage parts were in relatively short supply, although a production line was set up at Peenemünde in the north-east of Germany.

At approximately 1840 on 8 September 1944 there were two gigantic explosions. A number of buildings disappeared in Chiswick and trees were shattered in Epping. Both had been replaced by 40 ft craters. The German ultimate vengeance weapon was now ready, and it would rain on British targets for many more months. It could not be set for an air burst, it detonated only when it landed.

The V-2 programme had been the single most expensive development project by the Germans throughout the course of the war. Each one cost in excess of 100,000 Reichsmarks, worth approximately five to the English pound. In all the Germans would build over 6,000 of them and launch around 3,225. This was another German weapon that would fall indiscriminately across Britain. It was simply not sophisticated enough to be targeted at a specific location.

The V-2s' direct route was just south of Clacton, Brightlingsea and Harwich; in fact it was virtually over Burham-on-Crouch. The British rapidly redeployed their radar stations from the south coast; five were positioned from Bawdsey to Swingate, near Dover. On any given day, if someone looked into the skies on a clear morning, they could see the silver vapour trails of the rockets. The worst part was the fact that from the time that one was spotted crossing the east coast of England it was four minutes from its target. The only thing that could be done was to bring the German launch sites under attack. But there would be many V-2s fired before that could be successfully achieved.

By 18 September 1944 twenty-five V-2s had landed on Britain. One had fallen into the sea off Clacton, another off Shoeburyness, one more had landed on Kent, six had struck Essex and sixteen had reached London. It is worth remembering that this was at the point when the He 111s were launching V-1s at targets around the east coast. The He 111s were now trying to avoid radar detection; they were releasing the V-1s about fifty miles off the coast and then turning back.

Probably the first V-2 to fall on East Anglia struck Castle Farm at Hoxney in Suffolk at 1905 on 25 September. It slightly damaged a dozen or so houses. On the following day a second one fell just eight miles to the north-east of Norwich, at Ranworth on the Norfolk Broads. The weapon struck a field and exploded at 1630. Most of these weapons were being fired by the *Lehr und Versuchs Batterie 44*, based on Walcheren Island, off the Dutch coast. Over the period 25 September to 12 October this unit alone fired forty-four V-2s, and thirty of them landed in East Anglia. The V-2s fell on Kirby Bedon on 27 September, on Thorpe on the 29th, at Hopton on 3 October, Hellesdon on the same day and at Rockland St Mary on the fourth.

The Allies had launched Operation Market Garden in September 1944, which temporarily meant the Germans shifting *Batterie 485*, which was based to the north-east of The Hague in Holland. With the immediate threat over, they too began firing, targeting London. On 3 October a V-2 landed on Leytonstone. By 12 October they were routinely firing weapons against London and Antwerp. The problem was that many of these V-2s also missed their targets. One landed at Fulbourn in Cambridgeshire, another close to Mildenhall and a third at Mundesley on the north Norfolk coast.

The Germans reinforced these batteries on 20 October, but it was still relatively difficult for them to increase the pace of firing. It took upwards of three days for the weapon to be ready, including its fuelling-up and checking of parts.

The Allies knew that something had to be done in order to prevent untold and unnecessary destruction on the British Isles by these terror weapons. Towards the end of October RAF Fighter Command was now launching sweeps of the Dutch countryside, hunting for targets. These aircraft were operating from the Coltishall area, and included Spitfires belonging to 229, 453 and 602 Squadrons. In the first five weeks, from the third week of October, they flew over 600 sorties.

The Germans were still able to keep up a barrage of three V-2s per day, primarily aimed at London. Between 26 October and 4 November, however, no fewer than forty-four V-2s struck Britain, and thirty-three of them hit London. On a nightly basis He 111s were still firing V-1s off the Suffolk and Essex coasts.

This phase of the air war reached a climax in the period October–November 1944. More guns were added to the Great Yarmouth area, and these went operational at the end of October, by which time there were over 1,100 guns in position. A prime example of their effectiveness can be seen on 4 November. No fewer than twenty-three V-1s were heading towards the east coast between 1909 and 1958. For the expenditure of around 1,600 rounds of ammunition seven were shot down by anti-aircraft fire, including one by the anti-aircraft guns at Southwold.

There was an even better rate of exchange over the night of 5/6 November. The Germans launched twenty-six of the weapons; twelve were shot down over the sea, and of the ten that reached the land six were shot down by anti-aircraft guns. The Germans certainly knew that this type of operation was turning into an abject failure. They fired just ten on the night of 6 November; all of them were shot down by gunners between Bradwell in Essex and Southwold in Suffolk.

Undeterred, this V-1 campaign continued. On the night of 10/11 November the Germans launched twenty-six V-1s. The bulk of them made for the Felixstowe–Southwold coastline. Each and every one that reached the coast was shot down. A single V-1 escaped the attention of the anti-aircraft gunners and flew on towards Chelmsford. But before it could land and do any damage it was shot down by a Tempest.

The Germans were not finished that night; they launched twelve more V-1s between Aldeburgh and Clacton from 0127 to 0159. One of them was shot down near Southwold, a fighter claimed another near Dagenham, one crashed into the River Blackwater and another at Great Warley. In little more than a half-hour period, from 1849 on 14 November, eighteen V-1s were launched. Eleven of them came within range of anti-aircraft guns and all but two were knocked out of the sky. A second salvo was fired over a fifty-minute period, from 0001 that night. Twelve were tracked; two of them fell into the sea, four were knocked down by the anti-aircraft guns and six managed to penetrate the defences. There was a third launch in a twenty-minute period, from 0529 on the 15th. Of the seven fired three breached the defences.

This pattern of attack continued on 17 November when eighteen He 111s fired a V-1 each, but seven of them almost immediately crashed into the sea. Of the remainder three were shot down by anti-aircraft guns.

The kill ratio was perfect on the night of 7/8 December. Over a three-quarter-hour period from 1827, twenty-one V-1s were fired by He 111s, and a third of them soon crashed into the sea. Nine of them reached the Essex coast. Anti-aircraft guns accounted for eight of them and the last one was shot down by a night-fighter near Laindon, close to Basildon in Essex. Another four that had been launched were shot down by anti-aircraft guns from Aldeburgh to Clacton. There had been a similar degree of success on 4 December when nine out of ten V-1s had been knocked down by the coastal artillery. The last one had been shot down as it made its way over East Malling in Kent.

Of the 1,200 or so air-launched V-1s little more than half had penetrated the new anti-aircraft defensive ring. The British were taking the fight right to the He 111s, and in fact in the period 16 September 1944 to 14 January 1945 the Germans lost seventy-seven He 111s. This is a combination of losses to British Mosquitoes, crashes and launch explosions. It was not just the anti-aircraft guns that proved to be such an effective defence against the V-1s. Royal Navy vessels had shot down ten and Tempest night-fighters, operating out of RAF Manston and RAF Bradwell Bay, had claimed at least fifty.

Ultimately it would not be the success of the defenders, or indeed the losses of the He 111s that would curtail the V-1 offensive against the east coast of England. Instead it was the loss of the launch bases, which by January 1945 had been virtually overrun. The last V-1 to make landfall on the East Anglian coast came down at 0200 on 14 January 1945. It crashed in Hornsea in the borough of Haringey. It had been air launched by an He 111.

But just as the V-1 threat receded at the beginning of 1945, the V-2 rockets were falling at a rate of around two per day. Unlike the V-1s, which were relatively slow and low flying, the V-2s were incredibly difficult to combat. In fact no workable solution had been arrived at by late March 1945, when the last V-2 was fired at Britain.

The Germans still persisted with their use of V-1s after the failure of the air-launch campaign. Three ramps were constructed in northern Holland; weapons fired from these ramps would be aimed at London. There was also intelligence that an additional three ramps would be created and that weapons from these would target Antwerp. The Allies assigned no fewer than four squadrons to make daytime interception, and another four would be used at night.

On the night of 3/4 March 1945, the Germans launched a combined operation. V-1 rockets were launched and a major offensive was mounted by German aircraft. Radar picked up around sixty Ju 88s and Me 410s heading towards the north Norfolk coast. It was just after midnight. In all, 140 had been launched that night, but only around a hundred of the aircraft actually crossed the east coast. The Germans' target was to attack Allied bombers as they came back to land at their home bases. The German aircraft attacked thirty bomber bases and managed to shoot down twenty-two RAF bombers over Lincolnshire and Yorkshire. In return just six of the German aircraft were shot down.

The first attack had come in against Rendlesham airfield, near Woodbridge in Suffolk. A number of high explosives fell at 0023. Seven minutes later a pair of heavy bombs were dropped on Seymour Road in Ipswich: nine people were killed and a large number of houses were damaged. Bury St Edmunds came under attack at 0054 as a strafing attack was launched. Bombs fell at Little Cressingham near Thetford in Norfolk and at Fulmodeston to the west of Fakenham, Norfolk, and machine-gun attacks were launched against East Rudham near King's Lynn, Hemsby near Caister, Lexham near Swaffham, Botesdale and at Rickinghall near Diss. Further attacks were made against Wetheringsett near Stowmarket, and Reepham and Cringleford near Norwich. A little later, bombs dropped at Docking near the north Norfolk coast, on the main road to Norwich at Chippenham near Mildenhall, at Swaffham, Colchester, and nearby Great Bromley, and at Bodney, near Thetford.

There was a close-run thing for an American Liberator that night. It was coming in to land at Metfield airfield in Suffolk when it was pounced on by a Ju 88. In the nick of time the pilot spotted the Ju 88 below him and he manoeuvred to escape its upward firing 20 mm cannon. The Ju 88 was forced to take evasive action and its wingtip struck the ground. The German aircraft broke into pieces and debris fell over a number of fields.

The British immediately launched over twenty Mosquitoes to chase the German night-fighters back home and destroy as many of them as possible. A Ju 88 was shot down by 68 Squadron ten miles to the north-east of Cromer. No. 125 Squadron shot down another Ju 88 a little further to the east. Carrying the fight onto the continent, the Mosquitoes shot down another Ju 88 over eastern Holland (406 Squadron), and 307 Squadron shot down yet another Ju 88 just fifteen miles to the west of Bonn in Germany, on the River Rhine.

On the following night, 4/5 March, the German night-intruder operation was much scaled down. Approximately seven sorties were launched over Suffolk, Norfolk and Lincolnshire. One of the attacks saw a number of incendiary bombs drop over Beccles in Suffolk at 2010.

There was another attack several days later, on the night of 17/18 March, when eleven or so German aircraft operated primarily over East Anglia and Yorkshire. Great Yarmouth saw an intruder approaching at 2046; it was seen to drop bombs at Buxton, Norfolk. The aircraft also dropped bombs on Coltishall airfield and on Tunstead. It then headed back towards the coast, crossing over at Great Yarmouth. Metfield airfield was also attacked that night, as was Wisbech, where a number of bombs fell just before 2200. Machine-gun attacks had been launched against Swaffham, East Dereham and Wickham Market.

One of the last major attacks launched by the *Luftwaffe* took place on the night of 20/21 March. The first of ten German aircraft were spotted at 2020, still some sixty miles to the east of Orford Ness. Half an hour later, they began crossing the coast, but by then other aircraft were also crossing on an individual basis from Cromer down the coastline to Essex. The attack was short and sharp, and over in little more than two hours. Parham, near Framlingham in Suffolk, and the home of the US 390th Bombardment Group, was first to be attacked. All of the German bombs fell harmlessly on the outer perimeter of the airfield. The next attack struck Langham, near Holt in Norfolk. Bombs fell into fields either side of the road from Langham to Binham; this was at 2105. Seven minutes later Shipdham, near Thetford, was machine-gunned and bombs were dropped on the airfield at Swanton Morley. A barn was shot-up at Terrington St Clement, near the Wash and close to King's Lynn, and around the same time the small village of Sustead, to the south-west of Cromer, was also machine-gunned. Just before 2200 more machine-gun attacks were launched against villages to the south of Cromer, including Gunton, Roughton and South Repps.

There were still V-1s being fired at Britain, even at this late stage in the war. During these new night-intruder raids launched by the *Luftwaffe*, some 275 V-1s were fired off. Around 125 made it as far as the British coast, and of these only thirty-four managed to penetrate the anti-aircraft defences. The last probable V-1 to be seen on the east coast itself was dealt with by anti-aircraft gunners at Orford. It was shot down at 1243 on 29 March 1945.

Possibly the last sighting of the *Luftwaffe* off the east coast of England took place late on 30 March 1945. Five German aircraft were spotted; three of them ventured inland to attack Norfolk airfields and to launch an assault on a Mosquito that was just landing at RAF Coltishall. It is believed that they were Arado 234 jets.

As far as the war at sea was concerned, Nore Command still had a major role to play in the latter stages of the conflict. There had been a lull in operations following the Normandy invasions and the Allied push across France and into Belgium. On 9 September 1944 the major German North Sea naval base, Ostend, fell to the Allies. German E-boats could now no longer operate any further south-west than Rotterdam. The Germans left the harbour in chaos; they had sunk twenty-six vessels in the harbour mouth and in the docks, and detonated 150 land mines to wreck the quays. The approach from the sea had also been mined. On 19 September operations were well under way to clear these mines, and due to the tireless work of British and Canadian engineers the port was ready to be reopened in five weeks. Ostend now became a Royal Navy base and became Ostend Sub-Command of Nore Command. It also became the base for coastal forces, including motor minesweepers and RAF high-speed launches for air-sea rescue.

Incredibly, Dunkirk still remained in German hands. The isolated garrison was resupplied at night by air and by Dutch trawlers and E-boats. Two motor torpedo boats from the Lowestoft-based 65th Flotilla intercepted the 10th E-boat Flotilla on 18 September 1944. They sank three of the E-boats and captured sixty personnel.

There was an attempt to prevent a German troop convoy from leaving Emden on the Dutch coast on 1 October 1944. Five motor torpedo boats of the 11th Flotilla left Felixstowe to catch the convoy as it passed Ijmuiden. Two of the motor torpedo boats out of five were sunk, but the Germans suffered several vessels being torpedoed and shot-up.

Efforts now focused on clearing the whole of the Scheldt Estuary of mines. A large force of minesweepers operated out of Sheerness and Harwich. There were a number of casualties; HMS *Duff* and HMS *Dakins* both suffered mine damage in December 1944 during operations. Ultimately a successful clearing of mines meant that a ferry service for the Army could be established between Tilbury and Antwerp and Ostend. A passenger service operated from Parkeston to Antwerp.

The Germans made determined efforts to try and close the Scheldt Estuary. They still had up to fifty E-boats operating out of Den Helder, Rotterdam and Ijmuiden. Three of these E-boats were cornered on the night of 22/23 December. Involved in the operation was HMS *Walpole*, a destroyer from Harwich, and the frigates HMS *Curzon*, HMS *Riou* and HMS *Torrington*. They were joined by motor torpedo boats operating out of Ostend. The British claimed that all three had been sunk, but in fact one of them got away. Despite this, in the period November 1944 to April 1945, the Allies lost twenty ships close to the Scheldt, as a result either of mines or of enemy small-craft action.

The Germans, using their E-boats, carried out a major minelaying operation on the nights of 13/14 and 14/15 January 1945. The E-boats made an even bolder move in the early hours of 16 January, and again on 23 January. They penetrated the Thames Estuary and were brought under fire from anti-aircraft guns at Tongue Sand Fort, off Margate. On 24 January a German midget submarine was sunk off Great Yarmouth by minelayer 153. Three days later two German naval officers were plucked off Scroby Sands and brought ashore by HSL2507.

The German submarine *U-245* also operated in the North Sea in February 1945. It sank a merchant ship on 6 February and a landing-ship tank on 22 February. On that same night the German E-boats launched an attack on a convoy near Smith's Knoll, sinking *Goodwood* and *Blacktoft*, a pair of colliers. On 28 February the Harwich-based destroyer HMS *Cotswold* and the frigate HMS *Seymour* sank another E-boat off Ostend.

For some time the British had been trying to destroy the concrete shelters used by the E-boats in their Dutch bases. The US 8th Air Force launched bombing raids on 14 and 21 March 1945, dropping 3-ton bombs on the targets. The RAF also launched its attacks in early April. Meanwhile the Germans were losing more of their midget submarines: around twelve of them were sunk between 12 and 15 March. The E-boats were still very active, however, as were the midget submarines. On 12 March the merchant ship *Taber Park* was sunk twelve miles off Southwold. On 19 March *Rogate* and *Crichtown* were both sunk by E-boats. On 23 March SS *Newlands* was lost off the Kent coast and on the 30th the cargo vessel *Jim* was sunk near the Aldeburgh light float.

The attacks by German E-boats continued into April. Motor torpedo boat 5001 was sunk by an E-boat at Smith's Knoll on 6 April. However, the losses as far as the Germans were concerned were now becoming ruinous. In this period alone they had lost four E-boats, and, in all, their casualties throughout the war in the North Sea amounted to thirty-six. Fifteen of these had been sunk near the east coast of England.

The last major attack took place from 6 April, and involved small German submarines. Off Felixstowe on 16 April the cable ship *Monarch* was torpedoed. This was to be the last Allied vessel to be sunk close to the east coast during the Second World War. There would be three more losses over the next two days, but these were much further out to sea.

There was still more work for the forces of Nore Command. A bizarre story was told to shocked officials at Great Yarmouth on 10 April. The lifeboat *Joan Hodshon* had come in from Den Burg from the Dutch island of Texel. On board were sixteen Dutchmen and four former Russian soldiers. They explained that the island of Texel was garrisoned by Soviet soldiers impressed into the German army. The troops had mutinied and in retribution the Germans had shelled the island and then sent SS troops to deal with the survivors. Some 1,500 people had been killed, including Dutch resistance. Unfortunately it was too late for Nore Command to help those trapped on the island.

RAF aircraft, operating from Yorkshire, Lincolnshire and Norfolk, now switched their night bombing offensives to finish off German resistance on the Dutch islands and on the coastal fringes of the Baltic. On 18 April alone 1,000 RAF bombers dropped 4,400 tons of bombs on Heligoland. By the end of April and into early May, with Holland now liberated, operations now focused on the Baltic. Beaufighters operating from the east coast sank five U-boats on 3/4 May.

On 5 May news filtered out that German forces in north-west Germany, Holland and Denmark had surrendered. Full German surrender took place three days later. But for the vessels operating from the east coast of England their war was not yet over. They still had to clear the Dutch ports of hundreds of mines. Over the winter of 1944/5, 1,800 Dutch had died of starvation and cold. It was now vital that enormous amounts of supplies reached the Dutch population. For the next eighteen months the coastal forces of Nore Command continued to work tirelessly.

Little by little warships began to be built up at Harwich and placed into the Reserve Fleet. Many of the smaller vessels were either paid off or scrapped. Shipyards up and down the east coast continued to work to build or refit vessels to be used against Japan. Normality began to return in the shape of the fishing fleets operating off East Anglia and the Humber. Across the east coast landscape radar stations disappeared, airfields closed and the race was on to clear the enormous British minefields off the east coast.

The air war over the Nore was finished. The daily terror of enemy aircraft overhead dropping mines, bombs and incendiaries was a thing of the past, but it was not something that could easily be forgotten. Streets in towns and villages up and down the east coast of England had been scarred and devastated, people had lost their loved ones. Britain's eastern front had been held in this odd and impersonal war. It was a conflict that rarely meant the adversaries ever saw one another's faces. No German soldier had set foot on the east coast. The night-time terror of the drone of German bombers overhead, answered by ack-ack guns firing into the darkness, was no more. But as those who were there sixty-odd years ago confirm, it will never be forgotten.

Eileen Robinson, née Turner, was born on 1 January 1931 and was living in Pakefield Street, Lowestoft:

My brother and I were at a friend's house just past Pakefield church on the cliff edge when a German aeroplane suddenly appeared, shooting his guns all along the cliff. Jerry, our friend, frantically pushed my brother and me down into the Anderson shelter and jumped in on top of us. I was unhurt but furious and gave him a clip around the ear for his trouble. While walking down Pakefield Street early one evening there was suddenly the clatter of gunfire and loud aeroplane engine noises behind me. A passing sailor grabbed me and pushed me into the porch of the nearest house. He protected me with his body. He then helped me up and we both continued on our way. All over in a minute, and I wonder if I ever thanked him?

Pat Lilley was also a child during the Second World War:

A story recounted by my mother was of the time when she and my father lived in Lancaster Road (Great Yarmouth) and decided to walk to the Regal cinema at the top of Regent Road to watch the latest film. Because my father had to get to work (he was in the Auxiliary Fire Service), they did not stay until the end of the film. They walked home and just before they reached their front door, they heard a bomb fall somewhere fairly close. They later discovered that it had hit the Regal cinema and that two neighbours of theirs who had been sitting on the same row as them, had sadly been killed. They counted themselves extremely lucky to have left when they did. As a baby I was kept in a drawer of the large chest-of-drawers in my mother's bedroom, so that I could easily be transported to either the Anderson shelter in the garden opposite, or if they were at my grandmother's, into the Morrison shelter that my grandmother used as her dining-room table.

Bombing Attacks on Naval Bases

This table shows raids on many of the principal naval-based towns along the east coast throughout the course of the war.

Town or Area	No. of Raids	Bombs and Other Munitions Dropped	Casualties Killed/Injured	Buildings Destroyed/ Damaged/ Slight Damage
Brightlingsea	12	34 HE 2,380 incendiaries 2 mines 4 oil bombs 4 phosphorus 2 V-2s	2/21	10/274
Felixstowe	47	327 HE 1,200 incendiaries 5 mines 27 V-1s	7/42	29/71/789
Gt Yarmouth	126	1,070 HE 9,060 incendiaries 10 mines 10 firepots 10 phosphorus	217/588	1,836/2,016/ 19,840

Town or Area	No. of Raids	Bombs and Other Munitions Dropped	Casualties Killed/Injured	Buildings Destroyed/ Damaged/ Slight Damage
Grimsby & Cleethorpes	43	233 HE 7,300 incendiaries 4 mines 2,500 butterflies 25 firepots 101 phosphorus	148/250	400/600/ 5,000
Harwich & Parkston	62	446 HE 1,305 incendiaries 4 mines 1 oil bomb 5 V-1s 1 V-2	23/100	47/127/1,186
Hull	72	1,264 HE 15,000 incendiaries 122 mines 35 phosphorus 74 butterflies	1,062/3,000	4,354/15,378/ 66,983
Ipswich	48	316 HE 906 incendiaries 2 mines 15 firepots 9 oil bombs 310 butterflies 2 V-1s	78/407	180/5,500
Lowestoft	83	681 HE 4,644 incendiaries 6 mines 7 phosphorus 7 firepots 5 V-1s	266/690	578/13,000
Medway towns	78	838 HE 4,778 incendiaries 9 mines		

Town or Area	No. of Raids	Bombs and Other Munitions Dropped	Casualties Killed/Injured	Buildings Destroyed/ Damaged/ Slight Damage
		32 phosphorus 8 oil bombs 13 firepots 6 V-1s 1 V-2	201/570	800/2,500/ 15,000
Sheerness & Queenborough	22	100 HE 1,240 incendiaries 3 mines 1 firepot 1 phosphorus 2 oil bombs 1 V-1 1 V-2	2/10	80/220/1,500
Skegness	30	140 HE 400 incendiaries 7 firepots	11/80	101/120
Southend	85	567 HE 12,454 incendiaries 13 mines 185 butterflies 22 phosphorus 5 oil bombs 5 V-1s 2 V-2s	63/370	350/900/ 14,000
Tilbury	40	165 HE 1,622 incendiaries 2 mines 4 firepots 1 phosphorus	21/100	200/600/ 3,000

Air Raid Fatalities

By their very nature the following figures of air raid fatalities along the east coast can never be absolutely precise. These include service personnel and civilians, but they do not include casualties of those who were killed out to sea. It is worth bearing in mind that civilian deaths in London were around 30,000. Civilian deaths given for East Anglia, Essex, Hertfordshire and Greater London are approximately 2,108.

Location	Approximate Number of Fatalities
Aldeburgh	11
Boston	20
Bridlington	26
Brightlingsea	2
Burnham-on-Crouch	6
Caister	2
Cambridge	39
Chatham	58
Clacton	17
Colchester	54
Cromer	19
Dartford	59
Easington	2
Faversham	9
Felixstowe	7
Gillingham	53
Goole	3
Gravesend	36
Great Yarmouth and Gorleston	217

Location	Approximate Number of Fatalities
Greenhithe	7
Grimsby and Cleethorpes	148
Hadleigh	2
Happisburgh	2
Harwich and Dovercourt	21
Heybridge	4
Herne Bay	4
Hoo	1
Hull	1,200
Hunstanton	3
Immingham	17
Ipswich	78
Kessingland	3
King's Lynn	75
Kirby	1
Lowestoft	270
Margate	35
Martlesham	3
Melton	1
Nacton	2
Northfleet	41
Norwich	340
Oare	3
Orford	13
Parkeston	2
Rochester and Strood	95
Skegness	11
Sheerness	2
Sheringham	14
Sittingbourne	27
Southend	62
Southwold	10
Thurrock	131
Walton and Frinton	15
Whitstable	9
Winterton	2
Withernsea	15

According to British government figures some 60,595 civilians were killed as a direct result of enemy action between 1939 and 1945. A further 86,182 were injured. Of the total number killed 51,509 died as a result of conventional bombing, including incendiaries. A further 6,184 died during the V-1 offensive. Some 2,754 died as a result of V-2 long-range rockets and 148 died from cross-channel bombardment. These figures include civil defence workers, but do not include the Home Guard, merchant seamen or civilians who were killed as a result of enemy action at sea.

Air-Sea Rescue Units and Craft

Air Sea Rescue units and craft in Nore Command, September 1943, including Royal Naval vessels, were as follows:

Base Port	Unit	Craft Available
Bridlington	RAF 21 MCU	Pinnaces 1285 and 1292 Seaplane tender 439
Brightlingsea	Royal Navy	Air Rescue Boats *Patrician*, *Eclipse*, *Aro*, *Mike* and *Romany*
Felixstowe	RAF 26 MCU	High-speed launches 2555, 2557, 2558, 2562
Great Yarmouth and Gorleston	RAF 24 MCU	High-speed launches 185, 2550, 2551, 2506, 2570, 2707
Great Yarmouth and Gorleston	Royal Navy	Rescue motor launches 492, 496, 498, 499, 512, 514, 515, 517
Grimsby	Royal Navy	Steam harbour launch 304 Diesel harbour launches 4002 and 41107
Grimsby	RAF 22 MCU	High-speed launches 2503, 2559, 2560, 2579, 2594, 2677
Herne Bay	Royal Navy	Air-Sea Rescue boat *Dandy*
Lowestoft	RAF 24 MCU	High-speed launches 195, 2501, 2502
Ramsgate	RAF 32 MCU	High-speed launches 127, 149, 169, 178
Sheerness	RAF 31 MCU	Seaplane tenders 443, 444
Wells	RAF 23 MCU	Seaplane tenders 349, 350 Pinnace 1241

Corpo Aereo Italiano Order of Battle (1940/41)

Commanded by *Generale di SA* A. Corso-Fougier

Unit	Commanded and Based at	Sub-Units
13° Stormo BT	Commanded by *Colonello* Carlo di Capoa and based at Melsbroeck equipped with Fiat BR.20Ms.	Comprising: *11° Gruppo* commanded by *Maggiore* G. Mini and split into *1ª* and *4ª Squadriglie. 43° Gruppo* commanded by *Maggiore* G. Monteleone and split into *3ª* and *5ª Squadriglie.*
43° Stormo BT	Commanded by *Colonello* L. Questra and based at Chièvres, equipped with Fiat BR.20Ms.	Comprising: *98° Gruppo* commanded by *Maggiore* G. Tenti and split into *240ª* and *241ª Squadriglie; 99° Gruppo* commanded by *Maggiore* G. Battista Ciccu and split into *242ª* and *243ª* Squadriglie.
56° Stormo CT	Commanded by *Colonello* Umberto Chiesa.	Comprising: *18° Gruppo* (designated *18./JG56* by *Luftwaffe*) commanded by *Maggiore* Ferruccio Vosilla and split into *83ª,*

Unit	Commanded and Based at	Sub-Units
		85ᵃ and *95ᵃ Squadriglie*, based at Ursel and equipped with Fiat CR.42s; *20° Gruppo* (designated *20./JG56* by *Luftwaffe*) commanded by *Maggiore* Mario Bonzano and split into *351ᵃ*, *352ᵃ* and *353ᵃ Squadriglie*, based first at Ursel and then later at Maldegem and equipped with Fiat G.50bis.
179a Squadriglia	Commanded by *Capitano* C. Pirelli, at Melsbroeck and equipped with Cant Z.1007 bis for tactical reconnaissance.	n/a

Known Italian pilot loses during operations over eastern England, 1940/41

Name	Rank	Role	Unit	Notes
Felice Agnetti	*1° Avieri*	Aircrew	*242ᵃ Squadriglia*	KIA on 11 November when 242-3/MM22267 was shot down by enemy fighters.
Pietro Appiani	*Sottotenente*	Pilot	*243ᵃ Squadriglia*	Crashed with BR.20M 243-2/MM22621 on 11 November 1940 in Tangham Forest, Bromswell, near Woodbridge after combat. He and two or three of the crew were taken POW (the other two of the crew were killed).
Paride Astesati	*Sergente*	Air gunner	*5ᵃ Squadriglia*	KIA on 24 October 1940 when BR.20M MM21928 (5-8) crashed during take-off from Melsbroeck.

Name	Rank	Role	Unit	Notes
Lino Bettio	*Avieri Sc.*	Aircrew	*242ª Squadriglia*	KIA on 11 November when 242-3/MM22267 was shot down by enemy fighters.
Ernesto Bianchi	*Sottotenente*	Pilot	*243ª Squadriglia*	Shot down by enemy fighters and KIA while flying BR.20M 243-10/MM22620 on 11 November 1940.
Paolo Biziocchi	*Sergente*	Flight engineer	*5ª Squadriglia*	KIFA on 24 October 1940 when BR.20M MM21928 (5-8) crashed during take-off from Melsbroeck.
A. Brunetti	*Avieri*	Aircrew	*5ª Squadriglia*	MIA when BR.20M MM22257 was shot down by an enemy night-fighter on 20/21 November 1940.
Guido Buatier	*Sergente Maggiore*	Pilot	*243ª Squadriglia*	KIA on 11 November when 243-10/MM22620 was shot down by enemy fighters.
Oreste Campioli	*1º Avieri*	Aircrew	*243ª Squadriglia*	KIA on 11 November when 243-10/MM22620 was shot down by enemy fighters.
M. Cini	*Avieri*	Aircrew	*13º Stormo BT*	KIA on 29 November 1940 when BR.20M MM21908 crashed when trying to land back at base after mission. The aircraft was probably damaged after combat and hit some workers' houses at Diegem-Lo, burning out and killing the crew.
G. Columbano	*Avieri*	Aircrew	*13º Stormo BT*	As above

Name	Rank	Role	Unit	Notes
L. Dal Forn	*Tenente*	Aircrew	*13° Stormo BT*	As above
R. Giampieretti	*Avieri*	Aircrew	*5ª Squadriglia*	MIA when BR.20M MM22257 was shot down by an enemy night-fighter on 20/21 November 1940.
Giacomo Grillo	*Sergente Maggiore*	Pilot	*95ª Squadriglia*	MIA on 23 November 1940 when MM5665 was bounced by Spitfires from 603 Squadron off Folkestone and shot down into the sea.
Vittorio Lanfaloni	*1° Avieri*	Aircrew	*242ª Squadriglia*	KIA on 11 November when 242-3/MM22267 was shot down by enemy fighters.
E. Lesignoli	*Avieri*	Aircrew	*5ª Squadriglia*	MIA when BR.20M MM22257 was shot down by an enemy night-fighter on 20/21 November 1940.
G. Maruelli	*Avieri*	Aircrew	*13° Stormo BT*	As M Cini.
Guido Mazza	*Tenente*	Pilot	*83ª Squadriglia*	MIA on 23 November 1940 when CR.42 MM5694 was bounced by Spitfires from 603 Squadron off Folkestone and shot down into the sea.
Aldo del Monte	*Sergente*	Flight engineer	*5ª Squadriglia*	KIA on 24 October 1940 when BR.20M MM21928 (5-8) crashed during take-off from Melsbroeck.

Name	Rank	Role	Unit	Notes
Giuseppe Monti	*1° Avieri*	Air gunner	*243ª Squadriglia*	Killed after an unsuccessful parachute jump from BR.20M 243-3 near Courtrai on 29 October 1940.
Carlo Pagani	*Capitano*	Pilot	*5ª Squadriglia*	KIA on 24 October 1940 when BR.20M MM21928 (5-8) crashed during take-off from Melsbroeck.
Enzo Panicchi	*Sergente*	Pilot	*83ª Squadriglia*	KIA on 11 November 1940 when CR.42 MM6978 was shot down into the sea apparently by Flight Lieutenant Lionel Manley Gaunce of 46 Squadron.
S. Paoli	*Tenente*	Aircrew	*5ª Squadriglia*	MIA when BR.20M MM22257 was shot down by an enemy night-fighter on 20/21 November 1940. The body was washed ashore at Wassenaar, without parachute but with lifejacket.
Armando Paolini	*1° Avieri*	Radio-operator	*243ª Squadriglia*	Baled out of a BR.20M on 24 October 1940 over Belgium after the aircraft became lost. He was wounded in a foot. KIA when BR.20M 243-2/MM22621 was shot down by enemy fighters on 11 November 1940.

Name	Rank	Role	Unit	Notes
Ovidio Podda	1° Avieri	Aircrew	243ª Squadriglia	KIA on 11 November when 243-10/MM22620 was shot down by enemy fighters.
Pier Antonio Poggi	Tenente	Pilot	242ª Squadriglia	KIA on 11 November. Probably co-pilot in Sottotenente Enzio Squazzini's 242-3/MM22267.
Talete Rebuscini	Tenente	Aircrew	13° Stormo BT	As M Cini.
C. Rildani	Sergente	Aircrew	5ª Squadriglia	MIA when BR.20M MM22257 was shot down by an enemy night-fighter on 20/21 November 1940. The body was washed ashore at Wassenaar, without parachute but with lifejacket.
E. Romito	Maresciallo	Aircrew	13° Stormo BT	As M Cini.
Mario Roncali	Tenente	Pilot	352ª Squadriglia	KIA on 13 April 1941. Last CAI pilot to be lost.
Enzio Squazzini	Sottotenente	Pilot	243ª Squadriglia	Shot down by enemy fighters and KIA while flying BR.20M 242-3/MM22267 on 11 November 1940.
Arrigo Vardabasso	Tenente	Aircrew	5ª Squadriglia	KIA on 24 October 1940 when BR.20M MM21928 (5-8) crashed during take-off from Melsbroeck.

APPENDIX 5

V-2 Rocket Attacks

V-2 rocket attacks against the east coast of England, 1944/5.

Date	Time	Site Hit	Comments
25/09/1944	1910	Hoxen, Suffolk	Damaged twelve houses
26/09/1944	1630	Ranworth, Norfolk	Exploded in field
27/09/1944	1047	Horsford, Norfolk	Landed near Botany Bay Farm
27/09/1944	1625	Kirby Bedon, Norfolk	
27/09/1944	1755	Beighton, Norfolk	Landed on Acle Hall Farm
28/09/1944	1420	Horsey, Norfolk	Crashed into the sea
29/09/1944	1312	Hemsby, Norfolk	Landed on shoreline minefield, damaging a large number of properties
29/09/1944	1945	Horstead, near Coltishall, Norfolk	Landed in meadowland causing two minor injuries
29/09/1944	2042	Whitlingham, near Thorpe, Norwich	Landed in a field and damaged twenty-five nearby houses
30/09/1944	1214	Halvergate, Norfolk	Landed in open ground near Staithe Farm
30/09/1944	1922	Caister, Norfolk	Crashed into the sea
01/10/1944	1755	Bedingham, Norfolk	Landed on Sycamore Farm, badly damaging the farmhouse
03/10/1944	0932	Beeston St Lawrence, Norfolk	Damaged a church and five houses
03/10/1944	1441	Hopton, Norfolk	Landed near Valley Farm, damaging twenty-eight houses
03/10/1944	1655	Great Witchingham, Norfolk	Hit Mill Farm, causing damage to two farms

Date	Time	Site Hit	Comments
03/10/1944	1945	Hellesdon, Norfolk	Hit golf course and damaged 400 houses
03/10/1944	2010	Denton, Norfolk	Hit Darrow Farm causing slight damage
04/10/1944	1222	Great Yarmouth, Norfolk	Crashed into sea eight miles off coast
04/10/1944	1340	Rockland St Mary, Norfolk	Damaged a public house and twenty-six houses. There were eight injured
04/10/1944	1647	Crostwick, Norfolk	Damaged farmhouse and two cottages
04/10/1944	1736	Spixworth, Norfolk	Burst in the air, damaging a church and four houses
05/10/1944	0736	Great Yarmouth, Norfolk	Crashed into sea off coast
05/10/1944	0904	Taverham, Norfolk	Landed on grounds near Hall Farm
05/10/1944	1138	Peasenhall, Suffolk	
05/10/1944	1328	Surlingham, Norfolk	Burst in the air, slightly damaging thirty-six houses
05/10/1944	1609	Acle, Norfolk	Landed approximately a mile and a half to the north-east, slightly damaging three houses
05/10/1944	1744	Little Plumstead, Norfolk	Landed on the grounds of Heath Farm
06/10/1944	0925	Shotesham All Saints, Norfolk	Landed in woods to the south-west of the church, and damaged forty-two houses
09/10/1944	1045	Langley, near Cantley, Norfolk	One house damaged and livestock killed
09/10/1944	1050	Brooke, Norfolk	Slight damage to Brooke Hall
09/10/1944	1830	Orford, Suffolk	Fell into sea off Orford and Shingle Street
10/10/1944	0727	Frinton, Essex	Weapon air-burst six miles out to sea
10/10/1944	1600	Harwich, Essex	Air-burst off coast
10/10/1944	1735	Bramerton, Norfolk	Landed on edge of decoy site, damaging some cottages

Date	Time	Site Hit	Comments
11/10/1944	0810	Haddiscoe, Norfolk	Damaged a hall and four cottages
11/10/1944	1051	Rockland St Mary, near Bramerton, Norfolk	Fifteen houses damaged
11/10/1944	1421	Playford, Suffolk	Landed in field
12/10/1944	0247	Clacton, Essex	Air-burst three miles to the south-east
12/10/1944	0740	Ingworth, Norfolk	Landed in stubble field near Manor Farm
15/10/1944	0504	Chelmsford, Essex	Four houses badly damaged in Bellcross Road
17/10/1944	1550	Little Baddow, Essex	Wrecked six houses and caused two injuries
23/10/1944	0401	St Osyth, Essex	Landed in the sea
24/10/1944	0500	Rushmere St Andrew, Suffolk	Landed to the south-east of the church
26/10/1944	Unknown	Orford Ness, Suffolk	Came down in the sea
26/10/1944	1014	Welborne, Norfolk	Damaged a school and fifteen houses
10/11/1944	1504	Fulbourn, Cambridgeshire	Came down in a field near Valley Farm
22/11/1944	1327	Bradwell Marshes, Essex	
24/11/1944	1100	Braughing, Hertfordshire	Landed six and a half miles to the north-west of Bishop's Stortford
26/11/1944	Unknown	Orford Ness, Suffolk	Came down in the sea off the coast
29/11/1944	1510	Bradwell Marshes, Essex	
29/11/1944	1950	Poslingford, Suffolk	Came down in a field
02/12/1944	0735	Ramsholt, Suffolk	Came down on mud flats in estuary
03/12/1944	0930	Burnham-on-Crouch, Essex	Came down in a river to the west of Whitehouse
06/12/1944	0447	Woodham Ferrers, Essex	Slight damage to some buildings
07/12/1944	0210	Great Saling, Essex	Came down in a field at Anker's Farm

Date	Time	Site Hit	Comments
07/12/1944	1443	Chediston, near Halesworth, Suffolk	Failed to explode
14/12/1944	0505	Nuthapstead, near Royston, Hertfordshire	Missile air burst
14/12/1944	2343	Writtle, Essex	Came down in a field
18/12/1944	1632	Clacton, Essex	Hit the cliff face just to the south-west of the pier
19/12/1944	0130	Chelmsford, Essex	Killed thirty-nine and injured 152 when it hit a factory shop, the Marconi works and several other businesses. Many properties were seriously damaged.
19/12/1944	1130	Bradwell Marshes, Essex	
21/12/1944	0945	Bradwell-on-Sea, Essex	
23/12/1944	2350	West Row, near Mildenhall, Suffolk	Weapon air burst
03/01/1945	0330	Chelmsford, Essex	Caused slight damage when it fell to the south-west of the town
04/01/1945	Unknown		Southwold, Suffolk Came down in the sea off the coast
05/01/1944	0925	Layham, Suffolk	Weapon air burst
07/01/1945	1810	Brightlingsea, Essex	Slight damage to eighty homes
08/01/1945	0034	Sheringham, Norfolk	Crashed into the sea between Sheringham and Bacton
08/01/1945	0218	Cley-next-the-Sea, near Holt, Norfolk	Came down in the sea off the coast
09/01/1945	1720	Little Hallingbury, near Bishop's Stortford, Hertfordshire	Fell in a field
10/01/1945	1420	Henlow, near Shefford, Bedfordshire	
12/01/1945	1737	Trimley St Mary, Suffolk	Fell in a field beside the railway line

Date	Time	Site Hit	Comments
12/01/1945	1758	Writtle, Essex	Fell in a field
13/01/1945	Unknown	Orford Ness, Suffolk	Crashed into the sea
13/01/1945	0342	Halstead, Essex	Damaged 280 houses
13/01/1942	1640	Depden, near Newmarket, Suffolk	A farmhouse was damaged
15/01/1945	1600	Mundesley, Norfolk	Slight damage to some buildings
17/01/1945	1700	Hatfield Broad Oak, near Bishop's Stortford, Hertfordshire	Crashed into fields near Lancaster's Farm
20/01/1945	0858	Takeley, near Bishop's Stortford, Hertfordshire	Fell in a field to the north-west of Frimhall Priory
20/01/1945	0957	Earl Stonham, near Stowmarket, Suffolk	
20/01/1945	1005	Bishop's Stortford, Hertfordshire	Slight damage to some houses
22/01/1945	0704	Brightlingsea, Essex	Slight damage to some houses
22/01/1945	2010	Clacton, Essex	Hit the edge of the sea wall, badly damaging seven houses and causing slight damage to 200 more. There were twenty-seven casualties
23/01/1945	1050	Mayland, near Chelmsford, Essex	Damaged six houses
23/01/1945	1700	Chelmsford, Essex	One killed and sixteen injured when a timber yard, iron foundry and nine houses were badly damaged. Over 200 other buildings were slightly damaged
25/01/1945	1210	Hatfield Heath, near Bishop's Stortford, Hertfordshire	Fell near Lancaster's Farm
28/01/1945	0730	Kirby Creek, near Thorpe-le-Soken, Essex	Fell in mud flats
29/01/1945	0555	Bradwell-on-Sea, Essex	One minor casualty
01/02/1945	0230	Great Leighs, near Chelmsford, Essex	

Date	Time	Site Hit	Comments
01/02/1945	0915	Great Leighs, near Chelmsford, Essex	Some slight damage to some houses
05/02/1945	2343	Tollesbury, near Maldon, Essex	Fell into the River Blackwater
08/02/1945	0325	Writtle, Essex	Fell close to Reeds Farm
07/03/1945	1450	Brundish, near Framlingham, Suffolk	Fell near Clutton's Farm
12/03/1945	1115	Lower Kirby, near Frinton, Essex	Two houses flattened, a school and eleven other houses damaged. One killed and one injured
21/03/1945	0530	Boreham, Essex	Slight damage to some buildings
21/03/1945	2135	Bardfield Saling, near Braintree, Essex	Slight damage to some buildings
21/03/1945	2352	Stansted, Essex	Slight damage to some buildings
22/03/1945	Unknown	Great Yarmouth, Norfolk	Came down in the sea twenty miles to the south-east

Bibliography

Bates, L.M., *Thames on Fire*, Dalton, 1985

Benham, H., *Essex at War*, Essex County Standard, 1945

Bowyer, M.J.F., *Airfields of East Anglia*, Patrick Stephens, 1979

Bowyer, M.J.F., *Air Raid*, Patrick Stephens, 1986

Box, C.J., *Great Yarmouth, A Frontline Town*, Great Yarmouth Corporation, 1945

Brooks, P., *Coastal Towns at War*, Poppyland, 1988

Brown, R. Douglas, *East Anglia*, Dalton, 1980

Collier, B., *Defence of the United Kingdom*, HMSO, 1957

Foynes, J.P., *The Battle of the East Coast*, privately published, 1994

Geraghty, T., *A Northeast Coast Town*, Hull Corporation, 1951

Herbert, A.P., *The War Story of Southend Pier*, Southend Corporation, 1945

Jenkins, Ford, *Lowestoft Port War*, Lowestoft Corporation, 1945

Johnson, D.E., *East Anglia at War 1939 to 1945*, Jarrolds, 1978

Malster, R., *Saved from the Sea*, David and Charles, 1968

Monsarrat, N., *Three Corvettes*, Cassell, 1943

Rootes, A., *Frontline County*, Robert Hale, 1980

Smith, M., *Blitz on Grimsby*, Humberside Leisure Services, 1983

Sutherland, J. and Diane Canwell, *The RAF Air Sea Rescue Service,* Pen and Sword Books, 2005

Wallington, N., *Firemen at War*, David and Charles, 1981

Index